I'm
not
dead...
yet!

**Robby
Benson**

Also by Robby Benson

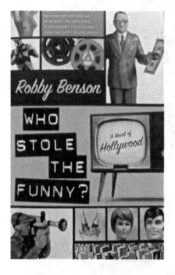

Who Stole The Funny?

Published by HarperCollins

"An irreverent and hilarious stroll down the dark alleys of Hollywood's TV landscape."— Peter Bart, editor in chief, *Variety*

The Los Angeles Times Best-Seller List (2007)

Open Heart

Published by Samuel French (2006)

"A sharp, uncompromising look at the value of true love.. The surprise ending will leave you stunned, sad, happy and satisfied all at the same time."— *Broadway.com*

WISH IT, DREAM IT, DO IT!

Oops...

WISH IT, DREAM IT, DO IT!

That's better.

I'm Not Dead...Yet!

or: *"The Corpse Moved"*

A medical memoir by

4-Time Open-Heart Survivor

Robby Benson

VALOREDITIONS.COM

Published in the United States of America
First Edition: August 2012

Library of Congress Cataloging-in-Publication Data is available upon request.
ISBN 978-0-615-41873-5

2 4 6 8 10 9 7 5 3 1

Cover design by **Concetta Halstead-Lord**
LordCreative.com

Portrait by **Sigrid Estrada**
SigridEstrada.com

Original Photographs
Robby Benson

Editing & Technical design
Karla DeVito & Dan Berlinghoff

Printed by CreateSpace

Author's Note

If you want to learn more about the medical conditions being discussed in the book, please go to The Cleveland Clinic website at www.my.ClevelandClinic.org

This book was originally conceived with film clips, photographs, slideshows and songs embedded *within* the ebook as an integral part of my story— media that would *enhance* your reading experience.

But I realize many readers would like to have a print copy of the book. So, now, let the book speak for itself. (Sorry… it can't 'speak' here, either… Soon, I hope!)

Thank you, r.

Karla Jayne

Forever

"It's just a simple song—
about eternity, infinity,
and what you mean to me..."

Contents

Preface

I WAS LYING IN A HOSPITAL BED looking up at the patterns in the ceiling, wondering how many people before me had morphed the ceiling tiles into faces and images. And because I'm practically blind without my contact lenses, I was seeing wonderfully imagined images: and, for a moment, I was sure I saw the face of a man whom I recognized. In my myopic stare, the ceiling tile became that man, a colleague who had asked me to help him get through his open-heart surgery just weeks prior, but the catch? Only if I could do so with discretion— secrecy actually— he wanted no one else to know of his diagnosis.

So typical, I thought. Been there. Done that.

Since 1984, when I had my first open-heart surgery, people in need have managed to locate me in order to ask all kinds of questions regarding open-heart surgery. They know we are all linked together as kindred spirits—people who will have their chests sawed open and then a stranger's hands will reach inside our torsos, touching and manipulating our hearts. No matter age, color of skin, or gender, we are all connected by this brutal association. It's almost like in a science fiction B-movie when the actors pass one another on the street and can tell with a slight nod that they have been captive by the same spaceship aliens.

I tried to remember, to recount all the people I have spoken to, tried to help throughout my four open-heart surgery 'career,' and how having someone to talk to can be so reassuring to both the patient and their loved ones. How many people had I spoken to about overcoming the daunting hurdle of open-heart surgery? Hundreds, thousands? I guessed— *but not nearly enough.*

As I stared at the ceiling tile, I realized I couldn't go another moment without sharing my experiences with other vulnerable souls. Even though I was an actor and in the public eye, my journey is similar to theirs— and maybe yours— because in the long run, the hospital gurney is: 'one size fits all.'

There is great urgency to life when you've faced death four different times. I made up my mind to write a book that would detail the ups, downs, the sideways, the falls, spills, yaws, the hurdles and the walls that we all smash into. I had to get my faux-pas and two paws to my computer as fast as possible. Maybe from my history recorded on paper or on a digital tablet, a father, husband, wife, mother, daughter, friend, or loved one who will be facing this ordeal will find something that helps or comforts them in my book. Or just makes them laugh.

This brings me to the first colossal, whale-like query that is ever-present in the theme of this book and in the theme of most patients' lives: Karla, my wife and soulmate, and I have been on a quest for most of my adult life, trying to find a hospital where we can enter and leave with hope. Does such a place exist? Once I had the nerve to face my demons, we went hunting for it.

And this is quite the journey.

Prologue

I WAS A MOVIE STAR...

in Hollywood!

I was a very happy husband.

I believed in true love   and was blessed to have my

pie   and eat it too.

I had the perfect woman  who was my best friend, lover, wife and partner for life.

We had a remarkable, healthy, baby girl, Lyric, who was barely a year old.

Joy... hope... love... and the brightest future, full of vitamin A:

We were inseparable.

I represented everything vital, young, strong, and athletic in our

pop-culture world. I liked and respected my fans. I loved all sports. Anything intellectually or physically challenging was exciting. I loved basketball to such an extent that I wrote a film, *One On One*, with my father Jerry Segal;

a great writer, an even better father.

As good of a ballplayer as I was, I was a horrible

skater. (I fractured my hip filming a hockey scene); but as a

baseball player (at 14), I owned the legendary street-rat distinction of hitting a baseball all the way from the old baseball field at Riverside Park, up, up, up, and disappearing onto the West Side Highway.

I was a marathoner running 3:05 in the 1983 New York Marathon. (Ahh! I didn't break 3 hours. I thought I'd get a second chance to shave that 5 minutes off my time.)

I excelled in some things, was a total failure in others, and tried to make up for my shortcomings with a work ethic that almost killed me.

My foundation was strong: my heroes were my two loving parents who met

young,   married young

and are still in love today. My sister, just a year older than me,

was smart, talented, loving and on her way to becoming an astonishingly successful fashion designer: Shelli Segal. (The real talent in our family.)

I had everything anyone could hope for: family, friends, a privileged life, a career and the greatest woman I had ever met as my wife and best friend. And I knew how fortunate I was, which made

it all the sweeter. Sure, there were career ups and downs, but with each day, life began with blissful optimism. The math for our family: strength plus intelligence times compassion plus tolerance equals my template for life.

I don't mean to brag but:

So honestly, I was one very lucky guy.

I did have one minor problem:

I — couldn't — breathe.

I would need a cow valve placed in my heart to keep me alive.

Funny  how one minute you think you're

on top of the world, and the next you may be

under it. I thought I was doomed.

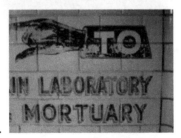

Doomed…

I BEGAN WRITING THIS BOOK TWO WEEKS FROM THE DAY the anesthesiologist asked me to count backwards from 100 and moments later, the surgical team was sawing down the middle of my chest (for the 4th time), blossoming my rib cage to get to my veteran surgically repaired heart. I imagined the past surgeons leaving graffiti-type notes on my heart saying things like: 'How's it going?' 'My email has changed.' 'Good seeing you at the Heart Conference in Vegas.'

One can look at open-heart surgery as life's defeat; a reminder that we are so mortal and moments away from death; a morose and painful time that marks the end of the best years of our lives.

Or, one can experience this as a chance to live on borrowed time, because in truth, aren't we all living on borrowed time? Sometimes it takes a life and death situation to remind us how lucky we are. For me, I feel like I've experienced a chance to live on as I approach the best years of my life.

I hope once the pain subsides, you see your experience as a rebirth, because it is a miracle that I can sit and write this and then go for a run. Maybe I'll see you there... and we'll nod to one another— as if we've been on the same spaceship together.

54 years-old, two weeks out of my fourth open-heart surgery,

about to swim in the Atlantic.

This can be you!

You may be a lot better looking and a better swimmer,

but *this can be you.*

This song is a bit corny, but... why not?!

"Good Guys Win"

In The Beginning

I HAD A GREAT CHILDHOOD, but I was a sickly kid (and didn't really know it). As an infant, I needed a metal brace between my legs to force the bones in my ankles to straighten. As a toddler, I was under an oxygen tent and I remember my dad bringing me the coolest little cars to play with— the hospital didn't seem like such a bad place. One of my earliest memories is of a doctor telling my parents when he listened to my heart he heard a murmur. I thought that was pretty cool. He reassured my parents, telling them I'd grow out of it— that I'd live a long life and would probably never have to worry about the murmur in my heart.

My life as an actor began when I was very young. By age eight I was a pro. I was schooled 'old school.' As Oliver, the starving urchin in **Oliver,** I was malnourished in between shows (my choice). I was trained by wise and experienced performers in both summer stock and on Broadway. And my mother was a brilliant actor and my dad was an extraordinary writer-director. Both taught me old school.

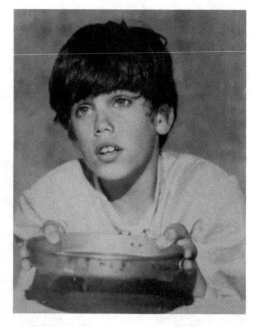

Instead of watching Saturday cartoons, I went to the movies— foreign films at the art houses, classics at the revival houses— it all fascinated me. I was hired to dub children's voices in many movies: from *Godzilla* films to the 1968 release of the Russian *War and Peace,* and Vittorio de Sica's 1970 film, *The Garden of the Finzi-Continis.*

CAST AT TWELVE YEARS OLD, I made my Broadway debut in 1969 in the straight play **Zelda** with Ed Begley Sr.

and Lilia Skala at the Ethel Barrymore Theatre. The guidance and artistic education I was given represented everything I adored about theater. Theater was like sports: there was a brotherhood; teamwork; the implication of a traveling family. I eventually took on the work and the billing of a star, but I always believed in parity; equality. When actors are on stage or in front of a camera, we are all *equals*.

I was taught (never complain!) nothing mattered before the curtain went up or before 'Action!' was called. The show not only must 'go on,' but you must *never* allow others to witness anything but the best performance possible.

I was taught (some may say 'programmed,' but that's a bit harsh) by a different set of rules, one of them being: 'Not showing or acknowledging pain or discomfort is virtuous; noble!'

I was a trained circus animal. I didn't mind. I loved it. (And was

proud of it: Look, I can stand on my trunk! Longer than anyone!)

Since 'life was a performance,' I could never let on how it affected my heart. And I've learned:

Everything Affects Your Heart

Zelda opened to a standing ovation. It got creamed in the *New York Times* and the following day there was a total of fourteen people in the audience. The show closed a few days later.

If everything affects your heart, I believe we need a way to quantize and calibrate the things in life that make our hearts sing; and at the other end of the spectrum, the things that do damage to our hearts. Although my journey is mapped with show business stories, it is similar to everyone's journey— our hearts respond to stress, to refuge; to abuse, to safekeeping; to hate, to love. We are all on our own journeys. This is mine.

BECAUSE I WAS SO INTROVERTED, things that felt like family were very appealing to me. One of the beautiful similarities between track and field events and acting is you are on a team with others, but it is really your inner will that propels you forward to a significant goal. And I believed the goal was not financial success, but artistic and creative perfection and since that is a rarity, it's a great goal because you're always trying to summit that creative Everest without oxygen (in my case…).

In sports, it meant only one thing: winning. I would die on a basketball court before I'd let someone beat me playing one on one. If I could walk off a football field after the final gun, then I did not give my best effort. If I were doing eight shows a week on Broadway, every show had to be better than the show before. That can be trickier because we are now discussing the art of acting and that doesn't necessarily mean exertion, it may mean complete control down to not batting an eye for an entire scene. When my dad told me the Australian track team ran up sand dunes to train for the Olympics, I ran the stairs of my high-rise— every night, up and down 30 floors, over and over again until I came back into apartment 28-D with no energy to shower and collapsed on my bed. Even though I was an athlete, I remained in the best shape possible because my heroes were Chaplin and Buster Keaton and the body is your tool to make people 'believe' you as an actor. If I got a huge laugh in a show on a Tuesday, I would work all week to understand each audience so that I could finesse rather than repeat my performance, thus 'earning' that laugh.

If I were to audition for a movie and knew I had the first appointment of the day, let's say 9:00 a.m., I would get there at 7 a.m. and sometimes fall asleep until the door was unlocked. If I were asked to come prepared to 'read,' I would memorize the scene and go one step further, I'd memorize *every* scene — then if I were asked to read another scene, I could put the script down and say, "Whenever you're ready, sir."

The laughs I'd earn made my heart sing. The games we'd win would make my heart soar. The behavior I'd witness and be a part of as a very young person in an adult world, earning an adult salary which came with the stress of an adult job, would make my heart... sore. "I did my best" was considered an excuse.

EVEN THOUGH I WAS A GOOD STUDENT, I loved show business because going to

work or auditions was a 'Get Out Of School Free' pass. Making a living at such an early age taught me responsibility and everything that came with earning a paycheck. During my audition for **The Rothschilds**, we were paired in groups on a Broadway stage. I was in a group with a bigger boy who was snotty and always an ass, no matter where our paths crossed. We were asked by the director to get into a minor shoving match. This bully shoved me so hard that I forgot I was at an audition and tried to take his head off. How I got the part of young Solomon Rothschild, I'll never know. But I did hear someone say, "He has the spunk we're looking for."

I worked eight shows a week in *The Rothschilds*, simultaneously, played Bruce Carson in the soap opera, *Search For Tomorrow*, and was on the basketball and track teams at school. I was also a latch-key kid; my parents trusted me and allowed me to be independent. I took the bus or subway home alone every night after the show (at midnight) from the seedy 1970s Broadway theater district. New York City at its most violent. The bus stop was in front of a porn theater. The subway was less exotic, more dangerous, but a quicker ride. (Odds were, I took the bus home more than the subway.)

I was jumped half a dozen times coming home in the subway, and one time was mugged and stabbed in my right hand. I was afraid to tell my parents— my dad was a Texan with quite a temper when it came to injustice; I thought he would go out hunting for the kids who jumped me or try to kill the kid who stabbed me. So I learned to eat with my left hand, and no one noticed.

Every night during the show, as I would go up the stairwell to my dressing room, I would round the corner on the second floor and two dressing room doors would be wide open. One dressing room was filled with the most beautiful women in New York who were dancers in the show— and they would change costumes with the door open. Naked. Eight times a week. My permeable young mind was being filled with an esoteric farrago of sexuality on a daily basis.

Every night I would see these gorgeous naked bodies standing 6 feet from me, who would catch my eye and just smile or wink. In the other dressing room, licking a lollipop, was a Tony Award winning predator, err— actor, who would wink as well, but eight shows a week he'd also whisper, "I'll suck your cock if you'll suck mine." Gorgeous naked women in one room and a pedophile in the other.

I felt I was expected to behave with an 'old school' attitude; my performance and allegiance to the show came first. If I told anyone what this man was saying to me, it would make its way back to my father— and my father would simply kill this man. There was no doubt about that, so silence was necessary. I was becoming a pro at being silent.

One day in between shows, I was bouncing a ball in front of the Lunt-Fontanne Theater and a man in his 30s, dressed in a cheap pinstripe jump suit came out of a club next to the theater. He was escorting his 'woman' and to impress her, accused me of trying to hit his 'woman' with my pink hand ball. As a New Yorker, I began to say 'F.U.' but couldn't even get to the last consonants of the curse word before his fist connected so solidly with my chin that my head exploded on the side of the curb. When I awoke minutes later, I saw the entire cast of *The Rothschilds* staring down at me in horror. I tried to look around. I was covered in blood, and chunks of skull and pieces of hair were close to my head. The real fear was hoping to somehow hide this from my dad. If my dad found out, he would kill this man. No doubt about it. Of course, my parents eventually found out.

"Hello, Ma? Dad? Don't worry. I'm okay. I only needed 15 stitches and I shouldn't go to sleep tonight after the show because the doctor thinks I may have a concussion."

"Robby— what are you talking about?"

No one from the theater bothered to call my folks. The man in the pinstripes was never heard from again. I couldn't help wondering if my dad called in a chit with the people he was writing comedy material for— 'old school' in that world meant the mob— and some of my dad's clients were managed by the... 'old school-teachers.'

The most exciting thing that happened to me during *The Rothschilds* was appearing on *The Ed Sullivan Show*. Back in the late 60's and early 70's there were two shows on TV that I'd never miss— *Walt Disney's Wonderful World of Color* (on our black and white TV set)— and *The Ed Sullivan Show*.

Today, The Ed Sullivan Theater is where David Letterman tapes his shows, but back then it was where everyone from The Beatles to Topo Gigio would perform and all of America would watch. And now I was going to be singing live on *Ed Sullivan!*

During rehearsal Mr. Sullivan shook *The Rothschild's* Tony Award-winning star Hal Linden's hand (a wonderful actor and a better man), but not any of the boys who played the young sons. Since I was the 'alpha' actor among the boys, I got up the nerve to go to the great-and-powerful Mr. Sullivan's dressing room, knock on his door, and ask if he would call us over and shake our hands as well when the song finished.

Before my entrance on live TV, I was sweating and noticed I couldn't move and I could not feel any part of my body. It was the most stage fright I've ever had. I heard my cue... The next thing I knew I was singing and making people laugh with a little crack in my voice that I invented as a comedy bit because my voice was changing— so why not get a laugh?

When the number was over, Ed Sullivan called Hal Linden over and began to shake his hand. Just before he threw the show to commercial, he smiled, looked at *me* and waved the boys over— and I got to shake Ed Sullivan's hand on national television.

A few months into the run, a very handsome woman in the chorus, in her early forties, offered to stay late and give me singing lessons in the empty theater. Let's just say, I got a whole lot more than 'singing lessons.' Broadway. Old school.

I'm not sure of the affects to my heart and my spirit, but call it even when it comes to *The Rothschilds*. Kind of like a long game of tug-of-war with my heart. No one really wins but the heart has plenty of stretch marks.

Valuable Life Lesson: Survive at all costs. Ed Sullivan was a man of his word. Singing lessons actually don't have anything to do with the area of the body below the diaphragm. Oh— and don't take candy from strangers.

WHEN I WAS ALMOST 15, along came an opportunity to play a cowboy, ride horses and star in **Jory**, a movie that was to be shot in Mexico. Could it get any better? More exciting? More romantic? It was one more 'Get Out Of School Free' card— but I had to get the part first. I literally camped out at the office of producer Joseph E. Levine, who had just made *The Graduate*, and this was to be his next blockbuster. For every audition and every call-back I'd get to the office before the cleaning crew. I memorized the entire script.

An actress I was working with on *Search For Tomorrow* had a farm in upstate New York, and I asked if I could ride her horses. (I didn't tell her I had never ridden a horse before.) She said okay, if I was willing to paint her barn. I rode her thoroughbreds without a saddle because I didn't know how to put a saddle on a horse, and these were English saddles and I was doing a western, so— a saddle? Unnecessary. I didn't know how to put on a bridle or reins either, so I learned to ride by holding onto the mane of a 100,000 dollar horse, galloping out of control through the woods and onto the paved street. I once almost rode onto the freeway.

From the producer of "Love Story" ...for those who love adventure.

He hung up his guns at the age of fifteen.

Joseph E. Levine presents An Avco Embassy Film

JORY

JOHN MARLEY B.J. THOMAS ROBBY BENSON

Based on the novel by MILTON R. BASS • Screenplay by GERALD HERMAN and ROBERT IRVING
Directed by JORGE FONS • A Wonder Karobone Production in association with Cinematografica Marco Polo, S.A.
Executive Producer LEOPOLDO SILVA • Produced by HOWARD G. MINSKY
AN AVCO EMBASSY RELEASE

From sheer determination I got the title role in *Jory*. That same determination fascinated the Mexican caballeros who took pride, pleasure and gambled to see if I could do more and more dangerous tricks on a horse, some of the tricks the stuntmen wouldn't try (which made it more appealing to me), and eat the hottest jalapeno (which I did, and still do!). By the time the movie was over I could do every trick I've ever seen in a western, including riding at a full gallop while standing on the horse's bare back, jumping off and back on again— while picking up my cowboy hat from the dirt. This came at the expense of once flying head first into cactus. I picked out every needle and no one ever knew. I did learn that the poison in the needles of a cactus can sting for days. But it was best to just never tell anyone.

Every morning for breakfast, I ate homemade tamales sold from the back of a bicycle by an older Mexican lady. I got food poisoning at least once a week. But I still ate the tamales to the delight of the Mexican cowboys. I also went nose-to-nose with Mr. Levine, and with pure determination got him to fly in Linda Purl as my love interest. I had worked with Linda in Japan doing *Oliver* at the Imperial Theater when I was 13. I had a big-time crush on her and I wouldn't let up. Finally they flew her in, all the way from Japan to Mexico, and gave her the role. And I *never* lost a contest to the Mexican stuntmen when it came to 'who could eat the hottest jalapeno.' That was nothing more than a war of wills. I would never lose that battle. No skill involved, just personal pain. Pain? Ha! No problemo. I had that covered, to their delight.

John Marley, who received an Oscar nomination as the dad in *Love Story* (but is best remembered as the studio chief who wakes up with his horse's head in his bed in *The Godfather*), was in *Jory*. He became my mentor and a dear friend. He taught me so much about the film business. (Old school. He was a John Cassavetes favorite.) He also told me the worst thing that could happen to any actor in show business was "being known for having heart trouble." John Marley was fighting that fight when I first met him. He said if anyone ever found out he had a bad heart, he could never be insured and his career would be *over*. He smiled that pock-holed smile and rubbed my head and told me, "Thank goodness you'll never have to worry about that, kid." I agreed... silently!

My memory of the doctor telling my parents I had a heart murmur came back to haunt me. I was *scared*. I had to be quiet— *never* tell anyone about the doctor or my **Heart Murmur**. Never. Shh...

Valuable Life Lesson: If you are determined to fight for what you believe in, you might actually get it. And don't eat tamales that come from the back of a bicycle. Oh— and *never tell anyone that you have a heart problem*. That could be the end of your career.

JEREMY WAS A GREAT OPPORTUNITY to star in a movie made in New York City... and get out of school.

I was cast as Jeremy at age 15 by writer-director Joe Brooks. He had hired me to sing and play guitar on a string of national commercial jingles he had written, and our mailbox at 165 West End Avenue was usually jammed with residual checks from my work with Joe.

Long before filming began, he asked me to work with him on the script. Joe sat at his typewriter and asked me questions like:

"What would you say here?" I'd speak— he'd type.

"What would the girl say?" I'd speak— he'd type.

"What would happen next?" I'd speak— he'd type.

This went on for the entire writing of the shooting script. He never gave me a writing or story credit, but I did learn an invaluable lesson: I could write a screenplay that was good enough to be made into a movie.

Four days into shooting the film he fired me. It was his first directing job and we had worked for four days and we were four days behind. Age appropriately, I thought that we were friends, so this firing was devastating; *heartbreaking*. I felt completely betrayed. A few days later the financiers made Brooks re-hire me. I told him: I wouldn't be surprised if you'd fire your wife. (He did. Four times.)

I did my first nude scene with a beautiful, kind, young Glynnis O'Connor. (Why ever go back to school?) The day we shot the scene Brooks said, "Okay— time to get undressed." I was still remarkably shy, even after my 'singing lessons.' We both took off our clothes and stared at each other, scared, in our underwear.

"You're in your underwear!" Brooks barked. "I said take off your clothes! It's a nude scene. You're making love for the first time!"

There were no social workers on the set, no parents, no SAG rules or representatives— no supervision of minors whatsoever. To be a child working in New York at that time, all they needed was a permit from City Hall.

I called home. My mom and dad conferred and decided 'if I was okay with it, they were too.' They really did trust me. Unfortunately, they also trusted Joe Brooks and the people making this film.

So, off came the underwear. It was... traumatic. I tried to use my body to shield Glynnis from the eyes of all the set's lookie-loos. Suddenly Joe Brooks yelled "Cut!" during our naked onscreen kiss. "Robby, you don't know how to kiss a girl— let me show you," and the next thing I knew he was kissing an obviously uncomfortable Glynnis. Creepy? Actually life-changing. From that moment on I did not see Glynnis O'Connor as an actor anymore; I saw her as someone I had to protect, heart and soul.

Of course, Glynnis and I fell in love during *Jeremy*. Back in the day there was only one phone in my apartment. We'd be on the phone for hours, causing my father to say, "Are you gonna just listen to each other breathe all day?"

When a rough cut of the film, an X-rated version showing minors' genitalia, was purposely shown to Joe Brooks, he did exactly what the producer knew he would do: Brooks disassociated himself from the film and took his name off the movie— which also meant he relinquished his points if the movie made money.

The "PG"-rated *Jeremy* was an international success; it won an award at the Cannes Film Festival, and I was nominated for a Golden Globe for 'Most Promising Newcomer.' The odd thing was that at the Cannes Film Festival press conference a man I never met told the press he was the writer/ director of the film, and that the movie was based on his life story. I arose from my seat and in front of the international press and blurted out (I couldn't help it— it was so wrong), "You're a liar. I've never met this man before. He didn't write the movie or direct it!" My response was exactly what the producer was gambling on— we became an instant manufactured press item and one of the big stories of Cannes that year. But I did get to go to the south of France with my girlfriend and co-star, and François Truffaut called us his "American Parfait!" Truffaut!

First love... A bond was formed between me and Glynnis, and even though we rarely see each other anymore, we are friends for life.

(Joe Brooks, who won an Oscar in 1978 for writing the song "You Light Up My Life," was indicted in 2009 on ninety-one counts of sexual misconduct when he was caught holding fake auditions for beautiful women.)

Valuable Life Lesson: I learned— I was a writer! I later got a 3-year deal as a writer at Universal. But seriously, what's up with these powerful men who get their sexual rocks off in such disgusting ways?

Francis Ford Coppola (Part I)

I WAS CAST BY FRANCIS FORD COPPOLA as Al Pacino's son, Anthony Corleone Jr. in **The Godfather Part II**. It was thrilling to be a part of one of the greatest movies of all time. I had one scene. The last scene of the movie. At the very end of the film when Al Pacino sits in a chair, alone on the lawn, looking out at Lake Tahoe, I would enter the scene and have a brief conversation with 'my father,' telling him that I didn't want to be a lawyer— I wanted to follow in his footsteps and be the next Godfather.

We shot the master (the wide shot that establishes geography) and the scene went beautifully. But when it was time to move in for coverage (tighter shots, singles, over-the-shoulders) it began to rain. Mr. Pacino and I went into a nearby truck to wait out the storm. We talked. I knew him from the days when he was in *Panic In Needle Park* and hung around the theater to be with Jill Clayburgh in *The Rothschilds*. He was a really good guy.

The rain lasted all day and finally the scene was rescheduled for the next day. When I went into the house that looked out over the lake, they were trying to get the scene where Fredo is shot in the rowboat on Lake Tahoe. As they were setting up, I heard a loud argument. Finally, out of the room in the house, came a frustrated Francis Ford Coppola, behaving as a son, not an Academy Award-winning director, saying, "Momma, will you please tell Daddy to leave me alone? It's my movie, not his!" Wow, I thought— this happens to everyone! We waited two more days for the light to be perfect in order to cover the final scene (it remained overcast and the beautiful light never returned), until the producers decided the cost would be in the millions if the company didn't make the move to the Cuba location. (Unfortunately, weather became a running theme with me and Mr. Coppola.)

I was told that the reshoots would happen in a matter of months and we'd pick up the scene then. Sometime later I received a call from Mr. Coppola telling me how sorry he was, but his worst nightmare would be to make a "Godfather Part III," so he found a way to end the movie without setting it up as a 'franchise' film. A powerful and introspective way to end the film: Al Pacino sits alone on the lawn of his compound... so alone...

I thought it was the right move. I was thrilled to be a part of the film, even if I never had the chance to shoot the entire scene. I still feel that way today. Disappointed, sure, but still honored.

Valuable Life Lesson: Always be a team player. Always do what is best for the project. *Always.*

DEATH BE NOT PROUD WAS A TOUGH SHOOT FOR A METHOD ACTOR— it took a lot out of me. I will always be grateful to director Donald Wrye. He fought the network executives who wanted another actor. Mr. Wrye went to the mat for me. He was as honest with me as any director I've ever had. When something didn't work, he came over and simply said, "I didn't believe you." My goal became to make every moment of my performance believable.

ARTHUR HILL · JANE ALEXANDER
ROBBY BENSON

DEATH *Be Not* **PROUD**

"*. . . simply magnificent . . .*"
— Sue Cameron, THE HOLLYWOOD REPORTER

I felt I owed that to John Gunther. The book was required reading for high school students across America. Even though I was a young guy who didn't understand my own medical problems, I felt a kinship with his journey. How he handled himself throughout his ordeal gave me an entrance into his battlefield, fighting to save his life.

Back in Philadelphia on the pre-Broadway tour for *The Rothschilds,* I ended up in the E.R. with excruciating headache pain. An inexperienced doctor told my parents it was probably a brain tumor— only to find out I had inherited classic migraines.

For the first time as an actor, in *Death Be Not Proud* I came face-to-face with a *true* story, a medical story that didn't have a happy ending. I felt so close to Johnny Gunther because he understood the 'darkness' yet tried with every ounce of his soul to embrace the life he had left.

This understanding (even if it was prefabricated on my part) allowed me to get deeper and deeper into the role until one day during the shoot, at a San Francisco hospital, when we broke for lunch, a security guard thought I was 'escaping from my room' (I was still in wardrobe and make-up) and I had to get a producer to tell the guard I was an actor and I only wanted to eat lunch with the rest of the crew. That gave me a great sense of confidence because a complete stranger believed I was deathly ill, yet I felt true shame when I looked back and saw a building full of sick people who weren't acting.

I also had to learn to play lacrosse for this film— and I remember my heart began to 'play tricks on me' during the filming of the lacrosse game. If you see the film and wonder why I'm so out of breath, I'm not acting...

When *Death Be Not Proud* screened in Los Angeles, I was totally unprepared for the response. As the film reached its climax and my character was triumphant even days before death, I heard... primal sounds coming from the audience. People were doing the best they could to stifle

cries and sobs. Two seats away, my mother (one of my toughest critics), finally burst into tears. At that moment I knew how powerful this medium could truly be.

Valuable Life Lesson: Live life to its fullest— and all jokes aside, there are some really good people in Hollywood.

DESPITE AN ALL-STAR CAST, with Gene Hackman, Liza Minnelli, and Burt Reynolds, **Lucky Lady** was one of Hollywood's biggest flops. (Fun fact: it was written by the people who gave us *Howard the Duck*.)

When I auditioned for Stanley Donen, the famous co-director of the classic film *Singing in the Rain*, he asked me how tall I was and I said, "Five eleven, sir." He walked out of the room saying, "If you stand up straight you'll find you're really six feet tall."

Why they wanted me for the part of the skipper of the "Lucky Lady" I'll never know. I was bald because my head had been shaved for *Death Be Not Proud* and I was far from a sailor. As a matter of fact, I was perpetually sea-sick for almost five straight months on the movie.

Mr. Donen wanted to shoot the entire film on the ocean rather then use a stage or miniatures for the battle scenes. The one battle scene, where my character gets killed— mowed down at point blank range by John Hillerman's character— and then falls straight down a metal flight of stairs on an oil tanker while bombs are exploding all around us, was my introduction to big time movie-making explosions.

Just off-camera, a stuntman was prepared to grab the muzzle of the machine gun aimed at me if it went above his hand— and spare me the painful misery of getting shot in the face with what we call full-load blanks. There are half-loads, quarter-loads— but for this, only three feet away from my face, someone wanted John Hillerman's machine gun to shoot full-loads. Full-loads — full-loads have killed people. I should've said something but it wasn't in my m.o. to make trouble, although I did think that the actual mechanics of this stunt were odd. I thought— hmmm... grab the machine gun if it goes above his hand? Won't that be a moment too late? I thought it, but never dared say it.

When the machine gun blasted me I felt warm blood from my upper lip, which was torn apart, flow down my face. At the same time, always acting (using it!) as my squibs went off (explosive charges inside my shirt filled with blood) I threw my 'dead body' down the metal flight of stairs, while the bombs and the heat from the explosions and fires were getting more and more intense.

Suddenly I realized my arm was on fire. I didn't break character or move as if I were alive— I 'flinched' from the pain of my arm being on fire, to which Stanley Donen exasperatedly yelled through his megaphone:

"Fuck! Cut it! The corpse moved! I can't believe it! The fucking corpse moved!"

I was very sorry and repentant, and had to have my lip sewn back together, too. As punishment, I was never allowed to take the speed boat back to base camp after a full day of filming on the ocean. No matter how sea-sick I was, Mr. Donen made me stay with the Lucky Lady and take the long sailboat ride home as he and the stars sped away in a motor boat. Finally, Burt Reynolds noticed how I was being treated and came to my defense. For the last month of shooting I was allowed to take the motor boat back to land with the other actors.

I was to be 'severely punished' by the production company for other *intentional* misbehavior. We had been without hot water for a whole week at the crew hotel— and I didn't believe the owner who claimed the entire city had no hot water. When I found out he was lying, it infuriated me— so I got naked and brought my 'Head and Shoulders' into the hotel swimming pool and took a nice warm bath to prove my point. Even though I got the hot water turned back on, no one was very happy with my stunt— or what I'd call my Right to Protest For Justice… or hot water.

The production company sent me to live in a one-room shack in the middle of the desert with no phone, no car, no TV (or radio). Burt Reynolds did ask if I wanted to stay at the mansion they rented for him, but I was such a loner and didn't ever want to be a problem for others, that I kept my mouth shut and stayed in a house three miles from civilization. I found out when I would be picked up for work when they sent a driver to shove a call sheet under my front door in the middle of the night. Burt did give me a radio. The American Armed Forces station became my only link to the outside world. When I would go into town for supplies I'd have to walk in the blazing sun jumping over scorpions and moving slowly away from rattlesnakes. It always felt like a longer walk back, laden down with more groceries than I could carry.

There were days on *Lucky Lady* where I became so ill that at night I would hallucinate, and my bed would be soaked from a high fever and vomit. I was sure they'd find me one day on the floor of the house in the middle of the desert, and to Stanley Donen's delight, 'the corpse wouldn't move.'

Valuable Life Lesson: Stick up for what you think is right, or learn to take cold showers. (I truly believed I was going to die on this film.)

ODE TO BILLY JOE REPRESENTED A TURNING POINT in my career and in my personal life. Max Baer Jr., who starred as Jethro in *The Beverly Hillbillies* and had written and acted in *Macon County Line,* had the idea of turning Bobbie Gentry's international hit song into a movie he would direct. Herman Rauscher *(Summer of '42)* wrote the script. I was cast in the title role. Baer auditioned and screen tested girl after girl for my love interest.

I did more than lobby for Glynnis O'Connor, I knew she'd be the perfect Bobbie Lee, but I also wanted a chance to get back together with her.

Glynnis had broken up with me a year earlier and I had not gotten over her... I think I discovered what real love meant when she told me she wanted to see other boys— because I understood and respected her wishes, and just wanted her to be happy. Now it was time to win her back.

Unfortunately, they put us up in a motel in Mississippi and Glynnis was given the room next to mine. When she spent the night with someone else, I could... hear. Everything. I began running 70 to 100 miles weekly on top of filming.

There was a clause in Glynnis' contract that she had to be under a certain weight or be fired. It was often over 100 degrees that summer and Glynnis would forego a glass of water, afraid she might put on weight. As per her contract, Max Baer had Glynnis weighed like a piece of meat every single day for the first two weeks of filming. When I couldn't stand the madness anymore, I went toe-to-toe with him, stood in front of Glynnis, and told him she was never going to be

weighed again or he would lose both of us. I made a friend for life, but never got my girlfriend back.

When the movie opened, we had an audience hit—and our stock in Hollywood was on the rise. I was happy for Glynnis, her performance, her boyfriends... But I was heartbroken, and foolishly punished myself by running and running in the smog-filled streets of L.A. to diminish the anguish.

Valuable Life Lesson: "If you love somebody, set them free."

I HAD THE HONOR OF WORKING WITH THE TEAM of George Schaefer (director), James Prideaux (playwright) and the incomparable Julie Harris in the public television production of **The Last Of Mrs. Lincoln**.

Before the rehearsal process was to begin, the actors sat around a table ready to read the two-hour version of the play. We had our manuscripts— thick, densely and beautifully written manuscripts— all open to page one. I glanced up at the remarkable talent, with Julie Harris appropriately sitting at the head of the table. George Schaefer rubbed his hands together and said, "Let's begin. Page one."

I noticed that Ms. Harris had not opened her manuscript. It just sat in front of her. Unopened. Closed. And she had what seemed like 75 percent of the dialogue in the play.

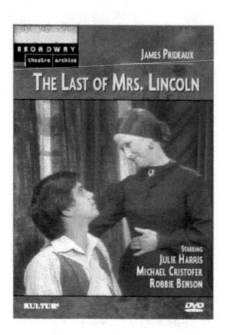

On Mr. Schaefer's command, Ms. Harris began. We all sat stunned— for two hours we read through the manuscript and Ms. Harris, the consummate pro, never once opened her script. Never once did she search for her lines. Never once did she falter, stutter, hunt for a sentence. She commanded the room, the group, the play— giving an astonishing performance, at times rising and 'playing the scene' at full speed.

When the read was over, Mr. Schaefer nodded mischievously, then gave us a five minute break. Mr. Schaefer, Ms. Harris and Mr. Prideaux gathered to discuss the play as the rest of us sat ashen. Ms. Harris had set the most exquisite precedent. The following day, none of us needed our manuscripts. We were all off book. 'Old school.'

One of the recurring themes in my career happened during this project. Hearing 'the call of the wild' (a basketball bouncing) at a playground the Sunday before we began shooting, I joined in a street game of basketball— I was always looking for the best ballplayers in L.A. I should have known better. As usual, because I could jump so high for a skinny white kid, I came down on someone's foot and snap— I broke my ankle. I was sure I had just eliminated myself from the play with Julie Harris, but when George Schaefer found out, he smiled and said, "Luckily, you're playing Tad Lincoln. He was a very sickly lad. I think I'll put you in a wheelchair." I did the entire play sitting in a wheelchair— and was not fired by Mr. Schaefer. This was the beginning of a wonderful friendship.

Valuable Life Lesson: You can never be too prepared. There may/will/should be someone who is more professional and prepared than you. 'Do your homework!' Oh, and stop playing basketball during productions. (I followed the first lesson to a "T." But I could never stay away from a basketball court— no matter what I was working on.)

IN *THE DEATH OF RICHIE*, the story has it that Richie is so out of control on drugs that his father eventually shoots and kills his own son. By this time I was as method as could be, but I refused to take any drug, not even an aspirin. At first, the director didn't believe that I had the rage in me to pull off the part, so I threw down my script and started acting with him. He seemed to be intrigued until I grabbed him, tore his shirt and threw him up against the wall. I got the part.

Eileen Brennan would play my mother; Academy Award-winning actor Rod Steiger was supposed to play my father (which is why I wanted the part so desperately), but the Friday before filming began Mr. Steiger had emergency open-heart surgery, and Ben Gazzara was hired in his place.

During the filming of *Richie* I found that if I starved myself and came to work dehydrated I could spin around and around right before the director called "Action" and be so sick and dizzy that I looked exactly like a drug addict (I also put Tabasco Sauce in my eyes to make them look red and bloodshot). But in one scene Ben Gazzara improvised— and punched me in the face. I felt the entire crew suddenly freeze. I stayed in character and finally the scene was over. The director asked for another take. I went to my mark and began my spinning routine and on "Action" the scene was off to another dynamic beginning. Once again, Mr. Gazzara threw a punch that landed squarely on my chin— this time almost knocking me out— but I stayed in the moment and finished the scene.

When the director asked for Take #3, a member of the crew stepped forward and said, "Mr. Gazarra, if you hit Robby one more time, you'll have to deal with me." And then another crew member stepped forward and said, "And me." "And me." "And me."

Valuable Life Lesson: Make friends with the crew. (And don't put Tabasco Sauce in your eyes.)

Francis Ford Coppola (Part II)

I MENTION **APOCALYPSE NOW** NOT ONLY because it was the second film I *didn't* make with Francis Ford Coppola, but because I went through an infamous audition— where the director and a camera operator went around the room filled with stars of all ages and had us improvise on the spot. I have never seen an audition held this way. Although he said he liked my work, Mr. Coppola told us the cast would be announced in a full-page ad in *Variety* and *The Hollywood Reporter*. I remember going to the news stand as if I was running to a bulletin board in school to see if I made the basketball team. And there was my name— I was going to be in *Apocalypse Now!*

For the usual insurance purposes, I was sent to see a doctor who was so concerned with the diseases we might catch in the Philippines that he didn't even listen to my heart. I did push-ups and sit-ups in his office as he was talking to me. I told him I couldn't allow even a moment to go by without getting more buff for the part. He looked at me like I was crazy (albeit in shape) and gave me vaccinations and horse pills for every possible disease, and malaria pills the size of Georgia. I spent what I thought was to be my last night in the U.S.A. with the gorgeous and gorgeous and did I say gorgeous Melanie Griffith, but I was so full of meds and anti-anything-Philippine pills that I 'couldn't perform' so we spent the night laughing ourselves to sleep. It was actually quite magical.

The next morning I awoke to the news that there had been a typhoon in the Philippines and all the sets were destroyed. Francis Ford Coppola's film would be delayed for months. But this time the weather was on my side...

One On One

I WAS NINETEEN, living in a 165 dollar a month apartment in Culver City where I sat at my small dining table and hand-wrote the first draft of **One On One** on a yellow legal pad. It was merely a year after my high school English teacher told me I would never amount to anything as a writer.

Luckily, she was wrong— but I hope every student who is told that they can't accomplish something by a teacher takes my story to heart. Because the next thing to happen was a phone call from my agent and friend, Rick Nicita, saying "Warner Brothers bought your script! They want to make *One On One.*" I remember looking down and realizing I was so excited I was standing on the table!

"**You're not big enough. You're not sharp enough. You'll never make it.**"

Did you ever want to make them eat their words?

Now there's a movie that does it for you.

One on One is the story of a kid nobody believed in except himself.

Discover

ONE ON ONE

The story of a winner.

LAMONT JOHNSON... ONE ON ONE
ROBBY BENSON · ANNETTE O'TOOLE · G.D. SPRADLIN ... ROBBY BENSON · JERRY SEGAL
MARTIN HORNSTEIN ... LAMONT JOHNSON ... CHARLES FOX ... PAUL WILLIAMS ... SEALS & CROFTS

I had to call my father, Jerry Segal, who was my co-writer. After the first few drafts, I realized it needed the help of a pro— and what could be better than to sell a script to Hollywood with your father as your partner? So we worked together, and my ideas coupled with his expertise and writing skills, resulted in a draft that was practically a shooting script.

Suddenly there was a real dilemma. I had been hired to be in *Apocalypse Now*, but this was my chance to make my own film. For the very first time in my career, I felt 'self-worth.' I was still a teenager, and now I was getting the opportunity to artistically express myself— to an audience of millions. And I got to play basketball too.

Rick made the deal: I would 'buy out' of my contract for *Apocalypse Now*. Unfortunately, Mr. Coppola was going through hell in the destructive typhoon weather of the Philippines and was quoted as saying "He is dead to me." Not exactly the way I wanted to leave things with one of the best directors in the film business... and someone I respected and liked as a man.

One On One was the first film to expose the inequities of the college sports system: how players are exploited and abused. I believe that if a player is going to take on the dual challenge of college studies and athletics— and perform like a circus animal in front of a stadium filled with 100,000 fans, and to millions of people watching on TV— these student athletes should get two things in return: they should benefit from the enormous income that is pouring into the school and the NCAA; and after their playing days are over they should have the right to return to college on a full scholarship to complete their degree. After unexpected injuries, these students can go from hero to has-been in a single tackle, rebound, or swing of the bat... They deserve a shot at success in life after sports.

We scoured L.A. and N.Y. for an actress to play Henry Steele's tutor and love interest. No one was right, at least not for me. Then Annette O'Toole walked into the office to read a scene with me. She was stunning— her acting was impeccable and her demeanor and presence was wistful yet never compromised the strength of the character she played. She was *perfect*.

But the studio and my director, Lamont Johnson, wanted to consider other names. I fought for the only actress I could ever see playing the part— and a big part of the success of *One On One* was her performance. I love it when pro ballplayers talk about the film. First they say: "There was some really good ball playing in that film;" then: "But that Annette O'Toole? Oh my God! Why couldn't I have had a tutor like her?"

We hired fantastic ballplayers; even at lunch we were playing ball. I had the idea to wear a helmet camera for the scene when Henry is high on uppers given to him by his roommate. Lo and behold, the director let me wear it and the footage was priceless. My father and I would sometimes do rewrites on the gym floor. I was in heaven— I was making a film and my dad was my partner. We had subverted the system! No big Hollywood writers or stars— just us. It was so rare at that time in the business. Every day I had to pinch myself— I was doing all of the things I loved to do, and sharing it all with my father.

One On One was a great shoot, but a physically demanding one. I also had to set an example for the other ballplayers who had never been in a film, so I was sprinting back to the number one position, ready for the next take without saying a word.

Wouldn't you know it— they followed me and we became a true team. I loved those guys. Our director, Lamont Johnson, was a crotchety guy who really knew what he was doing. I loved him like an uncle. I adored his wisdom, his experience. My nemesis in the film, G.D. Spradlin, stayed in character and nearly drove my dad and me crazy with his 'improvisations,' but he eventually read our dialogue as written, and his *dislikability* actually made him the perfect foil for me.

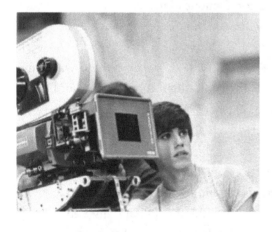

I had heard of a basketball team using ballet lessons to teach their ballplayers grace— to make them less clumsy, clunky and cumbersome on the court. This was a scene I couldn't pass up! So I took my dad and Lamont Johnson aside and we figured out how to shoot the team taking a ballet lesson— without our ballplayers being aware of what was going on. The 'ballet scene' works because it's spontaneous, and I cherish the honest and comic reactions of the athletes in our film.

When *One On One* first came out, we were placed in second and third-tier movie houses because Warner Bros. had two blockbusters in the best theaters: *Viva Knievel!* and *The Exorcist Part II*, starring Richard Burton and Louise Fletcher. I was in the limo with Ms. Fletcher (a wonderful actor, whom I later directed in the HBO series *Dream On*), piggy-backing the publicity for both our films, which opened on the same day in Dallas, Texas. We were silently reading our reviews. *One On One* received glowing reviews. *Exorcist II* was not only ripped to shreds, one review demanded that Louise Fletcher give back her Oscar for *One Flew Over The Cuckoo's Nest*. The scene in that car was a microcosm of the entire industry from an actor's point of view. I wasn't foolish enough to bask in my good reviews. I knew my day would come. No one is immune.

Because of their failure to attract audiences, both 'blockbusters' were pulled and Warner Bros. placed *One On One* in the best theaters all around the country. Our little film took off like a NASA rocket— ascending to heights far beyond studio expectations. We had a hit!

We were in Boston doing publicity for *One On One*, when I got a message that Red Auerbach (General Manager of the Celtics) wanted to meet me in his office. I was ecstatic. He told me he had never seen a basketball film before where the lead could actually *play*. Mr. Auerbach said he had an eagle eye for talent, and believed in my abilities to such an extent that he invited me to rookie camp. It was the most exciting thing that had ever happened to me.

Everyone thought I was insane to consider going to rookie camp with the Celtics— didn't I realize how lucky I was to be on a roll in the land of Hollywood? The next thing that happened was obvious: I got a film. To this day, missing that opportunity is one of my few regrets.

One of the hundreds of functions I had to attend was for the North American Theater Owners, who were giving me an award as 'Best New Talent' (a string of my films were making them a fortune). I was introduced to the man who ran all of the Loews Theaters. We were eating watermelon, and while the president of the theater chain was talking to me, I swallowed a watermelon seed and it went down my throat 'the wrong way.' My nose began to tickle and suddenly I had an unstoppable urge to sneeze. And I did. To everyone's horror, the seed shot out of my nose and landed on the president's plate. The liaison from Warner Bros. was apoplectic. The president of the Loews' Theater chain was at a loss for words— and I couldn't stop laughing as I apologized, over and over again. I started to think of my nose as a weapon. What else could I shoot out of my nose?

Fortunately, the watermelon seed didn't alter the business plan of the theater owner. People came to see our movie in droves. My father and I had done it. We beat the Hollywood odds! The bar was set... my career was about to jump to another level.

Could I?

Valuable Life Lesson: Like wardrobe that never comes off, never celebrate for more than ten minutes. Smile, but then get back to work, no matter what the triumph. In this business, do not believe your own press, good or bad. It's not real and it can be very painful. Stick to the work, the art and the passion to do it 'right'— the best you possibly can. It's the only way to survive. It's the work that counts— not the pontification that follows.

And always turn your head when you sneeze. Who knows what projectile might come firing out of your nostril! Even if I never did anything else in my life, I had accomplished something special and had shared it with my father.

The Audition and the Reality Check

THE REBOUND FROM *ONE ON ONE* WAS SO FAST it became a life lesson for me: I was now a true star in the business, but that also meant that some people might not want their film to become a "Robby Benson Movie." Case in point: *The King of the Gypsies.*

In February of 1977, New York City was hit with a wild, gorgeous and powerful snowstorm. I woke up to a city that had been completely shut down. The only problem was that in a few hours, I had a huge audition for the lead in *King of the Gypsies*. The role had come down to two actors: me, and a young Eric Roberts. They were looking for someone 'authentic,' someone who understood the life of a gypsy— someone who had experienced, as they put it, 'a lot of shit in their lives.' The word was, I was too 'soft'— an adjective I would deal with for my entire acting career. (Another: I was 'squeaky clean.' Well, at least I didn't smell... even though I did stink in a few films.)

This was the very first time a studio executive said "We just don't want it to be another Robby Benson Movie."

There was nothing I could do about being Robby Benson. But the perception of me as soft was completely wrong. I was tougher than anyone I knew— I just... had passion and was a romantic, too. Did I go out drinking with the boys after the game? No. I got ready and stronger for the next game. Was I intensively competitive? Yes. I was the boy next door, but *not* the boy next door who took heroin. I'd have to prove them wrong.

According to my agent, who I woke up in LA, the audition was still on even though the city was a frozen ghost town. There were no taxis, no buses, no subways running— nothing. Just new snow everywhere.

The audition was being held in a hotel on 60th street near Broadway where the director was staying, along with his co-producers. I had to make it there by noon and I'd have to walk from 70th and West End Avenue. They told my agent they didn't think I could make it. I looked down upon the city from my parents' living room windows; it was desolate and oh-so beautiful. But I had to toughen up— forget the beauty, I thought, and get into 'the gypsy.' (What the hell does that mean?)

I called my agent back and told him, "I'll be there. Nothing can stop me. Certainly not a little snowstorm." Now that was gypsy-like, dammit!

"But Robby, the city is shut down. No one is expecting you to be there. It's impossible."

"Impossible?" I laughed with a deep, Beastly set of macho-balls, "I'll get there *early!*" and hung up. Who did they think I was?

I dressed in a tacky 'gypsy-like' faux silk shirt with most of the buttons undone to show my macho, gypsy hairless chest. As I was leaving the apartment my mom, an actress, just looked at me and shook her head, "Are you sure you don't want a jacket? You could always take it off in the lobby of the hotel before you go upstairs to the director's room." I looked at her with a Scorsese *Mean Streets* affectation and said, "They don't think I can get there. Ha! Fuck 'em! Um... no offense mom. I didn't mean to curse."

And off I went, out into the wild, white gypsy yonder. There were drifts that covered an entire #104 bus. The snow was magnificent. I tried to tell myself it wasn't beautiful: 'Beautiful' couldn't be in my gypsy vocabulary. Fuck the snow! I was a tough guy! A gypsy! (Actually, it was hypnotic, otherworldly— absolutely the most beautiful and awesome sight) Fuck it! Shut-up! I had to be in character. A gypsy, dammit.

What a bunch of shit. A few lousy snowflakes and these pussies don't think I can get there? (I hate the word 'pussy.' I hope it's not in the script.)

Wait— are they actually challenging ⎍⎍⎍⎍⎍⎍⎍ my testosterone? (Man, it's gorgeous...) Thinking I can't make it ten lousy blocks? And *I'm* soft? They're probably ordering room service and eating poached eggs while I walk like a gypsy with an open shirt and no jacket to their hotel. They want macho?

I'll give 'em macho... (Man, this snow is incredible... I can't allow myself to forget what this looks like! I'll take a picture in my mind. It probably only happens once in a lifetime!) Fuckin' shut-up!

I made it to the hotel. It impressed them that I arrived early. But I was shaking and some thought I had frostbite. "Frostbite? Fuck it. Let's audition."

As I walked home, which was much less romantic because the city was beginning to come to life and some of the pure white snow already was layered with a blackish-gray New York City soot, I wished I had a jacket. The charade was over and now I wasn't so gypsy-like. I was an actor who didn't want to freeze to death, and what the hell— I *like* beauty. (Don't tell anyone, but I'm glad I'm not a heroin addict.)

As soon as I got back to the apartment, my freezing gypsy-macho self was sipping hot chocolate with mini-marshmallows. It was impossible for me not to notice that my heart was racing. I could barely speak because each word was interrupted with a fluttering heartbeat. I stealthily put my hand to the pulse on my neck and realized, doing the math, my heart was pounding over 200 beats per minute. (Take your pulse for 10 seconds; take that number and multiply it by 6 and you'll get your standing heart rate.)

My mom asked me what was wrong, and I was honest about one thing, "I don't think I'm authentic enough for this part. I'm not... gypsy-like. I heard Eric Roberts told them to 'go screw themselves' and didn't even bother to come to the audition. That's the attitude they're looking for... I'd never do that. It's unprofessional."

It only took a few hours for Los Angeles to get the news and relay it back to me: "The part's going to Eric Roberts. He's had a tough life. Family, drugs. You're just too *soft*, Robby."

"But I went to the audition— he didn't!"

"Exactly." (Huh?)

My heart raced at 200 beats per minute for six hours before it finally decided (like an on/off switch) to go back to 50 beats a minute. Too soft? Let's see Eric Roberts' heart beat at 200 beats per minute and give a performance that wouldn't frighten the people he loved.

I had to calm down. I needed to 'see' beautiful things. My heart was becoming a very real issue in everything I did. How long could I hide it from everyone? How long could I follow the advice of old pros like John Marley who warned, "If you ever have a problem with your heart, don't let these show biz bastards know— or you'll *never* work again."

Thornton Wilder's Pulitzer prize and Emmy Award winning play is brought to the screen by Hal Holbrook, Barbara Bel Geddes, John Houseman, Robby Benson, Ronny Cox and Sada Thompson. Here is the full poignant portrayal of love, life and death in a small American town that has brought pleasure to millions.

DRAMA   111

THORTON WILDER'S OUR TOWN

GEORGE SCHAEFER, WITH WHOM I HAD A WONDERFUL EXPERIENCE on *The Last of Mrs. Lincoln,* wanted to shoot the definitive version of Thornton Wilder's **Our Town** for television.

The cast would feature some terrific stage actors, including Sada Thompson and the great Hal Holbrook (who I later directed in *Evening Shade*). And it was another chance to work with Glynnis O'Connor. Maybe now we could be more than 'just friends'...

In a letter that Mr. Schaefer sent to the cast, he told us that we were to show up on day one having memorized the version of *Our Town* that Thornton Wilder was most proud. We all did.

From that day on, it was nothing but work... along with a slight hope that Glynnis might get back together with me again. But this was the definitive 'No.' I took it like a man. I cried.

I WAS REHEARSING THE PRE-BROADWAY MUSICAL *King of Hearts* when I got a call from my friend, Burt Reynolds, asking me to do a bit part in his film, **The End**.

I asked Burt, who was also directing, if I could come up with a few bits for my character, Father Dave— one of them being that the young priest is so enthralled hearing Burt's sins in the confessional that he takes off his collar and starts playing with it, nervously, making clicking sounds with the plastic against his teeth.

It worked, and Burt allowed me to 'do my thing.' A great guy, a wonderful friend and a very good director.

I went back east to the production of *King of Hearts* only to be informed that the director (Tony Award winner A.J. Antoon), and the playwright (Steve Tesich, who would win an Academy Award for *Breaking Away*) had been fired. They were the reason I was there in the first place, and they were my *friends*. So I followed suit, walked into the producer's office, and resigned. Joe Kipness was furious with me; he said he would ruin my career and actually threatened my life. I resigned anyway. Then he trashed me in the press, saying I'd been fired.

BECAUSE I WAS VERY SHY IN PERSON (even a bit backwards) I often seemed antisocial without wanting to be. I just didn't know how to interact with people unless I was working. But now that my career in films was taking off, the talk shows wanted me— and somehow (maybe because it was 'work') I had no problem with *that* human interaction. In my own way, I could be a pretty funny raconteur.

My first big show on national television was an interview with Barbara Walters on *The Today Show*. I did the local talk shows and was a regular on *Good Morning America*, *The Today Show* and *CBS This Morning* with every new film release. I even sang an original song from a film on *American Bandstand* hosted by Dick Clark.

If I were counting how many appearances I made on certain shows, *The Merv Griffin Show* would be in the double digits. The same for *The Mike Douglas Show,* including co-hosting for a week, and Regis with many different co-hosts over the years. And of course the pinnacle of late-night talk, *The Tonight Show with Johnny Carson.*

I had begun to do solo concerts on both coasts— in L.A. at the Troubador and the Roxy, and in New York at Reno Sweeney's. So when I appeared on talk shows to promote my latest movie, I was asked to perform. On most of these shows I would sing songs I wrote with Jerry Segal, my father.

When Burt Reynolds was hosting *The Tonight Show* (Johnny Carson and NBC loved it when Burt guest-hosted), he called to ask if I would be one of his guests and bring my guitar and sing "Mr. Weinstein's Barber Shop." Burt surprised me when we were on the air, by telling America about my ability to do sit-ups— into the thousands.

When we were working on *Lucky Lady* I looked skinny and frail in my wardrobe, not like the gym rat I actually was. Burt knew the amount of a sit-ups I could do without stopping and got a great idea: he would bet the stuntmen, and finally Gene Hackman, I could do more sit-ups than the best stuntman on the film. (That part was easy) But he kept getting more and more mischievous by placing bets saying, "I'll bet he can do... 1,000 sit-ups without stopping," and the dollar amount would go up. Then he would add, "Well, I'll bet you he can do 2,000 sit-ups without stopping." And the dollars began to skyrocket. He got the betting up to 3,500 sit-ups and the money on the table was probably close to 10 grand.

I did the sit-ups (somewhere in the 2,000's Gene Hackman realized he'd been scammed), Burt made a ton of money, and we were a 'team.' Kind of like being carnival hucksters.

That evening on *The Tonight Show*, Burt not only told the story, he told America and the studio audience that I could still do as many as he had ever seen without stopping. I was on the spot: national television and didn't want to disappoint my buddy, so I got on the floor and began doing sit-ups. The *Tonight Show* audience was amazed as they counted with each sit-up. When Burt threw the show to commercial I thought I could stop, but he wanted the gag to *continue*, so when they came back from commercial, I was *still* doing sit-ups and the audience was *still* counting.

Finally Burt stopped me and said, "Okay Robby— now go and sing my favorite song."

I walked over to the band area (thinking: 'Don't pass out') and picked up my guitar to sing 'Mr. Weinstein's Barber Shop.' As the song began, I couldn't catch my breath, and my abs were wildly spazing out. I somehow managed to sing— giving maybe my best performance of the song.

Valuable Life Lesson: Focus. Old fashioned focus. I had learned from so many remarkable pros (Burt being one) how to perform through pain and exhaustion.

ICE CASTLES

Robby Benson   Colleen Dewhurst   Tom Skerritt

When Tragedy Struck
Love Came to the Rescue.

PAYBACK TIME. Director Donald Wrye called saying he wanted to make *Ice Castles,* a film about a beautiful ice skater who has an accident and goes blind, but continues to compete— and no one knows she's blind.

I laughed and said, "You're kidding, right?" Silence...

He wanted me to play the love interest and there was no way I could say 'no' to my friend. It was one of the most absurd stories I had ever heard, yet it hit home to a generation of young girls— so I guess Donald Wrye and the studio knew what they were doing.

Never having skated before, I had to prep to be convincing in the hockey scenes. I worked with terrific taskmaster Barbara Williams, speed skating coach for the Stanley Cup New York Islanders.

The Islanders took to me as brethren— they liked the way I'd get up from a 'hit' and was ready to fight back. I just got up off the ice and took a run at the guy who knocked me down. No finesse here, but I learned enough to pull it off.

It was tough physically. I injured my hip filming a scene on the ice. At the hospital the doctor took X-rays and told me my hip was broken, and then asked when I had broken my other hip, as it had been fractured as well and had healed poorly. "Oh...um, well... can I go?"

Filming in the dead of winter in Minnesota, the only time to get the chill out of my body was at night, but now I had to sleep with bags of ice taped around my fractured hip to keep the swelling down so I could fit into my wardrobe. More and more ice.

To get my mind off the agony of the pain, I turned on the local 10 o'clock news and saw a scene of chaos and young women screaming, "I touched him! I touched him!" I thought, 'Cool. I wonder who's in town?' Then they showed a picture of me. 'Me? No way. Me? They're *crying*.' In my entire career I had no manager, no publicity firm, no assistants, no entourage. I was a solitary journeyman actor doing a job I loved. I never realized I was... affecting people. If I was affecting people, then a

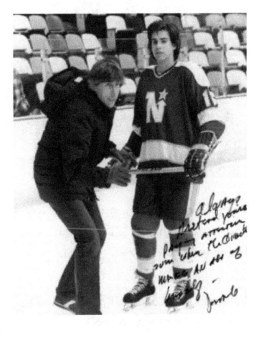

responsibility came with that ambiguous power.

For the last shot of the film, at the ice arena, I told the producers I would sign autographs for whomever came and donated their time to be in the crowd. They told me it could be up to 8,000 girls. I said fine, print 8,000 8x10 pictures and get me a lot of Sharpies. But first we had to shoot the scene. There were police and hired security, and the girls were screaming and breaking through the barriers. The producers were afraid for my safety. I said, "Take the police and the guards away."

"Are you kidding? They'll tear you apart."

"No, they won't. I think the barriers, the guards and the police are *causing*— no, allowing them to behave this way. Trust me."

The screaming stopped when I came out of my trailer alone and quietly said, "Thank you all for helping us with the movie. If you want a signed picture, I'll stay as long as it takes when we're done today to personally sign any and all pictures that you want. But right now, I need to go to work. Thank you."

Respect. Decency. The crowd was immediately well-behaved, went to their seats, and Lynn Holly Johnson (a U.S. National figure skating medalist) and I shot the 'We forgot about the flowers' scene.

After filming, I stayed until 2 a.m.— when the last young woman had her autograph. My hip was killing me, we were doing 'spring' scenes in the bitter cold (so we would wear next to nothing), and my heart never allowed me to forget that it wasn't happy. It fluttered throughout that movie.

Valuable Life Lesson: I'm not a skater. And: treat people with respect and they'll treat you with respect.

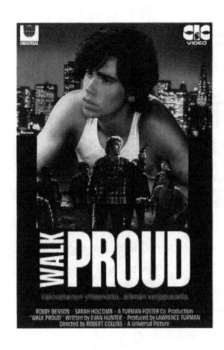

WALK PROUD WAS SCRIPTED BY EVAN HUNTER, the writer of the classic film *The Blackboard Jungle*. There was a huge uproar from the Chicano community and the liberal left— which I thought I was a part of, not a target of— over my casting as a young Chicano Gang member.

I thought, 'We're actors. The job of an actor is to become someone he's not. Why is everyone so pissed?' Well, because I was a white guy putting in brown contact lenses, taking a part away from a Chicano actor.

I would never take that part today, but at the time, my agent, the studio and the producers kept telling me almost every other role in the film was being played by Chicanos and "Gang" (the film's original title) would not be made unless I agreed to star. So I was a bit ...confused.

My fellow actors, Pepe Serna, Domingo Ambriz, and Trinidad Silva, treated me as a brother. We'd sit for hours going over dialogue. Pepe took me under his wing and made sure I was using the best accent possible.

The producers hired real L.A. gang members as advisors, but that only made the rival gangs more angry. On our first night-shoot in Venice, we were on a dinner break when I heard popping sounds. Still standing holding my dinner tray I wondered why everyone, including the security guards and cops, were hiding under the tables. Later we found out one of our gang contacts was shot and killed.

I learned two things quickly on *Walk Proud*: real gunfire doesn't sound anything like the stuff we see in movies, and don't be stupid— hit the deck and hide like everyone else with every drive-by shooting or old car backfiring.

One of the honey-wagon drivers (honey-wagons are the long trucks with dressing rooms attached) had been asking me to sign a lot of head shots. He said he wanted to give the fans my photo, and it seemed to make everyone very happy. I was furious when I found out he was bartering for blow-jobs from underage girls using my autographed picture as bait. I told the cops. The guy was arrested.

When the movie previewed the scores were very good for the film, but not so good for the musical score. The producers liked the two songs I had written with lyricist Jerry Segal for the film, and asked if I would like to score the entire picture. I had written temp scores for films in the past, so I jumped at the opportunity. The catch was: it had to be finished in one week. I'd have to work 24/7 until I could walk onto the scoring stage with an orchestra and deliver a full score. It was a great learning experience.

Because of violence at the opening of *The Warriors*, another gang-related film, the release date was held up. *Walk Proud* finally opened— to a favorable review in *The New York Times*— but all in all, except for my friendships, this film was a disappointment.

Valuable Life Lesson: Duck, stupid.

(As Karla so aptly states: "Man is stupid.")

Why? What's wrong with us?
Okay— me.

I was 20 years old and in remarkable physical shape...

...except I couldn't breathe.

This contradiction would make the paradox finally come to a 'deadly' moment on the film **Die Laughing**.

JON PETERS PUT THIS FILM TOGETHER with a charm that negated every story I had ever heard about him. His first film had been the blockbuster remake of *A Star Is Born,* and he was well on his way to becoming a notorious studio mogul.

I met him at his home in Malibu, and when I knocked on the door, Barbra Streisand (who is much smaller than you would expect) opened it, smiled, and said "Hi, Robby. I'm Barbra." After she took me to Peters, she brought us a tray of cookies while we talked.

Peters wanted me to star in the film he was developing, which had a very troubled script. If I signed on, the film would be green-lighted. He wooed me with the offer of co-producing and bringing in my father to work with me on a page-one rewrite. We all agreed.

A few weeks later, when my father had a heart 'episode' on a Friday and went to the emergency room, a cold, dispassionate Peters informed us that if he didn't see my dad and me working at the studio on Saturday he would pull the script from us. So *this* is the Jon Peters everyone was talking about— Hollywood at its worst.

My dad and I should've pulled out of the film on the spot. But we didn't discuss it because we each thought it was a great opportunity for the other. Father and son— what could be better?

When we were a few days behind in filming (because our director hadn't a clue how to direct, just edit Ms. Streisand's music videos), the most professional man on the set, our cinematographer, was fired— even though I lobbied and made every phone call I could begging them to keep the pros and get rid of the amateurs.

I still have visions of Jon Peters and the director tearing pages out of the script, crumpling them up and throwing them onto the street. Peters did everything he could to drive a wedge between me and my father and almost succeeded. He even banned my father from the set. I called my agent to tell him I wanted out, but he said I'd be sued for millions and be blackballed from the business if I abandoned the production.

There came a time when Jon Peters was playing so many cruel head games with me that I'd have to find private places near the set, a closet, an empty toilet, to literally break down. Sometimes I'd cry; sometimes I'd just punch the wall; sometimes I'd twitch uncontrollably and sometimes I'd freeze and stay in a mental limbo until I heard someone yelling my name to come back to to the set. I had absolutely no one to talk to.

When I wasn't having a private nervous breakdown on the set (then getting my act together so no one saw me weak), I'd come home from work and I'd run and run, just like I'd been doing for most of my life. Only during this film, it was the hills of San Francisco and I'd run until I'd vomit and couldn't take another step. I didn't know it was my heart that was causing me to vomit, I just thought I was in a living hell. But what else could I do? My fighting spirit took over, and I decided I had to do everything in my power to make the best film possible under the circumstances. It almost killed me.

One day, my job as an actor was to simply carry a wooden box with a monkey in it and sprint up a very steep street, running as fast as I could. The intent: my character had to get away from the cops. After running the hill, I would then turn the corner, which would signify the end of the shot, followed by the loud yell of 'Cut!' On 'Action!' (a command that brings a great deal of power and permission, no matter how meek the decibel or directive), I sprinted up the hill. 50 yards. 100 yards. I began to falter... even I believed in the fantasy of my Hollywood abs more than my mortal lungs and heart. I was becoming more and more oxygen deprived. On take three, my goal became simpler: merely run up the hill and 'make it around that corner... come on, man, just make it around the corner...'

I began to black out, but until I disappeared around the corner, I kept thinking, 'Don't ruin the shot! Whatever you do, don't ruin the shot!' As my world began to spin, I made sure the monkey and the prop-box were safely on the sidewalk, then grabbed the first thing I could find to stop my fall— a parking meter. Sliding down the meter, I vomited. The trained voice in my head said, 'Good: you didn't ruin the shot, you didn't hurt the monkey, and the prop box is safe. You did your job. I now give you permission to blackout.'

I stopped myself. 'Wait. Where is the Second A.D.? He should be standing with a walkie-talkie right where I'm passing out. It's his job to be here!' (Forget about blacking out— we're talking professionalism; somebody could steal the monkey!) 'He needs to take care of the monkey, the prop box and clear pedestrians so no one ruins the shot,' was my last thought.

As the blackness lifted in corneal sparkles, and dark spots littered my vision, I was at eye level with the sidewalk (nice looking sidewalk...). I saw my own vomit (pizza...). I still could not lift my head, but a pair of shoes entered my sight line. The Second A.D. at last?

"Can I have your autograph, Mr. Benson?" a strange voice asked. I could not speak. I did the only thing my motor function could handle: I signed my autograph.

Watching his sneakers leave, I heard the guy say, "Robby Benson! This is so cool. I can't wait to show my mother!" Then I heard, "Was he nice?" coming from a young female. "No," the guy quickly answered. "He didn't even look at me. One of those stuck-up Hollywood assholes."

Huh? Me? Well... I tried; I wrote my name. I couldn't look up— I couldn't lift my head. An asshole? Why?

Throughout my entire career my fans have been very considerate, compassionate people. But there is always... an exception.

FAN ALERT

- Stay alert for hard-hit foul balls and bats that might leave the field of play.
- ALL fans assume all risks and dangers incidental to the game.

By the time the Second A.D. came, I was able to stand. When he asked me if I was okay, I told him I had food poisoning and asked if we got the shot.

"Perfect," he smiled.

'Perfect,' I thought. 'See? I *can* control my destiny,' I told myself. *My career is safe!*

A few days later, we were shooting a scene on an oil tanker in the San Francisco Bay. The shot required a few stuntmen to jump about 40 feet off the tanker into the Bay. One stuntman balked. He said he didn't think the stunt was safe and told the director he wouldn't do the jump. 'Are you kidding,' I thought. Since I was co-producing the picture, and we needed the shot, I turned to him and said, "Take off your clothes."

"Huh?"

"Take off your clothes. Let's switch. I'll do the jump."

And I did. In street clothes and wearing boots, I jumped over 40 feet— which seemed to be an eternity. The water was freezing and the waves were huge; the current was powerful and I began to sink. I should've drowned. Sheer will got me to the awaiting tug boat. But maybe... just maybe... I didn't want to make it to the tug boat. I look back and think of how selfish that last thought is— but as a very young man, with all this responsibility, whose father was humiliated by Jon Peters, I was completely alone and powerless to help the ones I loved. I only knew large choices, and death seemed like an option. I would do battle with this demon again. (And again...)

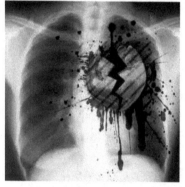

Valuable Life Lesson: Never, ever work for Jon Peters.

Attitude

Growing up, I was taught to 'Never give up. Never. Ever.' It's a very healthy attitude. For every job I got, I'll take a wild guess and say there were a hundred rejections in between. That's actually a pretty decent batting average. And since I'm using baseball, I've been up at the plate, 3 and 2, 2 outs, bottom of the 9th, the bases loaded and we were down by three runs. The next pitch came and was in my sweet spot. I launched it over the centerfield fence for a grand slam and we won a game we should've lost. 'Never give up.'

On the set or in the theater, attitude is contagious. A bad attitude can move through a show or a film like the plague. So attitude is something we should constantly do an internal check-up on— and make adjustments. The beautiful thing about an attitude change can be likened to the words, 'Cut!' and 'Action!' If the take was horrible, a new reality can begin with the next take when they call 'Action!' just moments later.

In other words, our attitude can change with a blink of the eye. It's up to us. I awaken, I feel grumpy, I realize I'm lucky to be alive and I kiss Karla— my attitude has just done a 180 in a matter of seconds.

But if you realize that you cannot change your attitude— if you come to the conclusion that you don't even *care* if you change your attitude— if you find yourself unable to jump-start any change in your attitude, you've got a serious problem and you should seek help.

My heart problems had me jumping through 'mental hoops' lined with barbed wire. This grief and torment is just as potent to a young guy who writes and acts for a living as someone who works in a law firm, a construction worker, a college student— anyone. It doesn't matter. If you have heart problems, we're on the same team.

I was the dummy who finally had to be hit with a 2x4 in order to face the fact that I was ill, that my heart was failing me, and it was healthy to find out why— and fix the problem. This is when I realized my situation. This is *not* when I chose to deal with it.

Denial

My behavior was the perfect example of denial. Looking back, I was totally irresponsible for not getting myself to a doctor. I thought I could *control* time and space— which is what any good filmmaker is taught to do; we create false realities that are very real to us. I naively believed my own fiction, living within my own reality, my movie star 'celluloid aspect ratio.'

Not one person knew the hell I was going through, so no one ever questioned my health. I needed help and was too proud, macho and *scared* to get it. Even when the warning signs were obvious, I foolishly believed I could control my own destiny.

I was fine. Mission accomplished. *Denial. Soft? Kiss my ass.*

The Slave Of Duty

***TRIBUTE* SHOULD HAVE BEEN** a wonderful film. Academy Award-winning actor Jack Lemmon was reprising his Tony-nominated role in Bernard Slade's play, and the cast included Lee Remick, Colleen Dewhurst and my old friend John Marley. Instead…

We shot the film in Toronto in the dead of winter. I worked out every single day at the local YMCA. The night before principal photography began I broke my ankle playing basketball. (Yup.) I tried to limp back to the hotel in the below zero weather. Not a single taxi cab would pick me up— hobbling, it looked like I was delirious and on drugs. I then had to crawl for more than a half a mile. I finally got a cab at my hotel to take me to the emergency room. Before my call-time for the first day of shooting (6:30 a.m.) I was leaving the hospital with the thinest cast that I could beg the doctor to put on my foot.

I went through the entire filming of *Tribute* with a broken ankle, no pain meds (still didn't believe in them), and only one person knew: the wardrobe mistress who modified my pants and shoes.

I was playing Jack Lemmon's estranged son— a very unsympathetic character with many affectations. And I did something foolish; I played the entire movie aiming at the one scene where you can 'see and understand' why this young man behaved so prudishly. It was a risk, but this pivotal scene would reveal my character's true feelings. When we shot that scene, I felt it was the best work I had ever done.

When I got back to Los Angeles, I received a phone call from Sherry Lansing, the President of 20th Century Fox, telling me she was overwhelmed with my performance and to expect an Oscar nomination.

What neither Ms. Lansing nor I expected was Jack Lemmon demanding my scene be dropped from the film. Without it my performance was... inexplicable.

To his credit, Mr. Lemmon called me and said that he owed me an apology. He explained that he had to take the scene out because it made my character more sympathetic than his, and undermined his performance.

He told me, "One day, when you've been around the block as many times as I have kiddo, you'll understand."

Funny thing— I understood immediately. But I can't watch the movie to this day. I understand, but I can't watch. It's a heartbreaker.

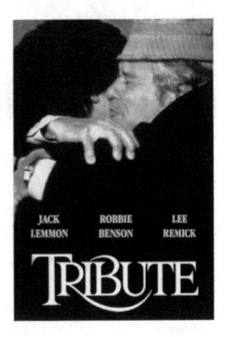

Valuable Life Lesson: Never believe the hype. And make sure they spell your name correctly. ("Robby," not "Robbie.") Another day, another indignity...

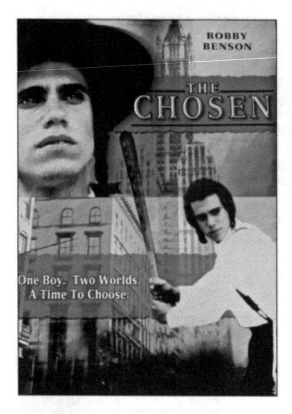

THE CHOSEN, CHAIM POTOK'S PERCEPTIVE NOVEL about two young friends, one Hasidic, the other a secular Jew, set in Brooklyn just after World War II, was my next film project.

The producers, Edie and Ely Landau, and director Jeremy Kagan offered me the part of Reuven, but I turned it down. I wanted the challenge of playing Daniel, the ultra-Orthodox boy brought up 'in silence.' The creative team agreed, and I finally got to work with Rod Steiger (healthy since his open-heart surgery three years earlier), who would play my father. Rod Steiger. Yes!

During filming, Mr. Steiger confided to me how the industry treated him after his open-heart surgery. "Death, kiddo. Death. I couldn't get arrested. Never tell anyone if you've got heart problems, kid. Never."

This resonated with me more than ever, now. I was really having ...symptoms.

Working on The Chosen became a challenge. A very talented but majestically selfish actor, Barry Miller, was supposed to be my best friend in the film. But Barry overwhelmed the set— he was so needy that nothing happened unless Barry was 'okay with it.' This isn't an exaggeration. The crew had a pool going— odds were set for 'Who would be the first person to punch Barry Miller in the face?' I was 2-1. Rod Steiger was even money. Even the great Maximilian Schell was 3-1. As fate would have it, Barry was taken down by a female Teamster who won over 500 dollars.

I did my final close-ups in the film, where I'm going off to college, to a piece of tape on the wall, rather than to his face. Not an unusual situation on a film, but a sad and avoidable one in this case. Fortunately, the magic of celluloid only showed us as the closest of friends.

Early one stifling New York summer morning, I was wearing heavy flannel Hasidic garb. As I sat in the make-up chair, 'picking my spots' when to gasp for that primal, fulfilling gulp of oxygen— which at best, would only be partially satisfying— trying to conceal my physical discomfort, the make-up man questioned me.

"Is there something wrong, Robby?"

"What do you mean?" I hesitated, and then looked deep into his eyes, reflected in the make-up mirror. Had I been 'caught?' Being caught would mean I wasn't *insurable*.

"You've been behaving like... Barry! Are you exasperated with

me?" the make-up man finally blurted out.

"Oh no, it's not you— I'm just a little tired. I'm so sorry."

Before every film, actors and directors have to take physicals in order for the studio to get *insurance*. Fortunately, the kind old doctors who did all the studio physicals liked me. We would talk, tell jokes, and I usually never had to take off my shirt. The toughest part of the insurance check-up was saying 'Ahhhh.' Not being insurable would mean I could no longer act in films. Not being able to do what I loved also meant not providing for my family, my future; everything I dreamed of doing in my life. Then what?

There was the cold reality that I didn't know how to do anything else! If I couldn't get past the make-up man, who was I really fooling?

I looked up, straightened my pious peyos and said, "L'chaim!" with confidence. "Don't worry, I'm as strong as a bull."

Bull...

And then I furtively gasped for air.

SOME OF MY BEST ACTING was hiding the fact that I couldn't breathe. After all, *The Chosen,* our small, beautifully directed independent film, beat *Schindler's List* and *Fiddler on the Roof* as 'The Greatest Jewish Movie Ever Made.'

(At least according to this book— I must've fooled someone!)

Broadway:

IN THE SPRING OF 1980, I HAD THE GOOD FORTUNE of being asked by Joseph Papp to play the role of Frederic in the New York Shakespeare Festival production of **The Pirates of Penzance** in Central Park. I had to decline because I was about to start the film *The Chosen*. But less than a year later, when the hundred-year-old operetta was a Broadway hit (about to be nominated for seven Tonys), he asked me again.

I had always originated parts and never considered replacing anyone in a Broadway show (honestly, I was a bit of a snob when it came to that)   but I was in New York with no more press to do for the special screening of *The Chosen* the following night.

As a kid I had always dreamed of seeing a movie I starred in projected onto the mammoth 3-story screen at Radio City Music Hall. By pure luck, the huge event for Israel's 33rd birthday included the premiere of *The Chosen* at Radio City. It was a dream come true.

I brought my dear friend from high school, Carleen Hussung, to the screening. When I was off doing films, she would take copious notes and help me study for tests. She was (and is) smarter than I am. But because I had a photographic memory, I could retain entire scripts and all the notes from biology, math and French, and therefore aced my exams. I was valedictorian based on test scores, but she's the one who deserved that honor, not me.

MY AGENT AND FRIEND Rick Nicita had told me, "Do - not - do - 'Pirates.' They'll forget you in Hollywood if you take over a role in New York. Hollywood has amnesia!"

My film career was very healthy and my agent was basically telling me the age-old story: I would blow all of the momentum I had worked so hard to achieve. At that time I had a three-year deal at Universal as a screenwriter— extremely rare for someone my age. 'Let's get real,' I thought— how could I sing eight shows a week without being able to *breathe*? Especially since the role of Frederic (the 'Slave of Duty') was the vocal workhorse of the show. And, a tenor. I'm a baritone, now.

So mischievously, with a night free, I asked Mr. Papp if I could see the show that was the hottest ticket on Broadway. I still had no intention of doing *Pirates*, but I wanted to see what all the fuss was about.

Well, 'the fuss' was about two of the best hours of entertainment I had ever witnessed, mainly because of Kevin Kline's performance as the Pirate King, Graciela Daniele's remarkable choreography, and a wonderful cast. But as the evening progressed, the young man who played the 'Slave of Duty' wasn't 'fitting into the show.' He had the voice of a Tenor God, but lost his character and was *competing* with the Pirate King when he should have been supporting him.

My father, who wrote jokes for some of the best comedians in the business, taught me there is an unwritten rule in comedy: there is the 'set-up' guy, and then the person who 'delivers the blow.' There are endless examples (in business and sports); basically, the set-up guy has a thankless job but should take great pleasure in getting the alpha comic a bigger laugh. If you weren't born with this understanding, then someone had better teach it to you. **EDUCATION IS OUR 1st PRIORITY** It's an art form. Think of the hallowed halls of comedy history: George Burns and Gracie Allen, Laurel and Hardy, Abbott and Costello. One nurtures the other and lobs the set-ups into the sweet spot for the comic delivering the punch line. It's... *noble* to be the straight man. It's the right thing to do. It's also a *sin* to compete with your on-

stage partner in the religion of the theater.

I could barely contain myself— I kept thinking, 'I've got to play this part.' I wanted to jump out of my seat and onto the stage! I felt my heart race; literally. It had done that many times before, but this time you could see my heart beating through my shirt.

By "Oh, Here Is Love" in the second act, I was ready to accept the challenge of the physical and vocal hurdles, and focus on making this a show where Frederic, the Slave of Duty, actually *fulfills* his duty.

When the curtain came down I thought 'Screw it all.' I was going back to eight shows a week. My true home. Theater. New York. 'Old school.'

Funny, but my heart immediately calmed down.

My agent couldn't believe it. I was in a position to start making big money. **CORPORATION RD** How could I take a Broadway show? But I never took a job because of the money; I made choices based on my inspiration to do a part. I wasn't a father and a husband yet, so I had that luxury. Broadway was the kind of hard work I adored; fine-tuning each moment in every performance; feeling the 'personality' of each audience within seconds of being onstage.

Back to New York. Back to *real* work.

When I accepted the role, Linda Ronstadt was about to leave the show. Joseph Papp and director Wilford Leach assured me I would love Karla DeVito who was given the ingenue lead and would be my Mabel. (I'm certain they had no idea how *much* I would love her.)

Karla had toured the world with Jim Steinman and Meat Loaf's original *Bat out of Hell*, creating the live "Paradise by the Dashboard

Lights."

Fulfilling a dream of starring on Broadway, she put her solo album on hold to become Linda Ronstadt's understudy when *Pirates* opened in January 1981— with a guarantee she would make her Broadway debut in the role.

It happened sooner than expected: on second reviewers night— just a few days after opening — with no rehearsal and 350 people from the press in the audience, Karla went on for an ailing Ms. Ronstadt. She sang like a dream, receiving a standing ovation from the packed house, and rave reviews from the critics.

To prepare for the role, I worked for two weeks with Dan Berlinghoff, the conductor, and Marge Rivingston, the ultimate Broadway vocal coach, finding ways to maneuver my baritone voice through the treacherous tenor shoals.

Then, during my first rehearsal, my life changed forever. A goddess walked into the room.

An  Angel!

A saint!

I felt like the theatre gods were looking down on me.
I lost all sense of time and space and completely lost my head.

She was

extraordinary.

She was funny   yet stunning!

She was Karla DeVito...

I fell in love instantly.

My heart felt like it was pounding again— but this time it was for a perfectly understandable reason!

Two weeks after meeting Karla, I told our conductor (Dan Berlinghoff; truly one of the great men/friends in my life) that Karla DeVito was the woman I was going to marry. (Of course, Karla had no idea of my feelings!) Dan was stunned by the speed of my decision and told me he thought "she may be in a relationship, but I'm not sure."

I felt like a dog,   but I couldn't stop expressing my love. I immediately began writing songs for her. I couldn't believe it— was this really happening to me?

KARLA HAD BEEN WORKING NONSTOP since she was nineteen and had never seen any of my films. I thought... 'cool.' When Karla took over the role of Mabel in May, the creative team were away opening productions in L.A. and London.

Rex Smith, who played Frederic, only gave Karla 15 total minutes of rehearsal before her official opening. A week later, he refused to take the set bow at curtain call with Karla: Frederic and Mabel; together— just as Linda Ronstadt had graciously allowed him to take his bow with her. Rex explained that he was competing for applause and the only way to tell 'who won' the night was to do his bow alone...

When Mr. Papp was informed he chided Rex that it 'wasn't in the spirit of the show,' and then filled Karla's dressing room with flowers apologizing for her leading man's behavior.

I learned a lot of the show from the orchestra pit and from Dan Berlinghoff. I wasn't one to schmooze and I always felt awkward if I wasn't working, so I stayed far away from backstage and getting in the way of those who had to do their jobs.

From our first rehearsal in the basement of the theatre (we both had colds and Wilford had us mime through our blocking), I was in heaven! Karla was a true pro: she was as passionate as I was about her work; she was 'in the moment' and when

I came at her with comic ideas, she said she felt like she was back studying at Second City. We incorporated all the new bits into the show with Wilford and Graciela's blessing, and Frederic, the Slave of Duty, selflessly gave Mabel many new laughs, as did Mabel for Frederic.

I couldn't believe it, Karla was a magnificent talent but she was giving and compassionate and never pulled a hint of the star power I was used to in these situations.

At every performance, when Frederic and Mabel pledge their love at the red center line of the downstage platform, our kiss was magical. Long after we had left, when *Pirates* closed, the stage hands saved that piece of the platform and shipped it to us as a wedding gift.

Karla and I played our first show together on July 28, 1981. Getting to work with Kevin Kline (and original cast members Estelle Parsons, George Rose, and Tony Azito) was a thrill— but all that paled next to being onstage with the woman I loved.

Love became the elixir for my heart.

'Oh, here is love... and here is truth...'

But was she in a relationship?

The relationship? Our love? It was a bridge we would have to cross.

A complicated, awesome bridge—

but it wasn't *impossible.*

I heard the basketball coach in my head:

I imagined carrying Karla away, high above the city. Just the two us.

I knew I wanted to spend my life with her.

I would carve her name into the earth!

I would wear sneakers with her name on them!

And then one day:

it happened!

Wow!

(Yes, that too...)

We were on stage, I was about to sing, and my heart, like an on/off switch, jumped to 200 beats per minute— and I could barely catch my breath, let alone sing. So I made the audience laugh... but all I kept thinking was:

 Help me! I can't breathe!  I – can't – slow – my – heart – down!

I – can't – sing! I – can't – breathe!

WHERE? IS! THE! FREE! AIR?

Tachycardia

Madly in love or not, over 2 million Americans suffer from **arrhythmia**. Mine was called tachycardia; this kind of arrhythmia is a rapid heartbeat (controlled by the heart's flow of electrical impulses) which obstructs the heart muscle's ability to contract appropriately. Mine would come with no warning and go on and off like a light switch. Be careful: it can be brought on by caffeine. I took Excedrin for migraines and drank strong black tea before each show, which no doubt exacerbated the symptoms. Applying pressure to the artery under your jaw and grunting (as if you are constipated) can sometimes stop the racing and put your heart back in sync with itself.

It's very hard to hide on stage, but if you've been acting long enough, there are ways to turn this dilemma into a 'bit' and no one will ever know you are a victim of tachycardia, which in extreme cases, caused by an underlying condition, can lead to sudden cardiac death. (They didn't have Google then—so what did I know?!)

SOME OF US ARE BORN WITH A MORSEL OF TALENT; stuck in the Peloton of creative mediocrity. I recognize my shortcomings and work like mad (Work ethic! Discipline! 'Old School!') to make the most out of the modest talent I have.

Karla, on the other hand, was born with a *gift*. It's as if someone in the heavens tapped her with a special wand and proclaimed, 'You will be an extraordinary singer.'

This is me: a manufactured falsification; an impostor with good slight-of-hand; in other words, a *fake* in a business of fakes.

And this is Karla: So few are gifted like Karla— genuine; legitimate. Being around Karla, I felt like I could survive anything! I had to spend my life with this woman, even if it took a miracle.

My heart was hers and hers alone.

Our Waterfall of Love

(Corny but no regrets. That director was right: for a gypsy, I wasn't authentic.
For a romantic, I'm your guy.)

Running Brave

KARLA AND I ONLY HAD A FEW MONTHS together in *The Pirates of Penzance*.

Karla had gone to the head of CBS records, Walter Yetnikov, to plead her case for accepting the lead in *Pirates* instead of committing to a summer tour with Meat Loaf (which she knew would not happen). Karla's debut album, *Is This A Cool World Or What?!*, had a November release date, and Epic/CBS International Records wanted her music videos to be shot in London.

Andrew Lloyd Webber's first wife Sarah had 'discovered' Karla, bringing her stellar performance in *Pirates* to the attention of Lloyd Webber who was looking for the perfect woman to star in a film version of his musical

Evita. Karla was called to meet both the Lloyd Webbers at MCA studios in New York and sang in a small practice room with Andrew accompanying her. He immediately called director Ken Russell to set up a screen test for her in London. Singing "Don't Cry for Me Argentina," Karla moved everyone to tears at her two screen tests at Pinewood Studios (except the lyricist, who had hopes for his lover to star). Karla was Russell's first choice for the role until the film fell apart, and he wrote about her performance in his autobiography, *Altered States*.

I met Ken Russell in 2007 when he was being honored with a Lifetime Achievement Award at the Asheville Film Festival where I was a judge. When he saw Karla, he held out his arms exclaiming, "My Evita!"

After Karla left *Pirates* I was devastated. Although we were crazy about each other, Karla was hesitant to take the next step.

One of the millions of reasons I loved her was because she was very sensible and never dated musicians or actors. Cool. My kind of woman. My kind of person! She was so smart and sexy without ever trying to be sexy— that was a new one in my business. And she was funny! Funny! Looking back, she held the fact that I was starring in films against me. I had faced that many times. People think you make movies so you must be a superficial jerk. I couldn't hold that against Karla. As a matter of fact, I admired her for it. It meant that she was waiting to see how Hollywood I was— how narcissistic, how self-absorbed. Who can blame her? Not me. These qualities made me respect her even more.

Pirates moved from the Uris (now the Gershwin) to the Minskoff Theatre on August 9th. Between shows on the first matinee day, I found Karla on a pay phone near the stage-left landing, and before she could move away, I had to tell her something that if it stayed inside of my heart and soul one more second, then I would be a hypocrite.

I went up to her when she finished the phone call and no matter what else was happening in the world, she had to know the most important thing that ever had happened to me: "I love you."

Karla was completely flustered and muttered something like, "Oh, oh...that's... great, gotta go." Not the response I had hoped for but it didn't matter— if this world were to end on that very day, Karla would know I loved her...

She quickly walked down the cement stairs; I wanted to stop her— I had been running the few stairs in this new building, but didn't think it was my right to tell her anything— I didn't 'own her'— I loved her. So I waited at the the door to the staircase. Like me, the 'stair-runner,' Karla went down the stairs only to realize we were in a new theatre and this was not an exit. (The cement staircase was a mistake. It went to nowhere. It had no exit.) Karla had to turn around and come right back up past me. I was hoping that in the small time she spent on the stairs, she would say, "I love you, too." Instead it was, "No exit. Gotta go."

When it came to love, my heart and true feelings were an unstoppable freight train and Karla was my destination. Up to a point; I despised men who forced themselves on others just to get their way. I knew when to step back— but Karla was the most extraordinary person I had ever met. And to prove it, here is what happened: She said she felt love for me, but also wondered if she had lost her mind.

Karla was in a four year long monogamous relationship with her best friend and manager, Sam Ellis. They met when Karla was hired for the original *Bat out of Hell* tour. Sam managed, designed and held together the theatrical live performances world-wide, propelling the album to historic status. Sam is the ethical compass of all who know him (including me... that shows you what an amazing man he is. I get jealous, and I found it impossible to be jealous of Sam Ellis. He was heroic...) Sam walked away from his share of the management profits for *Bat out of Hell* when he felt they were not doing business fairly. Karla asked Sam to manage her and they chose Winston Simone as their partner. The three of them had great fun guiding her solo career.

Back at the theater, Karla was tortured over the thought of telling Sam how she felt about me— and I had to trust her completely on this one. The very fact that she was loyal, understanding, a true friend and not the kind of girl who jumps from lover to lover (my past relationships... killer... but not Karla). But we fell into the purest love possible. I could hold Karla in my arms for all eternity and be satisfied.

Eventually those feelings were so powerful, so undeniable, Karla and I faced the truth and, as I call it, we went free-falling... and she said..., "I love you, too." *The greatest day of my life. To this very day, that was the greatest day of my life.*

When Sam married *his* soul-mate Valerie Silver in 1987, they invited us and asked Karla to sing and our daughter Lyric (4) to be their flower girl. Sam remains one of our best friends to this day. In many ways, he is a mentor; a teacher— a great man.

In January my stint in *Pirates* was finally over and I returned to L.A. But things were different this time— Karla had decided to take the plunge!

Co-starring with George Burns in the television film of **Two of a Kind** was an experience that sent my heart into the stratosphere of humility. I was so honored and fortunate to work with Mr. Burns, who was 86 at the time and still going strong (he lived to 100).

We had a sensitive script, by James Sadwith, a fine director, Roger Young, and a strong supporting cast, with Barbara Barrie, Cliff Robertson, and the adorable Geri Jewell. Karla made her first non-musical screen appearance in a small part as my counselor.

Before shooting started I researched my role, working with 'Dave,' a mentally challenged young man who selflessly helped me understand life from my character's perspective.

Wise people have said, 'Don't meet your heroes,' and I have endless sad stories to back up that maxim, but I can shout from rooftops that working with George Burns enhanced my life exponentially. During scenes when we had to sit in a car, he didn't want to get out while the crew would do the lighting for double coverage (mounting two cameras on the hood). He felt fine just sitting there with me and telling stories. He loved doing his routines for me because he knew I adored him and thought he was a brilliant comedian—and now my new, true friend.

One day he spotted a man in his fifties walking around slowly and complaining. Mr. Burns turned to me and said, "See that young man over there? He's auditioning."

"Auditioning for what?" I asked.

"Old age," he said wryly with perfect timing. "If he keeps acting like that, pretty soon he'll get the part."

When *Two of a Kind* first aired on October 9, 1982, our partnership received

exceptional ratings and earned two Golden Globe nominations: Best Motion Picture Made for TV and Best Actor (me).

Thank you, Mr. Burns.

THE *TWO OF A KIND* SHOOT ALSO HAD MY HEART ASCENDING to the heavens because every single day was one day closer to the day Karla and I were to be married.

Unlike any woman I had known, she never dreamed of getting married; she had a negative, visceral reaction to gold, diamonds, and wedding hoopla in general. Wow. We were similar. I believe we spent 189 bucks for both simple wedding bands.

I knew Karla was making an enormous sacrifice moving to California, leaving her New York-based career behind. Working there for eight years, she had no need for a car. As the song said: nobody walks in L.A. I wanted to buy her a new car — but what kind? Karla's favorite car had been her family's old '64 Volkswagen bug. A pure soul deserves German engineering.

Well, somehow I had to forget about growing up hearing how elderly family members would never purchase a German car. "No Nazi-mobiles for me! Never forget, Hitler rode around in a Mercedes!" And "God forbid you should ever marry... what did you say? Karla DeVito is half German?! Oy! Why can't you find a nice Jewish girl?" Yup. It's not just in Woody Allen movies.

I went across the street to the Volkswagen dealership during a break in shooting; there wasn't time to change out of my wardrobe— or even brush my hair. When I finally got a salesman to pay any attention to me, I asked him how much the convertible cost because I was going to drive it off the lot.

The salesman looked at me, dressed like a mentally challenged person, down to a fake tummy and shoes with different sized heels to help me with my 'stride,' and with contempt he said, "Money talks, bullshit walks. Why don't you get out of here and stop wasting my time." If he wasn't willing to be civil to someone who looked like 'Dave' I wasn't going to explain why he wasn't getting my money— today.

Taught to problem-solve at an accelerated pace, I ran (limped) across the street and purchased a new Mazda RX-7 in the speedy time of 10 minutes. I made sure that my 'performance' was in full view of the Volkswagen salesman, and as I drove the new car off the Mazda lot, I smiled and waved to 'mein Volks-vagen' salesman. Funny thing is, Dan Berlinghoff was my best man and Karla's mom Vivienne (a saint) was a Snyder. Here's how I broke it down for my grandparents: "Nazi, bad! German, good!"

ON JULY 11, 1982, three days after the movie wrapped, Karla and I were married at her Aunt Marilyn and Uncle Bob and cousins Bob and Andy Braeunig's home in Mokena, Illinois.

Karla Jayne DeVito and Robin Benson Segal thought you would like to know that they are getting *MARRIED* on the 11th of July, 19 hundred and 82 in McHenry, Illinois (because they love each other very very much)

We only had close family and a few best friends at the ceremony. My Mom and Dad and Shelli and Moshe flew in from L.A. Karla's mom Vivienne and Marilyn made the dinner. Our wedding cake was chocolate.

Karla was a few minutes late, and as I paced in a nearby cornfield with my best man, Dan Berlinghoff, I admit I was worried she wouldn't show up. But she came, with her brothers Mat, Ray, and Mark, and her 'best woman' and best friend since high school, the dynamic rock manager Billie Best.

I played guitar and we sang 'I Believe In Fate' to each other, and as my eyes welled up with tears, I almost botched our vows— an involuntary giggle kept coming out of my mouth when I was supposed to say "I do."

Little did I know, the ethereal, loving heart I was promising her for a lifetime, 'till death do us part,' was prophetic; because the heart itself was a tangible, substantial, medical mess. She thought she was getting a healthy, young romantic— and we both learned my romantic moral fiber was the best thing that could be said about my heart. My loving heart was plum; my practical heart was a lemon.

I know I am living on borrowed time. Then again, aren't we all?… I'm just lucky to be reminded of that fact with every heart beat and spend the rest of my life, with the love of my life.

To this day, Karla Jayne DeVito has stood by me, been my best friend and taught me that true love has nothing to do with appearances— only the soul. She should know. She has the purest soul of anyone I have ever met.

WE WERE STILL NEWLY-WEDS when Rick asked if I was interested in an offer to star in *Running Brave*, a film about a half-Native American, half-Caucasian runner who made it to the Olympics against all odds.

This remarkable individual is Billy Mills— who is still the only American to ever win the Olympic Gold Medal in the 10,000 meter (6.2 mile) race.

The film was being produced by Ira and Nancy Englander and financed by the Ermineskin Band of Native Canadians, and I was highly flattered to learn Billy Mills hand-picked me as the right actor and athlete to portray him. He won the race in Tokyo in 1964 in an astonishing fashion: he was bumped and knocked out of contention at the beginning of the last lap, but with a startling amount of athleticism and heart, he came roaring back, picking off

"You have to look deeper, way below the anger, the hurt, the hate, the jealousy, the self-pity, way down deeper where the dreams lie, son. Find your dream. It's the pursuit of the dream that heals you." (Billy Mills' father said to him from an early age).

Billy Mills
Oglala Lakota (Sioux)

TOKYO 1964

runner after runner in the last 400 meters— and in a stunning upset, won 'going away.'

I had been a runner ever since I asked my dad how a kid like me could ever go to the Olympics and compete for his country. My dad was very honest and told me how much training and sacrifice would be involved. He told me about the African runners who train endlessly and don't have an ounce of body fat. But he always gave me hope along with truth. If I had it within my spirit to make such sacrifices, I one day could be running for my country in the Olympics. Little did we know that the only way I would ever get there was as an actor in a film portraying an Olympic runner.

At least my training foundation began at an early age, running the stairs of our 30-story apartment building. I never allowed myself to stop because I believed, 'If you ever stop once, you'll stop again. Habit.' In good weather, I'd run the 220-yard cinder track at Riverside Park. A top women's track team from Harlem worked out there, and the coach allowed me to run with the 880-yard runners. The best I ever ran was 2:14 seconds. I was last in every race— I just didn't have the talent.

ROBBY BENSON
RUNNING BRAVE

The one athlete they least expected
outran all their expectations.

But I never stopped running. I refused to go for jogs—jogging was 'against my religion.' I ran, competing in every 10K race I could find. Before I left for Alberta, Canada to make the film, I got my time down to 36:00. Not bad, but not even remotely Olympian.

I believe in exercise; I actually love to exercise. It isn't just for the endorphin high, it's a belief that we are privileged to be alive, and movement and body conditioning is my way of saying 'Thank you for giving me life.' I think more clearly when I exercise. I feel I can overcome any physical problems by working my heart so it will be stronger and stronger. Some physicians may dispute this, but I believe that being able to run and swim and be very, very active after four open-heart surgeries is my heart's way of thanking me. We're a team.

When I had the good fortune of meeting and spending time with Billy Mills and his wife Pat, I realized what an extraordinary man he is. Many films are made about people who need Hollywood's help to make the effort worthwhile, but Billy

Mills is one man who truly deserved to have a film made about his life and accomplishments.

So heart symptoms be damned— I was going to portray Billy Mills and make him very proud of his film. I'd run my ass off and train harder than I had ever trained before.

Karla finished her theater commitments and joined me in Edmonton where filming was underway. We hated being apart— even if only for a few days. She flew in and after taking one look at me, began baking pies and making the most delicious healthy meals. I married her for love and had no idea she was the best chef I have ever encountered! (And because of my gas, I was able to run the 440 two seconds faster.)

I was putting in 120-mile weeks and rehearsing. When we were filming, I put in 75-mile weeks. Because we shot most scenes on the track, 440 yards at a time, I knew I had to work on my fast twitch muscles and began doing more speed work. I had such respect for true Olympic athletes, I was embarrassed to be winning an Olympic Gold medal as an 'actor.' I had to get over it — and cross that finish line first.

I adored my fellow actors, especially Graham Greene and Pat Hingle, who gave a great performance playing the coach from KU who tries to guide Billy through the 'white' sports world.

For one scene, I had to run in spikes on a cement oval, painted black for the film. We used the oval as a school track. My metal spikes got caught in a drainage grate, the spikes slid on the concrete, and I popped a quad muscle off my hip. I was lame— a doctor came to the set and declared it would be more than a month before I could run again, let alone walk.

To me, it was just another sports injury. Ice. I lived with ice wrapped around my left quad. I even went into ice whirlpools at night. I was running by the end of the week.

When we would shoot the track sequences we hired world-class caliber runners. But they didn't understand the work ethic of film: we do it until we get it right. Then we do it again. We would run 60-second 440's over and over. I had to set the example. I'd run faster during the take, and even faster after the take to get back to the starting position, ready to go again and again. I refused to leave an ounce of energy out of any take. The runners were gassed— they could barely keep up. This fueled my performance: I was no elite runner, but my 'heart' and work ethic had me trouncing them.

I had conditioned myself to run in the straight-up style of the great Billy Mills, and by the time we shot the Olympic sequence, got my one-mile time down to 4:32— which I knew would photograph honestly.

Almost all of the Olympic footage was shot at halftime during an Edmonton Eskimo football game with a crowd of 60,000 fans. The crew had to clear snow from the track to make it look like summer in Japan, and the runners had to be sprayed with glycerine to make us look sweaty in the freezing temperature. They couldn't find a souped-up golf cart fast enough to film me. But I wouldn't allow us to

'pretend' to be running fast— we would run fast. And because I was running 55-second 440's during the sequence, the fans turned from jeering to cheering. They 'got into' Billy's triumph, and that spirit is in those final moments of the Olympic race.

Of all the films I've made (except for *Modern Love*) I cannot help but cry at the end of *Running Brave*— because of the strength of character and silent beauty of the Native actor at the train station, when Billy triumphantly returns home. It's a great acting lesson. Without a single word, his dignity sums up the film— and the admiration and respect all of us had for Billy Mills.

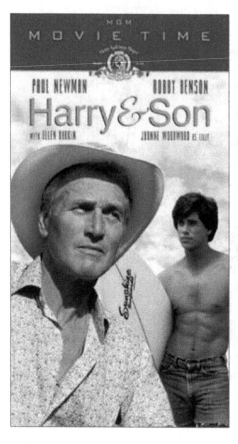

EVERY ACTOR IN HOLLYWOOD, From age 15 to 30, was fighting for the part of Paul Newman's son in **Harry and Son**. We all thought this would be a very personal film about Mr. Newman's relationship with his own son. (It wasn't.)

The film had a cast of exceptional people: Morgan Freeman, Ossie Davis, Ellen Barkin, Judith Ivey, and of course, Joanne Woodward and Paul Newman, who also directed. Paul Newman was my hero; my *idol*. I couldn't miss the opportunity to work with him.

Harry and Son actually began for me about a month before production. My first hurdle was trying to get through the script. It was... unreadable. I usually gobble up scripts with thoughts, brainstorms, and ideas I can't contain. In this case, I couldn't read five pages in a row without going for a run.

I had to learn to surf for the role. Every day in January I'd put on a wet suit, go out to Ventura County and watch other surfers, and try to mimic their actions. I was doing well until the weekend prior to a huge storm. The swells were ten feet and all the surfers were out in the ocean fighting for space. I took a huge wall of water and began to paddle, picking up steam, placing my board in the perfect spot for the perfect wave. I began to ride the wave in when I was cut off by a pissed-off surfer and went down. The wave took my body and hurled it into the coral reef and rocks. I was almost knocked out. My surfboard was tethered to my ankle with rope and velcro, and as I turned around a bigger wave was about to crash into me— but even more troubling was the surfboard, coming at my torso horizontally with no time to move out of its way. I broke a rib on the right side of my chest and the wave pounded me into the reef and rocks again.

I barely remember crawling out of the ocean. As I lay in the rocky sand, staring up at the stormy skies, I realized how lucky I was to have survived my self-taught surfing lessons.

The day before principal photography began in Florida, I was out for a run, testing my ability to breathe without gasping for air or showing pain from a broken rib. The next thing I knew, my foot came down on a rock, my ankle flipped (like an ankle that had been sprained dozens of times) and I immediately knew I had a severe sprain. (Yup.) My ankle swelled to the size of a grotesque grapefruit and I thought, "Well, you did it again. How?! Why?!"

I went to Mr. Newman and told him he should look for a replacement. He stared at me and then said, "No. I want you to do this part. We'll get you to the trainer of the Miami Dolphins."

The Dolphins had just lost the Superbowl. Their trainer was examining my ankle in an empty training facility (almost like a ghost town), when Don Shula walked into the empty room, stopped and stared at me. He looked at me like a man... who, well: had just lost the Superbowl, and said in a very nasal, angry voice, "What's he doing here?" The trainer explained and I was allowed to stay, only to hear him tell our first A.D., "Robby won't be able to walk for two weeks." 'Ha!' I thought. Heard that one before.

I began the old 'foot in a bucket of ice' routine, and showed up the next day without a sign of a limp. I'm referring to my ankle. My performance was another kind of limp. I tried to fix every scene I was in with unbridled enthusiasm. Bad choice.

Karla and I lived on a houseboat during the filming. Pregnant with our first child, Karla had to deal with morning sickness and sea sickness. Our 'house' never stopped swaying with the tide. One day Paul asked what baby book we were reading and Karla said *Pregnancy and Childbirth* by Tracy Hotchner. Well, it just so happened that Ms. Hotchner was Paul's best friend's daughter. Joanne Woodward knitted on the set between takes. She knitted our baby-to-be a little sweater. These were movie stars, but they were the most down-to-earth people I had ever met.

Our movie did have off-screen adventures. Paul loved to race professionally on weekends during the shoot, but one Sunday he had one of those 'Grand Prix' places, where everyone races each other in miniature cars, shut down— just so the cast and crew could let off some steam and have fun. The racing got competitive. It came down to Karla, five months pregnant, racing Paul Newman nose to nose as they headed for the checkered flag. Karla kicked Paul's butt. And that's the way Paul would want me to tell the story, because he was a prankster, a lover of life, and an all-around great guy.

There were many practical jokes we played on one another. In the emotional scene where I had to kiss him as he 'lay dead', Paul spent fifteen minutes before the shot rubbing ice on his mouth, getting his lips cold— just to see if his practical joke would work on me.

When I think of the movie *Harry and Son* I don't think of 'film'— I think of experiences and people we were lucky to meet and become friends with. Paul Newman, Joanne Woodward and their family have changed the world for the better; they have set a standard that we should all try and achieve when it comes to harnessing your good fortune with altruism. Their charities will live on long past any of us. When I'm in the grocery store and I have a choice, I will always pick Newman's Own over any competitor, knowing that the proceeds will truly help people.

I keep them close to my soul, as if Paul and Joanne are always laughing and knitting protection around my heart.

I COULD WORK MY BODY INTO 'HOLLYWOOD SHAPE' (without steroids, thank you). *I couldn't breathe* but still felt I had to give the impression everything was perfect. The irony was so... Hollywood.

We had been married for less than a year when we wrapped *Harry and Son* in Florida, and came home to the long hot summer in the San Fernando Valley.

Karla was the darling of Epic Records since the release of *Is This a Cool World or What?* Gregg Geller, the head of the A&R department, was convinced John Boylon was the only one to produce Karla's second album. She had been on hold for over a year waiting for a break in Boylan's schedule. Karla, Danny Lawson, and I had written (and I engineered and played on) demos of five songs Boylon loved. Finally free, that summer he had her recording nonstop in the studio until a week before her due date. She felt great and sang even better, saying pregnancy's natural muscle relaxing hormones actually helped her vocal chords.

From the day I fell in love with Karla I knew I wanted her to be the mother of my children. Our children. Throughout our first pregnancy, I had the luxury of being able to go to all doctor visits with her (great thing about an actor's schedule) seeing our all-in-one family/obgyn/pediatrician, Susan Stangl. She was the first doctor either of us had who answered our questions completely and with clarity. Karla knew more about cutting edge nutritional information than anyone I had ever met, and she practiced what she preached. She wanted a natural childbirth, and we read every book we could get our hands on, so we felt comfortable making jokes and having fun in Corky Harvey's LaMaze class— paying no attention whatsoever to the C-Section lesson. Why would we need that info? Karla was incredibly healthy and could sing louder than anyone since Ethel Merman— we assumed she'd hit a high note and our beautiful baby girl would come flying out into my arms.

Cut to: two weeks overdue, meconium in her water, induced with a Pitocin drip, twenty two hours of labor, and two hours of pushing, (inspiration for some imaginative moments in our movie *Modern Love*) and finally, me holding Karla's hand in the operating room as our exuberant and rhapsodic Lyric was welcomed to the world. Two 'authentic' romantics— now we were three!

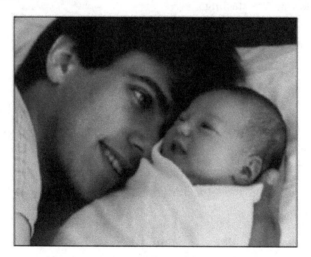

On the day Lyric was born, Karla's record label sent a beautiful congratulatory gift basket. That very same day, Sam and Winston (Karla's managers) received a call from an Epic executive saying she was being dropped from the label "because we don't believe she's a viable female rock & roll artist now that she's a wife and mutha."

If Karla had a child out of wedlock, that might've been rock 'n roll appropriate. An unwed rocker-mom is sexy.

I was pissed. I was angry. I could barely control my temper. My heart pained... but Karla was completely and uttterly blissed out— nothing could take away from the miracle of our daughter's birth.

I NEVER INTENTIONALLY KEPT A SECRET from Karla; she knew I was born with a heart murmur, but only heard the party line: It's not a problem. I gave no details about how I was feeling. Karla says she thought of me as this incredibly stoic, heroic, other-worldly being— with the humanistic values of the people she admired most: her mother Vivienne, her Aunt Marilyn and Uncle Bob. She had never known anyone so athletically or artistically driven, and she respected me too much to ask for more than I was willing to share.

Until one day, when I came in from a 16 mile run in the smog filled San Fernando Valley sweltering heat, and collapsed in a pile on our bedroom floor where she was breast feeding Lyric.

She gently said, "Darling, this can't be right."

She didn't understand my sense of denial; all of my absurd rules and regulations. I told her, "This is what everyone looks like after running 16 miles in 100 degree heat, breathing L.A. smog."

Nothing was going to stop me from running the New York Marathon.

Running Brave had been set to premiere just before the Marathon (Sunday, November 6, 1983), and it seemed like a great idea to tie in publicity for the film with me entering the race I had always wanted to run. My personal goal was to break 3 hours, and knowing that Billy and Pat Mills would be in town for the film, I felt inspired to take on the challenge.

When the race began, I did a very foolish thing. I got claustrophobic in the back of the pack of 19,000 runners and had to get away from the slow amoeba-type jog in the first few miles. This was before runners wore computer chips in their bibs or shoes, so unfortunately, I knew I had to make up for losing the first 10 minutes behind the mob of joggers before I even crossed the starting line. I ran a 4:52 third mile (and that was restraining myself). But because of the energy I wasted in mile 3, I was haunted by mile 23. I didn't hit the wall, I hit a tsunami. My goal of breaking 3 hours was 'dashed' when I crossed the finish line in 3:05:15.

Some people say, "Yeah, but if it took you ten minutes to just get across the starting line, you really ran ten minutes faster." Unfortunately, I don't believe that. When I crossed the finish line, the clock read 3:05:15. That means I ran 3:05:15. End of story.

When Karla got a call from her pal, 60s songwriting icon Ellie Greenwich, to star in the original version of her musical, *Leader of the Pack*, at The Bottom Line in New York, I became a house husband. I loved my new role, spending time with our baby and supporting Karla's career. She worked with the great Darlene Love and Paul Shaffer (as Phil Spector), and got a great review in the *Village Voice*: "The surprise was Karla DeVito, who sang 'Be My Baby' and 'Baby, I Love You' clearly and unaffectedly and then did a 'River Deep Mountain High' which was a credit to her race." That's Karla...

When *Leader Of The Pack* went to Broadway, Karla had to turn it down as she had to be in L.A. recording her A&M album, *Wake 'Em Up In Tokyo*. I had given Karla's Epic demo to Herb Alpert (the 'A' in 'A&M'); he loved it, and executive David Anderle wanted to produce her album in L.A.

THE MARATHON BECAME A WAKE-UP CALL for me. I was having more difficulty breathing— and didn't want to hide my problem from Karla. So I agreed to see someone. At that time in my life, I made the same mistake most people did; I assumed: 'Doctors know everything.'

Doctor #1: "You eat too much candy. Go home." I stopped eating candy. It didn't help.

Doctor #2: "You're under too much stress. Here's a prescription for anxiety. Go home." Too much stress? I was at my best under stress. I tore up the prescription on the way out of in his office.

Doctor #3: "You're a hypochondriac.. Go home and breathe."

I don't think so.

Doctor #4: "Eat more fiber. Go home."

So, I did.   It didn't help my breathing...

WE WENT TO NEW YORK where Karla was asked to host *Rock Influences,* the first music documentary series on MTV. And the people from the Broadway musical *Big River* wanted Karla to play a starring role in their show (Karla did that as well).

I was in the shower when Karla ran into the bathroom and squealed with delight, "Oh my god! Diana Ross is going to call you in a minute! She wants to sing our song 'Nobody Makes Me Crazy!' and put it on her new *Swept Away* album! Make sure you call her 'Miss Ross!' Do not call her Diana."

I looked at Karla with a head full of shampoo and thought, she is either batty or she's clairvoyant. And then the phone rang, as if on cue. 'Oh, my god,' I thought. 'My wife is not only the most amazing person I've ever met— she's a telepathic mystic! I married a shaman— no, a sha-woman! A sorceress! She can predict the future!' The phone rang again.

"Remember," Karla instructed me, "call her Miss Ross." (I'll do anything you say, Ms. Wizard!) With soap on my head and dripping wet, I walked slowly to the phone as it kept ringing. I was spooked by Karla's hidden abilities. What else in our future can Karla 'see?' I picked up the phone to speak to one of pop cultures true legends; a deserving legend. Could it be her? Really? And, can Karla predict the future?

"Hello?"

"Please hold for Miss Ross."

Holy shit. I then turned to Karla and my knees were shaking. 'I'm married to a Martian; wait— a Martian? What does a Martian have to do with genius and predicting the future? My wife is... telepathic! If this whole acting/songwriting/writing/directing/teaching thing doesn't work out,

there's always a cable show for Karla the Telepathist!'

"Hello?" It *was* Diana Ross! I mean... *Miss* Ross.

"Um... Hello? This is Robby Benson, but you can call me Robby. What an honor it is to be speaking with you... Miss Ross. My wife predicted you would call."

"Oh. Robby, I'm having trouble with the song you wrote.

"What kind of trouble, Miss Ross? I'll help in any way possible." I turned to Karla and mouthed, 'I'm-talking-to-Diana-Ross— but you know that!' I jumped up and down with excitement!

"Well, Robby, you know that note that jumps the octave?" As people have said to me before: she sounded just like herself! That famous voice on the other end of the phone was Diana Ross. Wow! I mean: WOW!

"Oh, yes. The payoff. It's the musical payoff of the song's theme. Didn't Karla sing that amazingly well on the demo? You should see some of the other stuff she can do, too!" I smiled a soapy smile at Karla. Karla shook her head.

"That's the note. I can't hit it. I want you to change it."

Of course, the story of my life. "*Miss Ross,* that note is why the music, the song— works. You cannot change that note. Sorry. No-can-do. Radeeeooo." (What was I saying?)

Karla punched me in the arm. I whispered, "I'm sorry honey— if she can't sing as well as you can, then *maybe she shouldn't sing our song.*"

"Are you insane?!" Karla whispered back.

"Well maybe you can cast a spell on her and she'll be able to sing the note."

"Robby," I heard Miss Ross continue on the phone, "do you have an alternate note?"

"Yes. Lower the key of the song so you can hit the note. The pay-off is *that note*. It's sonically... fun. And funny. It gives the song its quirkiness; it's personality. It shows the vocal gymnastics of the singer and how much 'nobody can make her crazy'— LIKE YOU DO! That is why there is a note that goes hand-in-hand with the lyrics. That's why, Miss Ross, you shouldn't change the note— or maybe you could VSO (variable speed) the master tracks so you can hit the note."

I thought I was doing pretty darn well. Karla looked at me with her mouth open wondering, "What kind of lunatic did I marry?"

"Do you want the song on my album? An album that is sure to go gold the day it's released?" Diana said with soft but 100 percent solid gold power.

"You know how I feel, so it's up to you, Diana."

After some backpedaling niceties, I hung up the phone. After all, it was *Diana Ross*, err, Miss Ross. And I'm just a schmuck composer who would sell my body parts to have my 'stuff' heard. Forget the money (see a pattern yet?), I just wanted to have my music heard— the way it was *written*. What's wrong with that?

Diana Ross sang the song the way *she wanted to sing the song;* changed the note— and it sounded great, just like Diana Ross! And both Karla and I had a song on the *Swept Away* album which did go gold. We didn't make a penny from publishing, but people would hear our song, thanks to our friend (she says so in this ad!), Miss Ross.

One of many misconceptions in today's pop-culture world: those of us who are successful have money. *Wrong!*

As I sat at my parents' house in Woodland Hills (trying to breathe), my mom, who had no idea about my symptoms, ironically decided it would be a good idea for me to see a cardiologist to lower my life insurance rate. After all, we agreed, I don't smoke, don't drink, never did drugs, have a body fat index of 6%, avoided fried foods, okay— I do love candy, particularly anything red or purple, but I have low blood pressure, and ridiculously low cholesterol (135!). I exercise faithfully every day and finished the New York Marathon in a time that put me in the top ten percent of competitors: shouldn't I be getting a break on my life insurance? Sounded logical to me. (But another doctor? Another waiting room? What a waste of life.)

I had to appease my mom; she and my dad had handled my finances since I was five, and she was the national spokesperson for Merrill Lynch, spearheading the movement in the late 70s and early 80s to teach women how to handle their finances. Karla thought it was a great idea to see a cardiologist, but I swore: this is the last doctor I would ever see. *Ever.* Period! Ha! I'm such a boob.

I had been exercising at Mid Valley in Reseda, and Karla and I grabbed a salad at the restaurant in the gym complex. Suddenly, I realized I couldn't chew my lettuce and breathe at the same time. I finally admitted, "We have to find out what's wrong with me."

Thanks to my mom we already had an appointment with a Dr. Peter Guzy, recommended by Dr. Kenneth Shine, the former head of cardiology at UCLA. Looking back now, as a parent myself, I realize that my parents were worried about my heart, and without saying so directly, this was their way to get me to the right doctor. It took being a parent to understand my folks' genius.

Karla and I went together; this pattern was set before Lyric's birth and has continued through our lives. (It is imperative to have an advocate in the doctors office with you when large issues are being discussed.) Once in the room I completely forgot about my symptoms and focused on the reason my mom made the appointment and I did (excuse the arrogance) some subtle yet powerful acting. My heart rate and blood pressure was marathon runner low, EKG looked great, he heard my health history and was impressed, and I thought we were on our way home with an approval from a top-notch cardiologist. (And I'd save some money on my insurance payments.)

Karla was honestly confused; when she realized I was ready to leave without saying a word about my ongoing symptoms, she simply said, "Robby's having trouble breathing."

I laughed it off and shot her our first 'dirty look.' I thought in my convoluted way, 'This is me. It's the way my body works. Let's stop 'paying the man' too much insurance money.'

The doctor said, "While you're here, let's get an echocardiogram," gave us the paperwork, sent us downstairs, then said "Don't worry, this test will give us a clear picture of what's going on with your heart. I'll look at it and my office will call you next week to set a follow-up appointment."

test kitchen

It was October 1984. My first real heart test was an **echocardiogram**.

I was naked from the waist up in an examination gown opened in the front. Before the technician came into the room I did what I had always done — anything humanly possible to make Karla laugh. I picked up every piece of medical equipment, even pretending to do the procedure on myself in areas that have nothing to do with the heart, to the point we were both laughing hysterically. It was some kind of comic pressure release for both of us, as my long kept secret was out— we now had experts in charge of my heart.

The cardiac ultrasound technologist walked in and lowered the lights. I was told to lie on my left side with my right arm over my head. She squirted cold gooey gel on the flat surface of a two-inch wide, six inch long 'wand,' and proceeded to glide it along my torso, around my heart, looking for ultrasound images on a black and white monitor and recording specific views of my heart, its chambers and valves (on VHS tape; old equipment in today's world, but cutting edge at the time). Every once in a while she'd turn up the volume and we'd be treated to the loud sound of my heart beating.

What we didn't understand (and the technician was forbidden to discuss with us), was the 'whooshing' sound after each heart beat. That was my aortic valve 'regurgitating'— unable to close properly, forcing blood to leak back into my heart.

The experience was cold and a bit creepy, but I decided to relax and just let it all happen. Karla held my feet the whole time and I fell asleep…

PREVENTIVE MAINTENANCE

Basically, an echocardiogram is harmless and painless.

The next morning the phone rang at 6:30 a.m. Karla picked it up quickly trying not to wake the baby. It was the nurse from UCLA saying Dr. Guzy wanted to see me today— as soon as possible. Could we arrive by 7:30 a.m.?

Karla said, "Yes. We'll be there." We stared at one another for about 15 seconds, both of us realizing this was not a movie and no one was going to yell 'Cut!'

We arrived at UCLA and I stared into Karla's beautiful, brown eyes. She looked so vulnerable, so young. This is when it hit me: *whatever was happening to me was also happening to the people I love.*

"Take any heart, take mine! Take heart, take heart: taaaaake heart!"

I could handle the pain; I could handle the fear; I could handle the unknown— because eventually I would become familiar with the unknown. This was going to happen to me whether I liked it or not. The unknown for me would become tangible. Karla, my parents, my sister— they would always be in a void of some kind. They would never feel the pain, only imagine the depth of it. I've learned the unknown is a much more frightening than being the vessel experiencing the corporeal. Feeling things physically was concise and substantial— whether it was pain, discomfort or mental anguish. I, at least, would have an understanding and familiarity with this dark unknown. On the other hand, my loved ones would always be in the dark, unknowing...

Whatever was about to happen to me became secondary. Whatever ordeal was ahead, my goal would be to keep my loved ones feeling safe. Never was there to be a single doubt; I would show no hint of fear. That was my duty. Now I truly was 'The Slave of Duty!' (Soft? No edge? Ha! The ironies in life are comical. I prefer my sarcasm served with a restrained tang of mockery.)

At 7:30 a.m, I watched the cardiologist carefully, studying him as he took a sip of water, smacked his lips, then looked 'beyond' us— avoiding any emotional connection— and with stolid temperament said, "Robby, you're going to need open-heart surgery."

My eyes went straight to Karla; she was trying to hide a flush of fright. I now had a real-life, highly dynamic task to use all my skills to protect Karla from her imagination. I began writing the script in my head (why couldn't Eric Roberts get *this* part?):

Close-up: Robby. We hear his (corny) voice-over.

ROBBY V.O.

> *From this second forward, no one worries. I'll be the*
> *best patient to walk the Earth and we'll get out of*
> *here as fast as possible. I'll heal and be back to work*
> *in no time. It will almost be as if I never had open*
> *heart surgery. And no one I love will ever feel*
> *vulnerable or frightened.*

That was my script. I was simultaneously writing it as the cardiologist was talking. Happy ending— we needed a happy ending. Sure, conflict was good, but this would be a Disney film. The surgery will be shot with no blood. I'll heal in a montage. We need old-fashioned, propaganda corn. One of my love songs, a pop love song, 'Classic Problem?' No— that's too 'soft.' How about 'Bang My Drum.' Better! With that song, we just grabbed a bigger demographic. Our first weekend will be boffo box-office and Karla is already smiling. That is a smile, right? Crap— she's wincing. What *is* the Doctor saying?

I watched his lips moving. "First you'll have to go through a series of procedures. Some will be slightly uncomfortable. Others will be invasive. We need to know everything we possibly can about your heart before we open up your chest."

"So, um…" Karla was trying to absorb that image and still ask good questions, "Robby doesn't have heart disease, he has something wrong with a valve?"

"Robby's arteries are perfect. But, he has a congenital defect called a bicuspid aortic valve. Instead of three leaflets, Robby's aortic valve has two."

Bicuspid Aortic Valve

It's actually basic mechanics: Simply put, a perfect aortic valve has three leaflets that open and close. This action allows blood to be pumped from the heart and sent to the the body as they open, and stops blood from leaking back into the heart chamber as the leaflets close. Because I was born with only *two*_leaflets, my heart was not performing properly and the pumping action progressively became highly inefficient.

Theoretically, this also explains why I felt better when I exercised. Exertion made my heart work harder and in doing so, it forced more oxygenated blood to the places that made me feel… alive. My valve was now so damaged and the leakage so severe, that my heart had become enlarged to the point of looking like a "saggy water balloon." (But I was not thinking about that, I was thinking: Maybe we should walk over and see what's playing at the movie theater down the street in Westwood. What I wouldn't do for some pop and a box of Hot Tamales… Thank God Karla is taking notes!) Somewhere in there I did hear the doctor say I'd need surgery in the next two weeks, as I was in danger of heart failure.

And all along I thought I ate too much candy, not enough fiber, was over-stressed and was a hypochondriac.

Dr. Guzy's nurse handed us a few ever-so-slim pamphlets about heart catheterizations, valve replacement, and open heart surgery— but my eyes couldn't stop staring at the diagram where the foley catheter goes into the penis and stays in the bladder, thanks to the inflation of a small balloon. It may be juvenile, but that… bothered me somewhat. Okay, a lot.

I kept thinking, 'It's amazing how little information we need for a surgery where they're going to saw my chest open and try to repair my heart. I'd get a bigger manual if I were buying a toaster.' And then Dr. Guzy gave us the most important information of all: if he had to have my operation, his choice for a surgeon would be Dr. Hillel Laks.

I looked at the pamphlets and wondered how Dr. Laks likes his toast...

Well Done

'Oh my god— my career!'

I HAD TO CALL MY AGENT. In Hollywood, this phone call usually came before the phone call to the parents. I did call my parents' first, then stayed at the pay phone and dialed my agent as I searched for more coins (no cell phones then…). My agent at the time was very, very powerful. We had grown up together in the business, I was his first 'big' client, and Rick Nicita was like a brother to me. When I finally got him on the phone, I began to laugh. It was a nervous laugh, a strange release of tension.

The perception of me had been 'the athletic, boy-next-door,' and as a young movie star who could never take his shirt off again, I would now be 'the athletic, boy-next-door-who-had-open-heart-surgery.' I realized I was screwed. I wanted to fight it— but I didn't know whom or what I could fight. I was fighting perception. And once they sawed me open, there was absolutely nothing I could do about the perception. Except never wear V-neck collars.

As all of this ran through my mind, I heard Rick struggle for words. I knew he cared about me, but there was a sense of ruin in his voice. "Robby, you may want to keep this quiet." By the time he circled back for a pep talk about how things would be 'okay,' Karla walked over, and I said good-bye, hung up the phone— and had the torrent rush of realization that my acting career was finished. Dead before the operation.

Was there a morgue for dead careers at UCLA Hospital?

(Probably…)

Let's invent the future.

I suddenly became energized! I would somehow put up a good fight. I would harness this energy and turn it into something positive. Karla deserved that. Our baby Lyric deserved that.

Vivienne quickly flew in from Illinois to take care of her little best friend Lyric while Karla and I dealt with making new kinds of decisions— not career choices (which now felt ridiculously unimportant) or new parent simple choices like which baby car seat to buy? We were in uncharted territory, and we needed a guide.

Karla and I went to meet Dr. Hillel Laks, the head of Thoracic Surgery at UCLA. Within the first few minutes in his office we knew we were in the right place. Not only a brilliant man, he was attentive, caring, confident, and had more quiet charisma than any movie star I had known. Dr. Laks said I would need a few more diagnostic tests prior to surgery, then proceeded to ask me questions unanswered by medical tests alone. He wanted to understand my temperament and life style. Dr. Laks saw me as a whole human being. No jokes or non-sequiturs from me in the presence of this man I would gladly have touch my heart. I held Karla's hand and listened intently as he showed us a model of the heart and gave us details of our options.

Mechanical Valve

The downside: a mechanical valve would mean having to take Coumadin (a blood thinner) every day for the rest of my life, as an artificial valve throws off blood clots. Monitoring blood levels weekly. Dietary restrictions. No more stunts or contact sports.

The upside: less of a chance of needing a re-operation. If perfect, the mechanical valve may last a lifetime.

Bio Prosthesis Valve

The downside: either made from pig or cow tissue, they have a limited life time and you will need another open-heart surgery to replace the valve when it begins to fail.

The upside: The body 'recognizes' the processed tissue and coats it like a real valve. No blood thinner needed. I would only have to take one aspirin a day.

Then Dr. Laks leaned in and said: "Robby, if I needed a valve replacement today at 40 I would want a bio prosthesis valve. At your age, knowing your athleticism and the nature of your work, I would advise the bio prosthesis— most preferably a bovine valve. Hopefully the size will be right for us to put in a large valve, offering you the biggest opening to accommodate your peak activity."

'Bovine,' I thought. 'Cow? Pink slime?' I returned my attention to his wisdom. He said if all went well my heart function would be better than it had ever been in my lifetime, and I could continue to be as physically active as I desired.

Then he broke my heart: "But no more marathons." He didn't think the stress of running 26.2 miles was good for anyone's heart, particularly someone with a repaired aortic valve.

"And no rowing. Studies of collegiate rowing teams show more cases of enlarged hearts than any other competitive sport."

Luckily rowing had never been high on my 'sports to conquer' list, but knowing I will never have a chance to shave 5 minutes and 15 seconds off my NY Marathon run and break 3 hours haunts me to this day. Karla, who understands me better than anyone, still doesn't quite get it. But 30 years years later, she knows why I have the blues come November.

We left Dr. Laks' office knowing I would have open-heart surgery in a little over a week and an animal tissue valve in my heart. It brought weird images to mind:

I had been the guy fighting to save the leatherback turtles and the baby seals...and then I remembered the word *bovine*:

a cow has *died* so I can live.

From that moment on, it has been very hard for me to eat red meat.

WE WERE SENT INTO THE BOWELS OF UCLA HOSPITAL to the **Nuclear Medicine** department. Karla had to wait outside behind a lead door, and I was shot up

Please Pardon Our Appearance While We Build Our Radiation Therapy Expansion Project.

with radioactive gunk (not a medical term),   then asked to lie in a small tube while pictures were taken to see how this radioactive stuff was flowing through my cardiovascular system. My twisted comic imagination was running wild. I was a human China Syndrome. A

walking Three-Mile Island. Karla didn't want our baby anywhere near the phantom rays of the microwave oven, but after this I'd be afraid to kiss her. Kiss her— would our next baby have two heads?! I shared my thoughts aloud with the nurses and technicians. Getting laughs from them for my real life black comedy was comforting. The technicians assuaged my fears immediately telling me I received more potent X-rays at a dentist office. (I later found out that this was not exactly true...) The only discomfort I felt was from lying in one position without moving, for 3 hours, which caused my back muscles to spasm. Time consuming, but otherwise completely painless.

I needed the biggie– Mr. Big— the "Rolls Royce" of all tests for the heart: The Heart Catheterization, also known as a Coronary Angiogram. It is the best way to 'see' inside the heart, test exact pressures, and make sure I did not have any problem other than my congenital valve defect. Karla and I knew this was the last test before my scheduled open heart surgery with Dr. Laks, so I was in my 'nothing can possibly go wrong/whatever it takes/bring it on so I can have the surgery and start healing' mode.

A nurse handed me a paper to sign which stated I understood there was a 4 percent chance I could die during this procedure. I was slightly spooked. (Today, with over a million heart caths performed every year in America, the odds of major problems now are less than one percent.) Naturally, as a responsible husband and father, I wanted to get all my ducks in

a row.

I called our lawyer to make sure my will was up to date, checked in with my life insurance agent (guess I wasn't eligible for that reduced rate after all), and called my dear friend and accountant Ed Lieberman. If I ended up in that 4 percent, I wanted Karla and our baby Lyric's future to be taken care of to the best of my posthumous ability. Later, I learned most of that 4 percent came from people who were very old and/or very sick and some were 'cathed' moments into a massive heart attack. So the extremely ill patients increase the dire odds. (If you were a gambler in Vegas, this would be good info. Bet on me living.)

The heart cath is an invasive procedure where a very long, narrow tube-like camera (on the tip of a catheter) is guided through an artery in either your arm or your leg (this first time, it was inserted through the femoral artery in my groin) and is gently pushed and channeled all the way into the heart. In my case radioactive iodine was flushed through the catheter so they could also see my arterial blood flow using a fluoroscope. I became hot, itchy, and nauseous as possible without vomiting. I was *not* having an allergic reaction to the iodine, these feelings were considered *normal*.

(Before my third open-heart surgery I realized if I asked them to administer the iodine slowly, it didn't make me sick. In 2010, when I had my last surgery at the Cleveland Clinic, I asked about it and they said they used an automated slow release system.)

The anesthesiologist had me happily sedated, yet alert and able to watch the video monitor and see the pictures, too. One of the reasons the Heart Cath Doctor wants you to be awake is he may need you to help by moving one way or another; coughing, etc. As a person in the film business, the pictures and images were absolutely stunning. My only problem: I'm a purist, despise video, and wished it had the magic of film. This, of course, is absurd, but I was in a state of chemically induced euphoria.

One sensation *was* very unusual— when the probe touched my heart, my heart *fluttered*. It felt like a tickle, and for a moment it took my breath away. Other than that, the heart catheterization was a breeze.

My advice: keep thinking positive thoughts, like how brilliant it is that they can do all this in order to save your life, rather than being consumed by fear. That attitude has always been my 'go-to' approach.

The discomfort for me came after the heart catheterization. To stop the bleeding from the incision in the artery at my groin, an orderly (where was Jerry Lewis when I needed him?) stood over me using his body weight to keep steady pressure on a 20 pound sand bag placed on my bandaged wound/groin. I wasn't allowed to move for six hours; not even raise my head, for fear of exerting my core muscles, popping the artery open, and 'bleeding out.' No big deal, just one problem: all of the iodine contrast dye injected during the procedure was now sitting impatiently in my bladder waiting to be relieved. In other words, I had to pee like a madman.  It would require me to pee while lying flat, in front of a... *stranger.*

 This was a dilemma.

It just so happens, I'm a very private person— a bit of a hermit, a recluse. (Exaggerate everything that comes to mind and you'll come close to who I really am.) And no matter how hard I tried, I could not pee. 'Sanctuary!'

What to do? My bladder was getting more bloated and the sensation of immense pressure was becoming overwhelmingly uncomfortable. Not pain, just basic human discomfort we all can identify with. You may want to

practice urinating from this position before you come face-to-face with the bladder troll. (I try and visualize... sometimes that helps.)

Unfortunately, I *could not urinate*. Thus began my love-hate relationship with the *other* catheterization. For those who have not received the pamphlet, a Foley Catheter is a tube with a deflated balloon at the end. In a male patient it is inserted through the penis opening and 'snakes' its way

into the bladder where the balloon is inflated, keeping it in place. Does it hurt? Not really. But it's no fun. Like when you were young, and the grown-ups think 'all kids like clowns' on their birthdays.

Clowns scared the living shit out of me. So in this situation, the clown arrives, scares the shit out of you, is inserted into your penis and there is momentary discomfort, and then the good part of the birthday: the present! You are immediately relieved of the urine through the tube into a bag,

and lo and behold, the clown is your friend.

Ahhhh…

Thank you.

After about six hours the doctor said my wound had healed, and they took the sand bag off my groin. A male nurse came in to take out my foley catheter and politely asked Karla if she'd step outside. Less than a minute later she heard an unfamiliar high-pitched scream. She ran to the door and saw it was her husband.

The young nurse was mortified, apologizing profusely. He blurted out, "I was so nervous to be taking out 'Robby Benson's' catheter, I completely forgot to deflate the balloon"— prior to pulling it out of my bladder.

Valuable Life Lesson: Ouch. Celebrity doesn't always bring perks. Just thinking about it hurts like hell.

WITH A CAMERA INSIDE OF MY HEART, I began to see excerpts of my life with great clarity. I saw many people, many 'moments in time' as if I had an ESPN instant replay. I had an epiphany: I realized every negative feeling towards another person could've been avoided. Suddenly, anger seemed like such useless energy; useless and very harmful energy. I saw how many of those countless times I was wrong. All I wanted to do was apologize to… everyone. I wanted to give these people hugs and say, "I'm so very sorry for what I've done. Whether I die or not— I'm so sorry."

And then I looked up at the monitor and saw my heart. Why oh why did it take a heart procedure to remind me I was mortal, and to realize how I behave towards others *matters significantly* while I'm on this planet? Why did it take a hint of death and an anesthesiologist's cocktail to recognize the need for more tolerance in my heart? The very heart I was staring at; a heart that was physically faulty— but had no excuses when it came to compassion and understanding.

I looked at the doctors, nurses and technicians in the room. All of them were behind sterile masks, but it was a very diverse group of men and women. No matter what belief, Muslim, Jew, Christian, Hindu, Agnostic, Atheist— from that day forward I needed to *see* with tolerant eyes.

While I was being so carefully handled by men and women who spent their lives learning to heal others, it was difficult for me to understand hatred, violence, and war. (I was always a 'hippie' at heart, but why was my epiphany reduced to sounding insignificant, superficial and silly?) We have the ability to be a civilized beacon in this world for others to follow by seeing our light; not our darkness. I realized I needed to let love be my guiding force. Love above all.

SURGERY

THE NIGHT BEFORE MY OPERATION, I was pacing my hospital room, pretending I wasn't scared, just 'exercising.' At 10:45 p.m. there was a knock at our door. No one came in. Odd; usually when there is a knock at a hospital room door, it is followed by the prerequisite, standard beat of 3, and then a nurse or a doctor enters the room. But no one came in— and then there was another knock. I looked at Karla, then went to the door and opened it. A well-coiffed woman, dressed in a pantsuit and carrying a clipboard, stood at the door.

"Hello, Mr. Benson. I'm from public relations here at UCLA Medical Center. NBC just called. They want a statement for the 11:00 p.m. news broadcast."

"What?" I looked at the clock it was 10:45 p.m. "How did they find out? I was promised that no one would know I was here!"

"I'm so sorry, Mr. Benson. There are many people going in and out of this hospital— any hospital— every day, who could use extra money by revealing things to the press."

In my career I never hired a personal P.R. firm. Press was for promoting work, not creating or preserving a persona. When asked to be a presenter at the Academy Awards before I was married, I appreciated the offer of a limo, but turned it down and drove my own crappy car, parked in a public garage, and skipped the red carpet part of the event altogether. (Best memories of the night before I went on: shaking the iconic John Wayne's hand backstage; and the talented and beautiful Jane Fonda, whom I had never met, calling out my name, grabbing me, and French-kissing me. A much better celebrity perk than pulling my inflated foley.)

"Well," I told the woman at my hospital door, "I don't have a prepared statement."

She apologized again, turned and left. I immediately got the classic aura for a migraine. A migraine the night before my open-heart surgery... oh man.

I don't think it's difficult for a non-performer to relate to the exigency of being revealed as damaged goods via mass media the night before your operation. This was Karla and my 'we forgot about the flowers' moment. We were focused on life and death issues at hand.

"Is this for real?," I asked Karla. "Let's turn on the 11 o'clock news and see. Maybe it was just Randy playing a practical joke."

I was the second story on the NBC news at 11:00. I guess if I had hired a press agent I might be miffed at being story number two.

As if on cue, there was *another* knock. I went to the door, even though I couldn't see it. The 'electric' aura from my migraine had reached its zenith. Aside from the excruciating pain of frequent migraines, I am a closeted fan of

the aura. I have a love/hate relationship with the visual recital. It's... spectacular in color and vibrancy.

I opened the door and a young UCLA med student stood in the electric prism of colors generated by my migraine.

"Would it be... possible to talk with you for just a few minutes, Mr. Bbbbenson?" he asked in a quivering voice.

"Sure, come on in." I put out my hand to shake his, trying to be as pleasant as possible, and noticed his hands were clammy; moist.

"You're sweating, man. Are you okay?" I pulled a chair over for him to sit down before he passed out.

"I'm just a little nervous. Or scared. And nervous. Scared."

"There's no need to be nervous. Scared." I tried...

"May I ask what this is about?" Karla sweetly, but pointedly inquired. "You know he needs to get to sleep. He's having surgery in the morning."

"That's just it! You see, I have a heart murmur— like you. A congenital, bicuspid aortic valve— just like you!"

"Cool. Lucky for you, you work in the perfect place—"

The young almost-doctor suddenly panicked and cut me off. His body (through the aura) stiffened and he was apprehensive; distressed. He grabbed and wouldn't let go of my hand. His grip tightened.

"No! I've seen what goes on 'down there!' It's horrible! I'm not kidding. I wanted to talk to you cause I'm so freaked out that one day, I'm gonna need your surgery!"

It was like having Gene Wilder from the original film *The Producers* in my room. He was hyperventilating, and... somehow I found this 'scene' playing out in front of me to be hysterically funny. Karla didn't.

"What?!" Karla said, her voice going from contralto to coloratura in one syllable. But that did not stop him.

"If I had to have that surgery tomorrow, I know what I'd do. I'd run! I'd pack up and run! I'm not kidding! I've seen what goes on down there!"

It was the kind of honest comedy anyone who studies the art of 'the funny' lives for: spontaneous, random— priceless. I began laughing hard enough to be incapacitated, and I couldn't converse with the terrified kid (who was probably less than four years younger than me). I felt rude laughing, but it was a prodigious release of tension. Karla on the other hand, was furious (which made it funnier and funnier— I became her audience) as she ushered him out the door. I mean, seriously, what could I do? I could either laugh, or be scared enough to leave. And I knew I wasn't going to leave, so why not laugh?

Later? Oh, the pain and throbbing from the migraine. I couldn't even take an Excedrin. A cup of strong black tea would've helped, but no liquids before the surgery, either.

It was a long night, leaving room for deep conversations with Karla about subjects usually unspoken. I wish every night was like the night before we face our mortality; that way, there would be much more meaningful conversations with the people we love... It was a great lesson; more of a gift than a burden.

THE FOLLOWING MORNING, I HEARD THAT *SOUND*... the metal table with the squeaky wheels— the sound of the prep cart coming down the hallway. Its

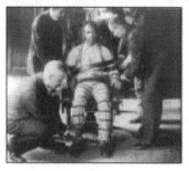

destination: *my room*.

I could still taste the migraine as I was 'prepped.' My inhibitions began to shed like the hair of a Golden Retriever on a suede sofa. I went from a private prude to an unwilling exhibitionist in a matter of minutes. Every part of my torso and groin were dry shaved with a Bic disposable razor by a male nurse who never spoke a single word to me, no matter what I said to him. Then he used a sandpaper-like substance to get the top layer of skin off my body. He rubbed and rubbed. The friction was irritating. Then he painted my torso and groin with cold Betadine. He pulled up my hospital gown and placed a Foley Catheter in my penis.

"Not even a kiss 'Hello'?" I joked.

No laugh. No smile!

"Gimme your arm," he said flatly.

He grabbed my arm, treating me like I was already anesthetized, flipped it over in a way that hurt, but I didn't want to show it (I didn't want to frighten Karla), and then he decided to put an I.V. into the top of my hand, just above the wrist. Pow. Done. Ow. None of this felt... good or pleasant and his company didn't help. Karla's deep concern only made me pretend that everything was 'A-okay.' What a sham.

Two other men in hospital garb pushed a gurney into the room.

"Let's get you over onto this gurney, Mr. Benson."

Suddenly, all I could think about was the hysterical student doctor from the night before telling me to "Run!" And that made me... calm. Because it was *funny*.

Keeping things light, I said, "I'm not the kidney transplant. I'm the open-heart aortic valve replacement."

"Your date of birth?" the unamused nurse asked me.

"One, twenty-one, fifty-six."

He looked at his paperwork. "Open-heart," he nodded.

Whoa— he took me seriously. And then— off I went.

"Wait!" I said in falsetto. I then deepened my voice, "I want to kiss my wife."

Karla looked into my eyes, kissed me, held my hand, and if ever I knew how lucky I was to spend my life with her, it was at that precise moment— except I wish she had chosen to hold the hand without the I.V. in it.

Energy passed through her and into me. Strength. Courage. Which reminded me of *The Wizard of Oz* and the beautifully written line that Professor Marvel tells to the Tin Man: "a heart is not judged by how much you love, but by how much you are loved by others." I looked at Karla. She loved me. How did that happen? I was not in the habit of 'Thanking God,' but I remember as I was being wheeled away that I thanked God for loving and being loved by Karla.

I would not let her down. Not her, or my mom and dad, my sister, my baby girl, or Vivienne— most of whom were already waiting in the visitors' lounge.

It was October 31st. Halloween.

Could I awaken from surgery and say 'Trick or Treat!' to my family as my first words? Could I assure them with those words— a pedestrian, gimmicky joke— that they had nothing to worry about? The only way I knew how was to focus and *visualize*, the same way I used to learn my lines; I would rehearse long monologues in my sleep. And when I would awaken, voila! I would know my lines backwards and forwards. Could I possibly do this with induced sleep? Could I accomplish this through all of the chemicals given to me for open-heart surgery? Well, I thought, 'I'll try.'

'Trick-or-treat. Trick-or-treat.' Don't forget! Black and orange. 'Trick or treat!' I thought, over and over and over again.

I was wheeled into the elevator and people in street clothes looked at me as if I were already dead. The passengers did everything they could to avoid eye contact. I searched their faces, but no one returned my gaze. There was a stale smell, like garbage was transported in this elevator— along with dead bodies— and clothes that stank of their owners having a smoke outside, thirty seconds ago.

Then I was wheeled into the operating room. What a contrast. The smells were now completely different; antiseptic— a chemical smell that was overwhelming and frightening. And the temperature of the operating room felt like those moments when I've looked deep into the refrigerator to find an old sandwich, way in the back, behind the carton of milk. I began to shiver.

"Would you like a blanket, Mr. Benson?"

"I'm the open-heart— right?" I smiled.

"Birthday?"

"One, twenty-one, fifty-six."

"Yup. Open-heart. Want that blanket now?"

"Sure. Thanks." The first kind gesture so far this morning… things are looking up.

People with blue smocks and paper masks on came into view. A clear plastic gas mask was suddenly being lowered over my nose and mouth; a bit of an ambush. I felt my pulse race like my first solo flight in a Piper Cub and thought, 'Yippee! Here we go!'

I was asked to count backwards from 100. I knew I'd never get to 95, so I went, "100, 99… 2, 1— Ha!"

"He thinks he's *funny*. Just wait 'til he wakes up. Let's see how funny he thinks he is then," were the last words I heard.

Trick Or Treat

WHEN I AWOKE FROM SURGERY (somewhere between deep sleep and a bad nap with water-boarding), I wondered if anyone had written down the

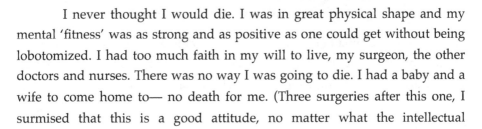

license number of the truck that hit me.

I never thought I would die. I was in great physical shape and my mental 'fitness' was as strong and as positive as one could get without being lobotomized. I had too much faith in my will to live, my surgeon, the other doctors and nurses. There was no way I was going to die. I had a baby and a wife to come home to— no death for me. (Three surgeries after this one, I surmised that this is a good attitude, no matter what the intellectual foundation.)

Remarkably, I felt like I had heard everything that had happened in the operating room. But my first agenda was to get these tubes that were down my esophagus *out!* I immediately yanked on whatever was in my mouth and pulled it from my throat. I heard a young woman's voice say, "Oh, shit— he just pulled his ..."— and then I opened my eyes. I was moving.

I made out the shapes of my mother and Karla for a millisecond. It took every ounce of will but I did manage to say "Trick or Treat!"

They literally squealed with delight, but then I was gone, unconscious again. The next thing I heard was a man vomiting, over and over. My eyes refused to open. I screamed inside my head, chastising my eyes and ordering them to open, but they yelled back at me: 'No!' I couldn't move a muscle but I could *hear* and remember with precision; the mental clarity was awesome.

I heard a doctor complain, "It really sucks that a guy who tried to O.D. was put in the cardiac ICU." And then I heard the man vomit again as they pumped his stomach. The same doctor said, "Look at this— he got blood on my new shirt! How am I gonna get this out?" And in unison my mom, my sister and Karla, with the wry sarcasm that makes up the trio that I love so much, said "Shout it out!" (mimicking the annoying commercial for the popular laundry product).

I heard my family talking and reading get-well cards. We may look unconscious, but we hear more than one might think. I've been with people in comas or in a deep drugged state due to cancer and was appalled at the way others would speak, as if the patient wasn't in the room.

Take it from me, *patients hear everything.*

The next thing I knew, a nurse was screaming in my ear: "Mr. Benson? Mr. Benson? Wake up! Do you know where you are? Mr. Benson, you just had open-heart surgery. It's time for you to wake up Mr. Benson!"

'My god, woman, stop screaming in my ear,' I tried to say

— but nothing came out. I had open-heart surgery not a middle ear cholesteatoma. Hmmm. Why would I know that medical term? Even though I'm drugged with anesthesia, I seem to have a heightened sense of intelligence, memory; a clarity that was fabulous— except for the fact I now upgraded my collision from a Mack Truck to a ROTEM K2 'Black Panther'

Tank.   Oh, my head! Another migraine? How can that be?

Who took a bite out of my head?   I noticed that my sense of smell was over-the-top: in survival mode. I smelled everything from B.O. to individual perfumes and colognes. I've always had a ridiculously heightened sense of smell, but now I knew exactly what this woman had for lunch: B.L.T., hold the mayo but gimme the chips. Cheddar cheese chips. And were they playing Bach in the operating room? I was sure of it! I'd have to ask.

"Mr. Benson, can you see me?" That was an ironic question. I am legally blind without my contact lenses: -11.5. I can't see anything but shapes. Shouldn't she know that?

"Mr. Benson, if you want to get out of the ICU, you're going to have to wake up, sit up and show me you are ready to move. Can you hear me? Can

you wake up? Are you awake? Can - you - hear - me?" she yelled.

'YES!' I screamed, but absolutely nothing came out of my mouth.

 I know she meant no harm, and I'm sure she had to do this every single day of the week, and maybe someone was waiting for my bed in the ICU, but it was painful to the *new* migraine. And then... there was the *REAL*

pain.  Not migraine pain— ***NUCLEAR PAIN.***

I worked hard to open my eyes and saw the blurry outline of the

nurse who had been yelling at me.

"Hello, Mr. Benson. How do you feel?"

'How do you think?' I thought. "Thirsty..." I managed to say.

"I'm sorry, Mr. Benson, you cannot drink anything."

'Then why did you ask me?' I thought.

"Okay," I said.

"Soon we'll be able to give you some ice chips to suck on, but until then, no liquids. We don't want to throw up and choke on our own vomit, do we?"

It was 'our' vomit? I actually said "No." Why? I don't know. Maybe because I could.

"The pain..." I managed to say.

"Yes. It hurts, doesn't it? That's perfectly normal. We'll give you some pain medication."

"No!" I said.

"What?"

"I don't want any."

Given her reaction, this was a new concept. I foolishly thought pain medication would destroy my ability to stop this explosion of hurt that lived in my chest. I could and would tough it out.

"You're going to need pain medication in order to heal, Mr. Benson."

"Says who?"

"Says me," the nurse volleyed. "Your body must relax to heal, and the only way your body can relax is with pain medication. The human body is a remarkable machine, Mr. Benson, and we have to give it every chance we can to help it mend itself. But you must listen to me and *do everything I say!*"

I was hurting like a victim in Peckinpah's *Straw Dogs*, or for today's audience, *Saw V.*

"Sorry," I said. "I don't believe in pain medication. I can make it through this without any chemicals."

I opined that taking pain medication would turn me into a fun-house tabloid story, mimicking so many other young actors who ended up addicted to drugs, and *idiotically,* I was convinced that taking pain medication for open-heart surgery would send me down the path of pop-culture self-destruction. I can't blame the anesthesia for that insane clunker attitude. I really was *ignorant* and scared out of my mind that drugs were like the flu. You could *catch* it. I had to do anything and everything I could— not to catch 'the drugs.'

Soon they had Karla by my bed. I could see better and I could smell her approaching. She had the most distinct smell. I can only quantify it with a non sequitur: she smelled *perfect.*

"Robby, darling, you must take pain medication. There is no reason for you to feel this much pain."

"I can't."

"Sweetheart, you're not a bad person for taking pain medication after open-heart surgery."

"I am."

"You're not!"

"To me, I am."

"To me, you're not." She could be strong for such a gracefully compassionate soul mate. "Do this for me, if you won't do it for yourself."

I almost started to cry. "I'll be a drug addict."

"You're not a drug addict for taking pain medicine after open-heart surgery, honey."

"To me, I am.

"To me, you're not!"

I was really upsetting her. And the whole point of "Trick or Treat!" and *not taking pain medication,* and everything else I was going to do, was to *prove* 'I was okay.' More than okay; I wanted to sit up and start walking before anyone— in the entire history of open-heart surgery on the planet we call Earth!

"Do it for me, Robby," Karla whispered in my ear.

Oh, this was a set-up.

She may be blurry, but I can visualize 'other things' too... She was my Goddess. I lived life for her and her alone! Nothing on the planet mattered more— and then the nurse held up a chart that was so fuzzy, it could've been

the original Magna Carta.   Instead it was a chart with *faces*, smiling and frowning. And next to the faces were numbers: 1-10. The number '1' meant I had no pain; '10' meant I hurt worse than castration.

"What number are you?"

"I'm not a number," I said. "I'm Robby. Robby the guy who doesn't take drugs!"

"He can't see the chart," Karla explained patiently to the nurse. "He's legally blind without his contacts."

"Oh, why didn't I know that?"

The nurse then continued in a tone that Nursery School teachers use on 4 year-olds. "If on a scale of one to ten, ten being the worst pain in the universe, and one being the way you feel when you go to the beach, what number describes the pain you're feeling now?"

"I hate the beach."

"Robby," Karla said, a bit stronger than usual. "Please tell her, darling."

"I'm not going to tell her or else she'll turn me into a 'shrum' addict."

"A what?" the nurse asked.

"Shrum! Shrum! Or Heroin!"

Okay— I said some pretty stupid things when I was coming down from anesthesia. As stupid as this sounded, and as much as everyone thought it was triggered by the surgical 'circumstances,' it unfortunately was the way I honestly felt. I was misinformed to such an extent that fear had burrowed deep into my knee-jerk reflexology.

"Shrum!"

Every time I was around drugs in show business (a lot), the only way for me to avoid being party to the parties was to brainwash myself. I believed — unmetaphorically, with graphic pithiness— I'd be a drug addict if I even looked at drugs, let alone allowed them into my system, my surroundings, vicinity, environment, background, foreground... Do not cross the border of my circumscription! (I vowed to live in my own urban legend.)

"Sweetheart," Karla whispered, "I've never asked you to do anything I knew was against your beliefs. I want you to take the pain medication. For me. For you. Do you understand?"

This was the biggest decision of my life. And because Karla asked me, the answer was easy.

"No."

"What?"

"I'm kidding. Okay. Gimme the dope."

I could barely make out the nurse shooting the ample hypodermic needle full of Lenny Bruce into the meat of my shoulder (remember, this was 1984; there wasn't a little button to press for morphine yet.) They didn't even give me the pain medication through the I.V. It went into the muscle like liquid lead. I began to wonder if I needed pain medication for the administration of pain medication.

Then it happened: I became a drug addict. Slowly, the pain in my chest began to dissipate. Then the aches in my stunt-ravaged body went bye-bye, too.  I began to think 'bye-bye' was the funniest word I had ever heard.

Karla was no longer a Goddess. She was God!

My surgeon walked up to the bed. "How are you doing, Robby?" he asked.

Dr. Laks was not only brilliant, he was so charming, good-looking and carried himself with such genuine magnetism that women would practically swoon as he would glide down the halls of the hospital. I thought if I should die during the operation, I'd want Karla to be with Dr. Hillel Laks. Okay, that's insane— but it showed my admiration for the only man I would never be jealous of.

"I'm ready to go home," I told him. "And I love you."

"Well, I'm glad you are feeling well, Robby, but it's only been a few hours since you came out of surgery. You still have drainage tubes and pacemaker wires in your chest and you'll have to do breathing exercises to keep your lungs clear and get up and walk before we can even allow you to go to your own room."

"I love you," I repeated. "And if I die, you can marry Karla."

"Thank you. And no more talk of death," he whispered back.

My drugged statements made him and the bevy of interns who followed him (like 'shrum' followed 'mush') smile, but there was darkness to my surgeon's mood. I couldn't tell why. He checked my chart and then moved on. I asked the nurse why he was troubled and she told me I was highly perceptive. And stoned. I told her I was an actor and a writer and I am trained to be highly perceptive. And yes, I was so stoned that everything sonically sounded like it was being produced by George Martin.

"Who's George Martin?" she asked.

"How dare you! How dare your musical ignorance! Have you no shrum?" I echoed and reverbed with a hint of flange and touch of warm analogue tube resonance. I managed to follow the form of my surgeon, an outline of his perfect posture standing in front of something about 15 yards away from me in the ICU.

The nurse leaned into me and said in a hushed voice, "He operated on a very sick baby..."

I had lived 28 years of a privileged life, yet a baby was struggling for life only 15 yards from me. I began to cry. I cried and cried. I understood that the pent-up emotions I had been carrying around for 28 years were being brought to the surface by my vulnerability. The beauty, happiness and silliness I felt only moments before were replaced by the equally powerful sorrow and the bottomless pit of despair where I was now falling… and falling.

"The baby will be fine, Robby," the nurse said.

"How can you know? How can anyone know?" My face was now entirely wet with a torrent of tears. Crying had become a grief-stricken calisthenics. This baby represented Lyric; Karla as a child; me; my parents fifty years ago; the entire population on Earth.

"Everything possible is being done for her."

IN ORDER TO HEAL PROPERLY, I did exactly what I was supposed to do and more; I inhaled into a little plastic 'toy' so a ball could elevate with every inhalation. It clears the lungs, and pneumonia is the last thing a heart patient wants, so I used the little toy, unprompted, over and over again. I sat up. I sucked on ice chips. I progressed by *forcing* myself to roll out of the bed, no matter how painful. Work ethic; discipline. I walked and walked the halls, pushing my I.V. I made trips to the ICU to check on the health of the baby in the small plastic, see-through cubby. Sometimes I'd just stand and stare at her.

Her name was 'Amy.'

Amy had bandages and tubes coming from everywhere. How on Earth could a surgeon work with such tiny organs, such small veins and arteries? It had to be impossible, yet my surgeon was known as one of the best pediatric surgeons in the world.

I prayed (this was becoming a habit). I prayed, begging God to heal this child. Is there a God? 'If there is, I beg of you— heal this little baby.'

I MADE IT TO MY HOSPITAL ROOM IN RECORD TIME because I was the Olympic patient I told myself to be. Joan Rivers was there with her husband Edgar Rosenberg in the room next to mine. He had open-heart surgery days before I did, and languished in bed, in pain.

Every time I walked past her, pushing my I.V., she would look up and say something 'encouraging' like "Robby— what took you so long?"

A day later came the moment of truth— the moment I call the ultimate episode of 'Robby Benson: come on down! *This Is Going To Hurt.*'

"What's going to hurt?" I asked naively.

"We're going to pull your drainage tubes."

Huh??

The drainage tubes were at the bottom of my vertical incision that began just under my sternum and went down to about 3 inches above my belly button. On either side were two, almost an inch in diameter, clear plastic tubes that drained the fluids from the trauma of the operation and every 'juice' that goes with open-heart surgery that includes liquids in places they shouldn't be.

Thus— *drainage* tubes.

I looked down at myself. I suddenly was very self-conscious of all the wounds, holes and crusty blood. It most certainly was Halloween. I no longer

needed a costume. For the rest of my life, I could go as *me.*

I inspected myself: the tubes disappeared into my torso. 'I wonder how far inside me they actually go?' I also thought I saw my skin and crusty blood, trying to grow around the tubing.

Two doctors went to either side of the bed. Both took the tubing in their hands and wrapped it around their grips the same way one does when

trying to pull the string and start a gasoline lawn mower.

And then, it happened. They placed their feet on the bed for leverage, one doctor nodded to the other, and the doctor on my right pulled the tube with a violent twist of his hips, as if he were swinging the hammer throw in the Olympics. Out came the tube.

Oh - my - god!

Where is that pain chart? Forget the chart— where is a megaphone? I need to warn every future patient that this was the most excruciating pain I had felt up until that moment in my life.

Then with little warning, and *no pain medication* to leverage the throbbing, hurt-of-all-time pain, exploding off the chart at 100+ (forget the 1-10 scale), a sensation so unbearably intense I wouldn't wish on anyone (not even Mel Gibson), Sadistic Intern #1 nodded to his Evil Twin— and I realized: *it was all about to happen again.*

GODDDDDDD! How can this be? Who thought up this horrible

OPEN HOUSE
DENNIS VILLAGE
CEMETERY

torture? Who thinks this way? These two young interns could've at least done me the favor of pulling out my tubes *simultaneously*. And as I agonized, they began to stitch my stomach up with no topical anesthetic. I realized how bad the pain from 'the pull' was, because being stitched up without anesthetic felt like someone was tickling me; pinching me, at worst. I'm watching the needle and the thread go through my skin thinking, 'This should hurt more...' Next, without warning, one of the doctors snipped, then pulled the wires from my pacemaker— wires that were coming from *inside* of my chest.

Wow. Big Pain meet Small Pain. All the broken bones, the 'stunts gone bad'— a car once driving over my legs in a get away scene— I never knew pain. Until now.

THE 'PULLING OF THE TUBES' (like its counterpart, 'The Running of the Bulls') may still go on at some archaic hospitals, but I doubt the procedure is the same. Now they have made it *easier* on the patient. But just in case, *you should know and be ready for it.* Ask the doctors and nurses to explain exactly what they are going to do when they take out your drainage tubes and make sure you tell them you do not want to feel excruciating pain— ask for pain medication.

Hour after hour, I got stronger and stronger. I even walked the stairs. I needed to convince my doctors I was ready to go home: I wanted 'out! I wanted to begin anew— immediately.'

But before I left the hospital, I went back to the ICU to check on 'Amy.'

Amy had died.

Recovery...

I WANTED TO GO HOME, but the reality of leaving the safety net of UCLA hospital four days post open-heart surgery was scary. I would be free of hospital 24/7 fluorescent lights, endless noise, and professional caretakers— no matter how well meaning— poking me every two hours day and night. Yet going home meant being on our own. Would we know how to handle a real problem? What might go wrong, and what is normal?

First I had to put on my street clothes. They had been in a plastic bag for only a few days but they seemed foreign, as if they were from another lifetime. I didn't want any help; Karla understood with just quick eye contact.

Completing each simple task, pulling up my pants, tying my shoes, getting into my T-shirt, was painful, but became a personal triumph.

At 28 I didn't look like the typical open-heart patient: there was color in my face and I gave the impression of being spry and limber. So when a volunteer came with the wheelchair asking if Robby was ready to leave the hospital, I turned to Karla and said, "Robby, no matter how good you feel, you have to get into the wheelchair. Really... It's a hospital rule— don't be stubborn!" The volunteer agreed with me, and after a few beats (just long enough to get a laugh but short enough so that no one felt stupid or manipulated) I finally gave in, sat in the wheelchair holding a pillow against my chest, and off we went. We were leaving the cocoon of safety and rolling back into the real world.

The drive home was awkward. I wasn't used to being out of control. I wasn't used to being a passenger in my own car. After open-heart surgery you're not allowed to drive for six weeks. This was the beginning of a learning curve: 'How to give up control and trust others— especially the woman you love.' That didn't mean I wasn't the most obnoxious GPS ever invented: "Slow down, turn right, prepare to merge, you're driving too fast..." (It took me three more surgeries to accept Karla doing the driving.)

I kept the pillow against my chest to protect my newly-wired sternum and fresh wound from the pressure of the seatbelt. Using a pillow to support the chest is something all open-heart patients need. A laugh is painful, and a sneeze without a pillow is excruciating— so a pillow went with me everywhere for the first few weeks.

On November 23, 1984, I was watching the Boston College game when Doug Flutie threw his famous Hail Mary pass for a touchdown in the end zone. I jumped up and down cheering him on at the top of my lungs and almost opened my incision. I grabbed a pillow, held it tightly against my chest, and continued to celebrate for Flutie. I was watching a *Saturday Night Live* parody of the massively successful Jane Fonda Workout. (Even tiny Lyric would exercise along with Karla, crying "More Jane Fonda!" when the tape ended.) The skit was the 'Henry Fonda Workout.' In the poorest taste, they had a coffin opening and closing, with a voice sounding like Ms. Fonda saying, "Yes! Make it burn!" Maybe it was the drugs, or maybe it was just funny— but thank goodness for the pillow...

During the first two weeks at home I would I get night sweats so badly Karla had to change the soaking wet sheets as I shook from the chills like a bobble-head doll. As soon as I'd changed, and Karla brought extra blankets, the cycle started all over again. Maybe it was my body working overtime trying to deal with my healing heart and sternum. I found out later many open-heart patients have night sweats. Research has shown it may be an after-effect of the Heart Lung machine. Night sweats can be a symptom of an infection, which is serious for any open-heart patient, particularly one with valve replacement. My temperature was normal— no fever, no infection. But all I had to do was lean down to rest and it was as if I had an altimeter that triggered water to pour from my pores— and the next thing I knew I was completely soaked and shivering, trying to understand (like a five year-old) 'when is this going to stop?'

I remember, as will many of the readers, the first time I went into the bathroom and stared— truly just stared— at my scar. Many open-heart patients remember the moment when we come face-to-torso with reality. It can come at any time, but for me, this was my moment when I just stared blankly at my scar in our bathroom mirror. This was the bathroom I wrote *Modern Love* in because we made a beautiful little bedroom for Lyric in the only other room in the house. As scars go, it was definitely not a 'cool' scar. I had plenty of those, with great stories from each stunt in a film that sent me to the E.R. But this scar was very different. It was a thick vertical ropey line of crusted blood. There were two more smaller scars, each a slit about an inch long. These were horizontal and were almost symmetrically placed above my belly-button. These scars were from the drainage tubes. Unfortunately, instead of making peace with the fact that someone had saved my life and now I was facing a different phase in my life, I looked at my scars and too many questions began swirling around as if someone had done a CGI moment and you could actually see hundreds of questions with question marks that were luminous in bright orange colors— the type of orange I learned to hate from medicine I took as a kid. These questions were whizzing around and around my head and my gut. Am I going to scare children? Will Karla be grossed out when we're together and pretend that everything is actually alright? Why am I not proud of this scar? I'm a guy, scars are cool. This scar was a sign of weakness. Was I really that backward? Do little children know to be scared of these wounds or will Lyric accept me as I am?

Whoa, I needed to get past this self-inflicted, indulgent vulnerability at once. Now, I thought. as I looked at myself in the mirror— it must go away — whoa— holy cow— my nipples are... askew. Askew? Nipples? Is it possible? Was one higher than the other? This can't be. I think they put me back together again worse than Humpty-Dumpty. My right nipple was higher than my left. Or was it the opposite? Whose opinion could I get? I thought... No one! If it were true, what could I do about it? Nothing. I would never have any kind of plastic surgery for narcissistic reasons. And who would I ask? Karla? We were just married a couple of years ago. Now we had a baby. What am I going to do, come out of the bathroom and ask her if my right nipple is higher than my left nipple? Who would do such a thing?

"Karla," I shouted. She was my wife but she was also my best friend. She was the only person to ask and to trust.

"Yes, sweetheart?"

"My right nipple is higher than my left nipple, isn't it?"

She never made me feel foolish. It was as if she understood immediately and wanted to be honest and at the same time put me at ease. We stared at my torso for about five minutes.

Finally she said, "I don't know, but it's kind of sexy."

She kissed me and we talked, but I tried to stay away from anything that was winey or indulgent. Then I told her I was going to take a shower and I would put plastic over my wound so it didn't get wet, per my hospital orders. She asked if I needed help but I explained that this is the kind of thing that must become second nature and I needed to deal with it on my own. So, with the kind of kiss I remember to this day, she left me to my own devices. (Bad call...)

Now my scar became an enemy— another hurdle to clear and my next thoughts came from my show business side of the brain. Which side of the brain is that? The one that begins in your ass: How would I ever hide this scar from the cameras? Was there a make-up artist on the planet who could take the scar away? I was so ashamed of my real feelings.

When Karla left the house to run a quick errand, I grabbed the keys to our other car and even though I wasn't supposed to drive for another five weeks, I drove to a make-up store in the San Fernando Valley called 'Frends Beauty Supply'. Every make-up artist that I knew had always used Frends so I went to the store to see if they had make-up to cover scars. I was given about six different bases and cremes and pastes and I bought them all. I didn't have time to waste— I had to get back home before Karla got back from her errand. And I did. I went into the bathroom as if I were going to shower and then locked the door. Secretly, I tried to come up with the best solution to hide the scar. Hide it not only physically, but mentally— this never happened. But what *did* happen was that out of every combination of make-ups only one worked: 'mellow-yellow.' This seemed to blend in with my skin tone and somewhat hide the scar.

Water was not supposed to touch the still slightly open and scabby 'scar,' yet now I had to remove every drop of make-up given to me by experts, on a wound that was still oozing and healing. I gently used make-up remover but that didn't work. So, I got out the peroxide and poured half the bottle on my chest. I let the bubbles foam up and finally I wiped away most of the make-up. But even that didn't work. I grabbed the bottle of rubbing alcohol from under the sink, took a deep breath and put a towel in my mouth to bite down on and then proceeded to splash the bottle of rubbing alcohol, on the oozing wound. The sting, the pain was almost laughable compared to what I had been through. The only thing I was worried about was infection. So, I emptied the alcohol bottle on my open wound, and with the help of some gauze, I got all of the mellow-yellow out of my scar.

I finally showered (ironically, with plastic covering my scar). But washing my hair was *orgasmic*. What a luxury, I thought— and then laughed at all of the things we do on a daily basis that were now heavenly to me: being with Karla; going to the fridge to get a snack; walking outside and feeling the sun on my face...

ONE OF THE HIGHS OF SHOW BUSINESS is when the phone rings unexpectedly with good news. I was still in pain and self conscious about my wound bleeding through my shirt when we received a phone call from Karla's producer, David Anderle. Karla's album for A&M Records, *Wake 'Em Up In Tokyo*, had not yet been completed and David asked if we'd be interested in writing a spec song for the soundtrack of the new John Hughes film. This was just what I needed; a chance for us to focus on a fun musical assignment. Keith Forsey was overseeing the soundtrack and invited us to the editing room to meet the iconic Mr. Hughes and watch an early cut of a dance montage, shot to an electronic click track.

Suddenly, I felt that I had purpose. Life in the arts was not over for me; I had hope.

When we got home I couldn't sleep. Lyrics and music literally poured out of me (even with the night sweats!). By the time we got into the studio, Karla had a blast blasting it out vocally, and it did what a song *should* do in a film: it energized the moment and moved the narrative forward. Mr. Hughes loved it. Karla sings "We Are Not Alone," the moment in *The Breakfast Club* when the kids finally connect

and dance in the library. My music 'got out there.' Karla DeVito sang our song. What more could any songwriter want?

WE WERE THE FIRST IN OUR PEER GROUP to have a baby; fortunately, Karla's mom Vivienne flew to L.A. and was ready, willing, and able to help us fill in the blanks. But, when it came to open-heart surgery, there were no family members or friends to call on to discuss the feeling of inadequacy; no one to talk to; no one to reason with; no mentor or expert to help get me through a topic even the doctors didn't like discussing: What happens after open-heart surgery?

I was prescribed pills. I went to a couple of sessions that were called cardio rehab, but that was just learning how to stretch and keep moving. Every inquiry I made through my cardiologist was returned with a well-rehearsed sentence or two about *time*. 'Time heals all wounds.' I felt like time was my enemy, and I didn't want more rest or to learn how to stretch. They screwed with my heart— I only had 'so much' time. I went back to the only way I knew how to deal with problems of the mind and body: exercise. And exercise at my pace. My first goal was to prove to myself that I was better than ever, which could not be accomplished without old-fashioned hard work. Hard work. At least I understood what that meant. You get what you give. So I (foolishly) gave a lot.

I went back to the gym immediately, forgoing protocol and creating my own cardio rehab. I pushed myself hard, training for a 10K race to be run exactly eight weeks to the day after my open-heart surgery. Every time I'd hit a painful moment in the gym I'd visualize the outcome— and the 'future images' kept me pushing past the pain, putting the operation behind me as if it never existed.

The race was held at midnight on New Years Eve, running off-road and sometimes crossing streams on a nature path. Karla wasn't worried because my best friend and teammate since grade school, Randy Gunter, was going to run and he'd hold the flashlight for us. In the past he had never beaten me in any race. Now I was running 8-minute miles, not 6-minute miles, and he not only could keep up, at about the 5K mark, he decided to 'put me away.' I had no problem with that— except he took the damn flashlight with him. I spent the last 3.1 miles running in the dark. Karla was upset with him, but I love Randy. He is like the brother you can't ever get pissed at— this was his chance to beat me, and he did. Fair and square. (I crushed him in the next race. Fair and square.)

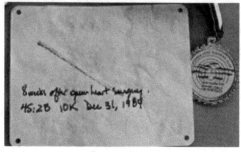

Accomplishing my goal through physical exercise was my only tangible way to show family, doctors, my agent and anyone paying attention I was physically capable of continuing at my former pace. Would it have been worse if I came home from the hospital and sat on the couch doing nothing? Yes. I believe you must get up and move. But really— what kind of idiot was I? A big one, constantly thinking I knew best. I didn't. I could've killed myself in the gym. And if not killed myself, I could've done serious damage to my chest.

Now, after four open-heart surgeries, I have come to an understanding that we must consult the experts and set realistic goals for ourselves after surgery. Unfortunately, back in the 80s, I didn't have anyone willing to discuss or consult with me about anything. But today, doctors and surgeons understand that what we do after the surgery is just as important as life before the surgery. My self-designed cardio rehab was insane. I was thinking with my testosterone, not my head.

The upside? I was in tremendous shape. Rick called, happy to relay some good news: I was offered the lead in an ABC TV movie **California Girls**. Charles Rosin's fanciful script was solid, and I still adore Rick Wallace, who directed, but I took the part because there were scenes where I would have my shirt off in the sun, and my chest exposed. This was a test; make-up would have to be applied over my still tender and scabby scar. But I knew the the right make-up to use, and as it turned out, the make-up artist agreed: mellow-yellow.

I took the challenge to prove to myself I could still carry a film, albeit a TV movie (with a harder schedule than a feature film because it's shot in less time). I had my doubts. Did I have the stamina? And what would I look like with my shirt off when the film came back from the lab?

It almost worked, but if you look closely, you can see the 'zipper' going from my sternum vertically down to inches above my belly-button. (In my mind my scar was the still the size of the Mississippi River.) Most importantly: I passed the physical with flying colors. With my new bovine valve in place courtesy of Dr. Laks and his team at UCLA, I was *insured*.

Less than a month later we were out of town working on a small project in Rhode Island. I awoke having tremendous chest pain with every breath, every heart beat. I *never* felt this before. I scared Karla when I said 'yes' to her suggestion we get to an emergency room. Normally, I'd just shrug it off. But I knew something was wrong.

I told the E.R. doctor that Karla was having chest pains. It was hysterical (even in pain) watching Karla try to convince the doctor I was the one in severe pain. (She's such a good sport! And I'm an ass. But making jokes or messing with the scenario seemed to calm everyone down.)

The doctor immediately put nitroglycerin under my tongue. Now Karla and I were both scared— nitroglycerin? That standard TV-doctor Rx made me think I was no longer just someone born with a bad valve that was fixed. Was I having a heart attack? Actually, nitroglycerin: was I going to blow up?! I could see the headlines in *Variety*: "Benson Goes Boffo Boom!"

They put me on a heart monitor, did blood tests, and called L.A. to track down my cardiologist. I had no swelling in my ankles (a warning sign of many heart related conditions) and my heart function and sinus rhythm were normal.

The pain was caused by my first in a long series of bouts with **pericarditis**, an inflammation of the heart sac. My cardiologist explained when the heart sac is cut during surgery, cells released into the blood stream appear foreign to the body's immune system and the response can cause the inflammation.

They prescribed a high dose of Prednisone for three days. After the first day's dose the pain was gone, but by the end of three days I was *nuts*. It works differently with different patients but the doctor told me there was a chance this drug would make me feel indestructible; elated; dismayed; gracious; hateful; benevolent; homicidal— oh, all at the same time. Prednisone is a very powerful drug (a steroid, which they no longer prescribe for this) and it did what it was supposed to do, it took down the swelling around my heart. I was thankful... and an incredible asshole.

TELEVISION SERIES PRODUCERS Paul Witt and Tony Thomas, liked my character in *California Girls* so much they asked me to play that same kind of guy as a young detective in their new untitled TV series. If I was willing to sign on they had a six-episode commitment from CBS. This was a difficult decision for me. It had just become acceptable for a film actor to do a television movie now and again, but a TV series was the 'elephant burial ground' for a film star's career. From a career standpoint, I was desperate. Desperate and looking for a magical cure. Witt-Thomas promised me the moon to star in their 'dramedy,' saying I would be involved in every major decision. I did not know what my 'heart' future would hold, and here was a chance to be a *working* actor again, get my Screen Actors Guild health insurance, and bring in a steady income for my family. The answer had to be: 'Yes.'

That was the last decision where I had a say. Once they had me— they owned me. When the powers that be decided to call it **Tough Cookies**, I knew I was in trouble. Instead of writing in the adorably feisty Elizabeth Pena as my potential love interest, they hired an actress who looked ten years my senior as my girlfriend. It's not that she wasn't talented, it just looked silly. The show was a mid-season replacement; it stunk, I got trashed in the reviews, and it was cancelled after six episodes.

One memory I will never get out of my loop of indelible images: Adam Arkin (who I would later direct in a series with my dear friend Joely Fisher), the warm and wonderful Lainie Kazan, and the entire cast and crew were huddled around a TV on January 28, 1986 watching in tears when the Space Shuttle Challenger exploded. It's a day I'll never forget.

Over the course of my career I had gone from 'the darling of the press' to a punching bag for journalists and reviewers. Even my name ending in a 'y' was fodder for their derision: 'Robby? When is he going to become Robert? How can you take an actor called Robby seriously?' (Too bad for Jimmy Stewart, Mickey Rooney, Danny Kaye, Johnny Carson, Jimmy Carter, Johnny Depp...) I worked my ass off for fifteen years at that point making a name for myself. I wasn't going to change my name to appease anyone. But I thought about it. I thought about anything that would somehow take the stigma of open-heart surgery away from a young actor.

Although I was an 'I don't read reviews' paladin in public, in private I would memorize the hurtful words and, for some bizarre reason, throw out the good reviews. I understood that 'soft' and 'edgy' are merely jargon-stamps that a superficial industry uses to make multimillion-dollar decisions. I realized I couldn't change my identity the way an actor can change roles; I came to the conclusion that it's best to show warts and all. Any deviation from self-awareness for reasons of vanity, ego or pride will eventually expose the very substance I'd like to conceal. In other words, I'd be a hypocrite.

But let's put things in perspective. Show biz stories aren't *deeply* painful. No one needs to be 'saved' in show business.

It's not an emergency or a life and death situation. It can be *artistic* death, or 'career suicide'— but, all in all, we're still here to watch the sun rise and set with our loved ones, and hopefully add to the planet rather than selfishly take away.

IN THE SUMMER OF 1986, Karla and I were on the road doing theater in Ohio, for "The Kenley Circuit."

The flamboyant and talented John Kenley was a true theater aficionado. Mr. Kenley was an extraordinary man; he built a summer stock theater business throughout Ohio and into Michigan using the great old theaters that are now hopefully not parking lots or strip malls. He lured talent into his summer schedule with major bucks and gave the people of Ohio good theater. John Kenley worked as a child in vaudeville; he was part of the Shubert's success in New York.

Mr. Kenley called and offered us a ridiculously large amount of money to do his summer stock tour of **Evita**. Although Karla had come close to starring in the film version, she had never done the show, and had only seen it once— when sent by Andrew Lloyd Webber and Ken Russell between her two screen tests in London in 1981. I hadn't seen it on Broadway, and frankly hated learning new material unless I loved the piece. I wanted to do *Evita* for Karla, but asked her about the amount of work I would need to do for the part of Che. Karla said, "Che's role is like the Stage Manager in *Our Town*— not that much to do." We immediately got on the phone and told John Kenley we were on-board.

Cut to us taking a trip to see the National Tour of *Evita* in Long Beach. After the first fifteen minutes I turned to the woman I adored in the theatre seat next to me and said (as quietly as possible), "You - will - not - live - past - intermission." Che was a babbling, angry nutcase who also sang song after song. Yes, I thought— kind of like the Stage Manager in *Our Town* on crystal meth, running around and singing every line in intervals that made no sense.

Karla's explanation was, "In London I had tunnel-vision; I only saw one thing: Evita!" She pleaded guilty to the classic actor analysis: My line. My Line. Blah blah. My line. My line. Blah blah. My line.

We contacted our friend and vocal coach, Marge Rivingston, and she recommended Kevin Farrell (who had conducted *Evita* for Lloyd Webber) to work with us. I studied the part— begrudgingly— at times questioning if Mr. Lloyd Webber had gotten bored and threw the cat on the piano searching for the intervals Che had to sing. I learned the part while cycling on a stationary bike listening to Mandy Patinkin. He had a gorgeous voice and I wanted to know I could get through the score while my heart rate was above 160. I had to test myself daily so that when I was onstage, what would be difficult for others would be a breeze for me.

We called Vivienne to see if she would consider taking another leave of absence from work to join us on the road spending time with her best little pal, granddaughter Lyric, turning three. She said yes!

MY MOTHER-IN-LAW WAS THE MOST SELFLESS PERSON I have ever met (except for Karla— it all made sense now for me). Vivienne was so joyous and full of life, with a great sense of humor, a laugh that could shake the rafters, and such a kind and giving heart that she was an inspiration to all who knew her.

Vibrantly beautiful at 18, with a great soprano singing voice, Vivienne was spotted by Jack Benny's agent and offered a screen test in Hollywood. Her parents said no; they needed her to work in the family restaurant. With no regrets, Viv said if she'd had great ambition she would have gone anyway.

Viv made it clear she would support any career decision Karla made — only wanting her children to find happiness in life. Karla's father Sebastian (who fought in WWII, looked like a combination of Tyrone Power and George Clooney, and was known for his great personality) was the love of her life. He died of cancer at 38 when Karla was eight, leaving Viv with four children to raise between the ages of three and thirteen. Viv was unstoppable— filling the house with love, laughter and music. Karla never felt there was anything a woman couldn't do because her role model worked full-time, was smart and talented, and able to repair anything— from a broken lamp to a leaky toilet. Viv even helped Karla's Uncle Bob and Aunt Marilyn build the house the family moved to in Mokena, Illinois after Sebastian died.

Vivienne never remarried. When we had Lyric, she came to live with us for a month, and then whenever she could, or if we were in a bind. She was in her glory— thrilled to be Grandma Vivi.

EVITA WAS SUCH A SUCCESS that Mr. Kenley extended the season and offered us another show, a favorite musical among Catholic audiences entitled *Do Black Patent Leather Shoes Really Reflect Up?* Karla promised her agent in L.A. she'd be back in L.A. for pilot season. We decided I would stay on, while Karla, Lyric and Vivi headed back to California.

I was on stage rehearsing when I received a phone call from Karla, and when I heard her voice, I knew something was wrong. Karla's mom Vivienne was in the hospital with heart pain.

I left telling Mr. Kenley I would be back when we all felt Vivienne was in good hands. He could've tried to persuade me to not leave (which wouldn't have mattered) but he didn't. Opening night was in five days, but John Kenley *understood*, even if it left his show without its lead actor.

In the early evening Vivienne had sudden, powerful chest pains. She was stoic— she wouldn't have said anything if she didn't know there was a real problem.

Karla called my cardiologist— she and Lyric had just spent the day with his wife and daughter at the L.A. Zoo. Should she drive Viv to UCLA?

He said no, get to the nearest E.R. immediately and have them call him from there.

Our house was in the winding hills of Tarzana, and Karla thought she could drive to the hospital faster than waiting for an ambulance— so she helped Viv and a naked Lyric (she didn't stop to dress her fresh from a bath) into the car.

(Karla says this was her first mistake: she should have called an ambulance. The EMTs would have relayed their assessment to the hospital and Viv's condition would have received immediate attention.)

She had Viv in the E.R. within 10 minutes of her first chest pain. Karla signed her in and gave them my cardiologist's number saying he needed to speak with them to recommend a colleague to be Viv's doctor.

They did not call him. They admitted Viv to their Cardiac Care Unit and assigned the doctor on call.

Karla met the assigned cardiologist briefly in her mom's room. He gave her no information about her condition, not even committing to say whether she was having a heart attack or not, just that they were doing blood tests, etc.

Then she never saw him again. Karla asked a hospital official if Vivienne could be transferred to UCLA. He said no; not until her condition stabilized.

My parents lived nearby and came to support Karla. They took Lyric home with them.

Karla spoke to my cardiologist several times by pay-phone and asked him to speak with the doctor, but since he was not affiliated with this hospital, he was apprehensive about protocol and stepping on toes. He said for his colleague to take over, Karla would have to *fire* the doctor assigned. Karla balked. It was the 'Cardiac Care Unit.' Wouldn't he be giving her the proper care? He told Karla to ask if Vivienne was receiving 'everything possible given to someone having a heart attack.'

The doctor was nowhere to be found, so Karla asked the head nurse in the Cardiac Care Unit, and she responded, "Absolutely. Everything possible is being done for your mother."

(Karla knows this was her second biggest mistake. The first 30 minutes of a heart attack are critical. If things don't seem right, *immediately* ask for a another opinion.)

When Vivienne asked Karla why was she still having so much pain, Karla asked *again* to speak with Viv's doctor. The Cardiac Care nurse said he had left the building, gave her his pager number, and sent Karla to a pay-phone.

When she finally reached him he said, "Miss DeVito, people experience pain for up to 48 hours after having a heart attack." It was the first time anyone acknowledged Vivienne was having a heart-attack.

Karla told him she was firing him and hiring a new doctor.

Less than two and a half hours after Vivienne's first chest pain, Dr. Oblath, my cardiologist's colleague, walked in and looking at the situation yelled to the Cardiac Care nursing staff, "Why wasn't this woman given Streptokinase?" It was then administered immediately, and Vivienne's pain began to lessen.

The next morning the young resident who had been working in the E.R. when they had arrived came up to Karla and quietly said he would have given Viv Streptokinase if it was his call. Karla thought, 'Protocol... Why didn't you tell me this when I could have done something?'

(We learned that although Streptokinase was approved for use in cardiac hospitals, the doctor was required *to be there* and a special nurse had to be brought in.)

I arrived and Viv's sister Marilyn flew in from Illinois. Vivienne had finally stabilized and we all were able to follow the ambulance transporting her to UCLA. This was the hospital that had saved my life. My cardiologist would take care of her; my brilliant surgeon was here. We were all feeling relief.

Karla helped Viv out of bed to use the bathroom and she said with a laugh, "Oh my Karlie, I thought I was a goner!"

We all kissed Viv goodnight and went home with plans to see her first thing in the morning.

As soon as we got home the phone rang. My doctor called and told us to come back immediately. Two days after her first attack, Vivienne was having a *second* heart attack at UCLA. They were taking her to the Cath Lab.

Waiting in the family lounge, I kept watching the clock... it got later and later but the tiny seconds-hand schemed and deceived. I was now a healed heart patient at UCLA, healthy and alive, living a normal life. The seconds continued to tick. I watched Karla, exhausted, trying to sit up in the waiting room, but eventually closing her eyes, unable to keep herself awake after three days without sleep. The clock refused to stop. Marilyn was reading every magazine in the waiting room, nervously. Time kept moving forward. I looked at Lyric, now three, playing quietly with hospital toys, her life moving forward.

I heard the hospital P.A. system announce, "Mayor Koch to the Cath Lab. Mayor Koch to the Cath Lab, stat!" Mayor Koch— no 'Code Blue?' Was this an attempt to avoid startling loved ones? Tick, tick. I stared at the clock. I was hypnotized by the seconds moving forward, life continuing, patients in the hallway recovering, men and women walking with purpose but seemingly unaware of the clock— their lives, second by second— on a collision course to their last tick.

I stepped out of the waiting room and looked down the hall. My cardiologist was walking toward me. He did the oddest thing. About fifty feet from me, he stopped (no urgency whatsoever) and took a drink from the water fountain. I remembered the day he told me I needed open-heart surgery. Before he told me, he took a sip of water from a paper cup.

My body froze. I managed to get Karla— not knowing what to say, except that the doctor was walking our way. I exchanged a look with Marilyn, a look I'll never forget: we both understood the tragedy unfolding. I was born with a creative mind and I used that mind to guide me through life. This scenario didn't require creativity— it was already too obvious and awful.

I can't remember what the doctor who helped save my life actually said to us about Vivienne's death, except near the end they cut Vivienne's chest open and gave her a 'heart massage' in a last-ditch effort to save her life. That visual was unbearable: the pain and vulnerability Vivienne, only 60 years old, must have been feeling, all alone in the hospital, away from her home in Illinois, lying on a cold table, surrounded by strangers, knowing she was dying...

I held Karla, Lyric and Marilyn tightly. Lyric cried because we were crying. We all went to a private office where we kept asking the same questions every family asks when something tragic and finite happens. The sounds we all made were sounds I never want to hear again.

We visited Vivienne's body. We collected her belongings. And Karla lost her mother... September 2, 1986.

THERE WAS NO REASON FOR ANY OF US TO STAY in L.A. I wanted to be with Karla but she urged me to go back to Ohio to *Patent Leather Shoes* because the show was going to open the next day without its lead... Karla and Lyric flew with Marilyn to Illinois, with plans to join me in a few days.

Karla was at Vivienne's condo organizing her mother's belongings for her brothers, crying and cuddled with a sleeping Lyric on her bed. The TV happened to be on the *Lifetime* channel. A program about advances in heart care came on, telling all about Streptokinase— the 'clot buster' drug— and how it could save lives when administered within 30 minutes of a heart attack. Dumbfounded by the irony, Karla realized if she had seen the program a few days day *before*, it would have saved Vivienne's life.

We learned from the autopsy Vivienne only had one artery with atherosclerosis, but because that doctor let her lie there without any intervention at Tarzana Hospital, a clot did irreparable damage to her heart muscle. At UCLA she was taken off Heparin (a blood thinner) in preparation for an angiogram within a few days. Without the Heparin, another clot formed causing the second heart attack and the heart muscle, so damaged two days before, virtually shredded. Vivienne's death changed the protocol for taking heart attack patients off Heparin at UCLA.

Karla did not rant and rave like a lunatic to get attention; she didn't throw a fit or hurl curse words or even raise her voice. She behaved with the respect her mother had instilled in her; she did everything she possibly could do to get someone to pay attention to Vivienne's chest pain— *without being an asshole*.

I'm here to tell you, sometimes *we have to be assholes*.

Why are many of us afraid to 'make waves' or 'step on someone's toes?'

... as patients, as caregivers, as loved ones. We cannot afford to be victims, because in this game, losing means death.

And please, *learn* from our mistakes. This was a very new time in our lives. We had weathered so many changes, many of them life-altering. This was a time to reflect; to think; to ask myself, 'Why was I the lucky one when it came to my heart and not Vivienne? Could it be because I was a popular actor and got better and more attention when I needed it than she did?' Unfortunately, the answer to that question will always be 'Yes.' That should make all of us reflect. That's just... wrong.

Valuable Life Lesson: It was about this time in my life where I realized, *every little thing* is a 'Valuable Life Lesson.' I began to comprehend that valuable life lessons were not sentences of wisdom that came in fortune cookies. Every breath is a journey into my sponge-like spirit if I manage to keep my eyes open and actually see what I'm looking at. Every blink of the eye is a chance, a golden opportunity to become more educated, compassionate, selfless, overwhelmed with the bigness of it all. I'll refuse to understand the word 'boring' from this day forth.

Modern Love

OUT OF THE BLUE, I got a phone call from Burt Reynolds asking me if I'd go to Italy with him and be in his film with Liza Minnelli, ***Rent-A-Cop***. (Man, when it comes to show business, that phone is a blessing.) He said he'd send the script over immediately. Work! Yes! Script! Oh, no...! I didn't know what to do. Burt was one of the greatest friends anyone could have, but this was just... awful. And it took place in Chicago in the dead of winter. I had no idea where the romance of making a film in Italy came from, but it wasn't anywhere on the pages.

I called Burt. Before I could say anything, he told me how much fun we would all have in Italy. Me, Karla, Lyric, him... I eventually hung up thinking I must've missed something. Somewhere. When did we go to Italy? I reread the script at a turtle's pace trying not to miss anything. Chicago. Chicago. Chicago. And the script wasn't getting any better.

"Burt, there's one thing I just don't understand— you keep saying how we'll all go to Italy, but the film is set in Chicago."

"Oh— I forgot to tell you, it's actually cheaper to build the interiors in Rome at Cinecitta Studios than it is to shoot them in Chicago."

"Oh."

"We'll do the exteriors in Chicago and all the interiors in Rome. So, are you in?"

"Karla and Lyric will have tickets to Italy, too?"

"Of course!"

"I'm in."

Work... with my friend. And since Karla's mom had just passed away, this might be a good thing for all of us. (Man I wish life were that simple...)

And so we went to Italy, where I promised Lyric we would see 'The David' in Florence, and the inside of the Sistine Chapel in Rome. We took Lyric everywhere. I would pick her up in her stroller, carry her up and down the Spanish Steps, and all the way up the cramped circular stairwell to the *Cuppola* of St. Peter's Basilica.

I did all of this with the new frame of mind that there was absolutely nothing wrong with me or my heart. We had a blast. Because my schedule was so light, we went to Venice and Florence and took the bullet train. It was grand. All was well.

All was so well that when the production finally came back to Chicago, Burt, Bernie Casey and I were invited to a Bull's game with Michael Jordan, and I was asked by the management of the Bulls to throw up an 'honorary jump ball.' I was told that the players loved *One On One* and coach Doug Collins was the biggest fan. Of course I said 'Yes.'

Before the teams were announced, someone from the Bulls came and got me and had me wait at the scorer's table— court-side. My adrenaline was pumping. As a ballplayer, I thought it was pretty lame to throw up a jump ball — that was so 'Hollywood'— so I asked if I could take an honorary free-throw. That was more... 'Indiana.' Not New York, but still, not American Samoa.

"Sure, why not."

They finally introduced the teams, but it all came down to introducing Michael Jordan. And when they did, I felt what it must be like to be Michael Jordan. Standing on the basketball floor with the lights suddenly off, the arena dark and the sounds beginning to rumble, all at once a light-show began and as thrilling as it was, there was an energy of thousands of fans beginning to pulsate and it felt as if the entire building was shaking. The plangent cheers for Michael Jordan were so loud I thought he could go deaf from the decibel level—louder than all heavy metal bands combined. And Michael Jordan and company heard this every night. Wow, game after game.

When the lights came up the crowd was still in hysterics and already a bit drunk. The P.A. announcer mentioned my name, "...from *One On One*" *was all I heard*, and then he said the words, "...honorary free-throw." There were boos and cheers, but all I heard were the boos. I thought, 'Yeah, I'd probably boo, too. Honorary free throw, that's so... well, now it seemed so 'Boston.' Screw that. I walked toward the free-throw line, took a dramatic step back, then back again to the 3-point line. Now, that was so... 'New York!' The first thought in my head was, 'Robby— you haven't really been playing any kind of ball since your surgery. Your chest is tight. Your shoulders have been pulled forward by the scar; your basketball posture is bad. What are you doing?'

'Shut-up,' my New York self said to my now Duke subconscious. Actually it would be more like UNLV - but this is a strange basketball mentality that only hard-core players will understand.

And then I felt the basketball in my hands. I felt the leather. I became one with the ball. I remembered the most important thing about being a shooter: a shooter shoots. We don't 'chuck' the ball up, we 'feel' the shot. We 'reel' in the basket from the 3-point line until it is inches from our face; we focus and visualize the ball going in— we never get tight. The better the shooter, no matter the distance, it has to be effortless. And confident.

Then I heard John Paxson laugh and say, "Oh… preeeeessure, Robby. Pressure."

I looked at the Bulls Stadium basket as if it were in the playground at P.S. 199, reeled in the basket until it was inches from my face, and the next thing I knew, I shot the ball… effortlessly… and… swish. Nothing but net. And as I used to say to Karla when I would practice and after every 'swish', "Isn't that the most beautiful sound you've ever heard?" Nothing but net.

The crowd went berserk. So did Doug Collins, Paxson and the rest of the Bulls. But the supreme compliment came when Michael Jordan ran over and slapped me on the butt. I went back to my seat with Burt and Bernie as the conquering hero, but all I kept thinking was: 'Michael Jordan patted me on the butt.' I now had a golden butt. If nothing else, I possessed the butt M.J. slapped. *My* butt. Oh, yeah. "Oh, by the way, Burt and Bernie? Michael Jordan patted me on the butt." I don't think I've ever seen Burt Reynolds happier. And he was happy for me.

I WAS INVITED TO TESTIFY before the Senate Appropriations Committee in Washington D.C. in the spring of 1987. I spoke on behalf of the National Institutes of Health for heart research funding and education. Representing the American Heart Association, along with Surgeon General C. Everett Coop and Senator Ted Kennedy, I also spoke in support of the ground-breaking Kennedy-Hatch Bill attempting to ban the promotion of cigarettes to minors and prevent tobacco companies from advertising at sporting events. (Bye-bye, Joe Camel.)

I DIDN'T REALLY LIKE TO DO THINGS OUTSIDE MY REALM OF COMFORT, and Karla and I were not partygoers, but if Burt Reynolds asked us, we went. He was the man, to me— also, Hollywood 'A-list'— and Hollywood at its finest.

Karla and I were always the youngest people on the guest list. Making an appearance with Karla clutching my sweaty hand helped me get through my fear of social events. We went to remarkable parties at Burt's where most of the guests were Old Hollywood, people we 'knew' from black and white films, coming to life before our eyes *in color*: like the great Fred Astaire.

Karla and I went back to another sold-out summer tour for John Kenley. Even Lyric had a part as our flower girl, and Cliff Bemis co-starred and directed. Cliff possesses a powerhouse voice and great comic timing. He had been a stalwart star at the Cleveland Playhouse, Cleveland Opera— he was virtually the 'king of Cleveland.' Karla and I convinced him to move to L.A. after the last tour and he has been our best family friend ever since. He slept on a pull-out bed in our living room for his first three months in Los Angeles. He was the best houseguest we ever had and we all cried when he he finally moved out. Cliff took Lyric on her first 'date' at three. She told her pre-school friend, "He's big and I'm little, but we don't mind the difference."

AT THIS POINT IN MY CAREER, I realized I would have to re-invent myself. The scripts I was being offered were not the kind of projects I wanted to pour my heart and soul into. I tried. I did my best but coming home from a straight-to-video faux sex thriller made me feel like I was a whore, prostituting everything I believed in, ruining every title that came before these films. But I had to make a living and I literally knew nothing else but the arts. Instead of whining about it, I decided to be proactive.

Maybe I could go back to school. I never took a break for college; I went from film to film after I graduated from high school. I dreamed of going to Harvard, in pre-med when I was in high school. Maybe I should really take a different path.

I had success as a screenwriter, but wasn't sure if I could make a living at it full-time. I knew, for some reason, an actor with a heart problem was an out-of-work actor, but a *director* with a heart problem was usually a respected director. Strange, I thought. *Perception*. I would somehow have to make the jump from actor to director if I were to continue with a career in the arts.

One of my favorite directors and mentors, George Schaefer, was the Chair of the Theater and Film Departments at UCLA. Maybe I'll contact him and ask for his advice, I thought. When we did speak, Mr. Schaefer suggested another option: he encouraged me to *teach*— eventually hiring me to give master classes for a semester at UCLA.

I INITIALLY PASSED ON ANOTHER LURID STORY of drug dealing and nude scenes with body doubles: "Hi, this is Amber. Amber get naked and sit on Robby's face." Nope— I just couldn't do that again. It may sound like fun but believe me, it's like the families at Disney World trying to stop their children from crying while the husband and wife fight. Something was pathetically sad and all screwed up at the happiest place on Earth.

I was offered the lead and could barely get through a script first entitled "Crack in the Mirror." The producers asked if I would reconsider if I *directed* the film as well. To be honest, it was a no-brainer. I love the education that goes with everything we do in the arts, and one of the most glorious aspects is that we are all students until the day we die. Without hesitating, I took on the role as the lead and as the director. This was my chance to 'step up' as we say in the business. Maybe I really could begin my career re-invention by directing this film. If so, I would have to do one helluva job with this script...

White Hot has the dubious distinction of being the first film to be shot on High Definition Video in North America. Which makes me an asterisk in a book of 'Triviality' as the first director to direct a feature in North America on High Def. At that time, the camera was the biggest hunk of electronics I had ever seen— kind of like a Mitchell Camera, but on steroids and camera growth hormones. Aside from its heft and bulkiness, it was permanently tethered to a truck with technicians calibrating and recalibrating each and every set-up, so I couldn't just say, 'Let's move over here and grab a cut-away

"There's only one place hotter than this."

ROBBY BENSON　　　TAWNY KITAEN

WHITE HOT

before lunch.' Making a move with that equipment meant 'lunch' turned into dinner and then overtime. Every move was science and history in the making. I kept telling the producers that no one is going to come to the movies to watch the technology— they just want to see a good film... err, video. "Can't you guys find a better script?" For some unknown reason, they stuck with the words in between Page One and 'The End' and it was my job to bring it to life.

We had absolutely no money to shoot the video... err, film, and I found myself wearing too many hats— even helping supply wardrobe and running to the Salvation Army to grab set-dressing. Our friend Cliff Bemis, who was great in the film, shared an apartment with me. We had no money to put him up anywhere. I went from 165 to 130 pounds in four weeks— not a bad 'look' for the film, but not good for my heart. I did my best to show how the character I was playing absolutely destroyed his life becoming a drug addict.

Acting and directing became bizarre in a scene where my character was making love to a beautiful drugged-out hooker to retaliate for his girlfriend's 'indiscretions.' Pretty campy stuff— except that real drug addicts told me they couldn't watch the film: it made them yearn to go back to the 'dark side.' Not exactly what I had in mind...

I staged this nude 'revenge fu--'... err, 'love-making' scene on an ostentatious black lacquer slide in an apartment that looked like a kid's playground from hell. The shot was set up so the camera makes a slow move in as my 'thrusting' gets more and more intense, then violent. As I acted the scene, my peripheral vision was on the camera— and I had to cue the dolly grip with my toes so he would know at what point in the thrusting he should start moving the camera forward. I also had to make the toe movement not look like a cue but like it was part of the scene. Now, here's the dilemma: this is my first feature as a director. I want it to look better than it reads.

"Action!" The more I became... athletically involved in the scene, the more the room began to spin. I kept telling myself, 'Don't ruin this shot. This shot took three hours to set up, and we can't afford to be behind schedule— so don't mess up... the... shot...'

The next thing I knew, I had passed out on top of the naked blonde actress.

When I came to (we were still rolling because I was the only one to call 'Action!' and 'Cut!'), I was nose to nipple with a strange woman's breast. I stared at her breast as alarm bells went off in my head: *'Oh my God! WHAT HAVE I DONE? THIS IS NOT KARLA'S BREAST! WHO DOES THIS NIPPLE BELONG TO? I'M NOTHING MORE THAN EVERY OTHER IDIOT WHO CHEATS ON HIS — WAIT— HUH?*

Then, peripherally, just barely out of the corner of my eye, I noticed the camera had hit its mark for the 'end position of the dolly.' And in a flash I remembered: *I was making a movie* (not love to a stranger), and yelled, "Cut!"

(Thank goodness. I really didn't think I was an asshole like that. An asshole in other ways, maybe— but never to cheat or hurt Karla. Never.)

I turned to the camera operator, and my way of trying to tell if the shot worked and also tell if anyone caught that I passed out for a second was to ask, "Was that as good for you as it was for me?"

He smiled and said, "It was perfect— I'd swear you even passed out in the scene. Perfect. Man— how do you do that? It looked so real."

"Well, that's why I make the itty-bitty bucks." (The technicians were probably making more than I was. This technology was new and these brainiacs weren't cheap. They weren't filmmakers, either.)

Another time I was standing in the pouring rain with Danny Aiello (and all his buddies who later were on *The Sopranos*), discussing how important it was to get this shot on the first take. In this gun battle, the actors all had explosive squibs hidden in their suits that would explode and expel blood, ruining their wardrobe and making it look like they were shot and killed in a 'bad-film-appropriate' way— and we only had one set of wardrobe. At that moment during my explanation, all of the squibs fired and all of us were surprised and goosed by the sound and the red gunky squibs exploding. We all wiggled in fast-motion as if we were really getting shot. When the 'gunfire' ended we all stared at one another, red Karo syrup dripping from our faces. We were flabbergasted, and sticky, head-to-toe. Time to problem-solve; no time to complain or even get angry.

"Okay, we need new jackets. I will personally pay anyone on the set full price if they lend me their jackets. Now!"

I got the jackets. Paid for seven or eight guys. We did the set up again, and the actors stayed— thanks to Danny Aiello, who told his pals, "Let's do it for the kid."

I WAS WORKING (AS A WRITER) ON A SCRIPT called *Modern Love* in January 1988 when Father Jerome Vereb visited our home and asked if I would come to the University of South Carolina to accept an Honorary Degree. I told him I appreciated the gesture, but I didn't believe in honorary degrees— I believed in degrees one earns.

When my mother found out I turned it down she tried not to cry.

"What's wrong, Ma?"

"Well, Robby, nobody from our family has ever graduated college."

"But Ma, I'm not graduating college, I'm flying 3,000 miles to pick up a piece of paper that I don't deserve. Even though it's in South Carolina, it's just small time Hollywood b.s."

"It's not b.s. They want you. They feel you deserve this honor."

"Ma, I don't deserve anything." I could see that she really was starting to cry. "Okay— Okay. No problem. I'll go."

When I finally said 'Yes' on the phone to the very persuasive President, James B. Holderman, he asked me what I'd like my degree in— and I told him 'Brain Surgery.'

The University of South Carolina was a remarkable place at that time. The President was a great fundraiser and a forward-thinker who attracted such notables as President Reagan, Kurt Waldheim, Madame Sadat, Helen Hayes, and even Pope John Paul II. Dr. Holderman turned the university from a party school in 1977 to the number one International Business graduate school in the nation— topping even the Ivy League Schools. He was the first non-southerner chosen for the position. Dr. Holderman was considered the most influential and powerful man in the state because he employed more people than any other public figure in South Carolina, including the Governor.

Dr. Holderman wanted me to teach at 'The Real USC,' as they liked to say (which predated that California school by about 80 years). He offered me an unlimited Artist in Residence professorship with M.F.A. students in the Theatre and Communications/Film departments beginning in the fall of 1988. It was tempting. And when I asked about creating a class that would incorporate students from both majors (something which had never been done before), he was very enthusiastic.

Dr. Holderman sent us on a tour of the campus, which was breathtaking. We were escorted to the flagship of the university, the 80,000-seat Williams-Brice Stadium where the Gamecocks played. Just like any kid, I wanted to run out onto the empty field for a touchdown, but was warned about the greenskeeper by our guide, "If ya did, he'd probably shoot ya."

At the end of our tour, I asked to see the film facilities.

"Sure thang." A door opened to a plush red-carpeted, gorgeously outfitted screening room. "Wow," I said. "This is perfect."

"Perfect? Nah," he said, then opened another door; "If you want to see perfect, take a look at the screening room fer the *de*-fense."

"So, can the film department use all of the film equipment?" I asked.

"Only if ya wanna git shot."

I was getting a college education after all.

I HAD NEVER TAUGHT FULL-TIME, and my script *Modern Love* was garnering interest in L.A., so Karla and I needed to discuss the pros and cons of such a big move. On campus there was an exciting, open dialogue about world views. But it was the South, and 100 yards off the campus grounds, you might find yourself listening to a discussion about why we lost the war— the *Civil War*. At that time they flew the Rebel flag over the State Capitol, which we Yankees found to be humiliating to of our friends of color. I wanted to change that, so I wrote a script about it entitled "Across the Tracks." I received good readers' reports, but no one wants to make a film that alienates the entire South.

We decided to 'go for it' and moved our family to Columbia, South Carolina to begin a new adventure. For me, it was like the entire world had been lifted from my shoulders. I re-wrote *Modern Love* and set it in beautiful South Carolina. I thought, "Why not make a film as a part of my class? It would be a terrific experience for my students to *work* (not just passively learn, but work and get paid) on a feature film, apprenticing professionals from L.A. and New York in every department, absorbing knowledge about the film industry the way I learned: by *doing*."

I received financing in a way that I'm pretty sure has never been duplicated. I went to SVS, a satellite arm of Sony, and said, "We need one million dollars and I need to know by November first because I have be in preproduction by the beginning of second semester."

They loved the script, and we got a green light immediately.

I had written the lead for Karla, and a role introducing our 5-year-old daughter Lyric. I thought it would be terrific to have Burt Reynolds in our film. When I called, Burt not only said 'Yes'— at his expense (he lost money— and did this for me), he arrived on set with his own trailer and support people.

Modern Love was a small film, but perfect for the class I was teaching— an opportunity of a lifetime for my Masters students at a university where the football team had state-of-the-art film equipment, but the film department had cameras more suitable for shooting home movies in the 70s. Now we were making a feature film with Panavision lenses.

We set up a student production office within the real production office. Twelve of my students were cast in the film and were given the opportunity to join the Screen

Actors Guild. One student became a Directors Guild of America trainee. My USC colleague, Professor Marsha Moore (who I later worked with at NYU), and Lilly Boruszkowski shot second unit for the 'kissing montage' at locations all over the state. Just the four of us got into a van and changed wardrobe and drove to beautiful locations for what I proudly call 'The longest kissing montage in film history.' (It was fun, too. I once had to fix the camera with gaffers tape, but the shot was gorgeous.)

I can never thank my hard-working crew, my friends and co-stars enough for what they did for our little film. Burt Reynolds, Rue McClanahan, Louise Lasser, Frankie Valli, our best friend Cliff Bemis, and my dear co-conspirator from *Pirates*, Kaye Ballard, who all helped me by giving their heart and talents to *Modern Love*... for scale.

The irony of this film was that I was still struggling with the sadness and guilt surrounding Vivienne's death. So I wrote and directed a comedy, a film that dealt with... life— and dedicated the film to Vivienne.

Lyric is adorable onscreen and off. The end credits are played over a scene with her in the bathtub that is priceless. (As a 4-year-old, she had a screen test with Martin Short and Nick Nolte, before we left for S.C. But seeing how the film's director treated her on set, I turned it down. We would not make that mistake; Lyric would have her childhood and make her own decisions about work when she was a grownup.)

I'm so proud of Karla DeVito, who gave the best performance in the film and got great reviews. The film is flawed; that's my fault. But it has some of the best work I've ever been associated with in my entire career. Because of our limited post production schedule, I made errors that didn't nurture the film, and even today I kick myself because *Modern Love* was the first film to show baby-boomers going through marriage and parenthood; funny and poignant— kinda like life.

Karla and I went to New York to promote *Modern Love.* We were ten minutes from going on the *CBS Morning Show* with Harry Smith when we received a phone call from Karla's Aunt Marilyn that Uncle Bob was in an accident. His truck had been sideswiped by a car. Shaken but still conscious, Bob had no signs of a life-threatening injury. "He was joking with the paramedics..."

Taken to the nearest E.R., the attending physician believed he may have internal bleeding, but said the hospital 'wasn't equipped to handle that kind of trauma.' Bob again joked with the paramedics as they placed him back into the ambulance. He was taken to three different hospitals over a five-hour period before they found a facility capable of dealing with the injuries Bob had sustained, only now Bob wasn't joking.

It was too late to save his life— he died en route of internal bleeding because of human ineptitude. As Uncle Bob, second father to Karla and her brothers, World War II bomber pilot, and captain for United Airlines with a flawless safety record would say, "It's pilot error."

I loved Bob. I was a private pilot too and we dreamed of building a plane together. Whenever I fly, I see him in the clouds...

So how do we avoid pilot error? *Knowledge.* Properly trained individuals, making the right decisions, taking responsibility for the 'flight plan'— that might have saved Bob's life.

Vivienne and Bob's stories are sobering examples of man's incompetence engendering death. If there is anything to learn here, it is to *be a vocal advocate.* Speak up until your questions are answered to your satisfaction. *Save* the people you love.

AS SOON AS WE RETURNED TO USC, we began rehearsals for an event starring Karla singing the music of Andrew Lloyd Webber. (The previous year, Karla had given a sold-out show, *Karla At The Koger*.) Featuring a 50 piece orchestra at the acoustically perfect 2500-seat Koger Center, this show was a celebration for President George H.W. Bush, Michael Eisner, and Andrew Lloyd Webber, who were receiving honorary degrees. (I guess their mothers cried too.)

Sam Ellis flew in from New York to produce the event, my father Jerry Segal conceived the running order and dialogue and helped direct, and the talented Kevin Farrell orchestrated and conducted. My MFA student, Stan Brown (who has one of the greatest voices I have ever heard, and later starred with us in *Open Heart)* was a featured singer in the group of talented students cast as ensemble members. USC's Dance Department and Black Gospel Choir joined in some of the numbers, and I sang masked as *The Phantom of the Opera.*

Performing nearly two dozen songs, Karla brought the house down. Andrew Lloyd Webber and Sarah Brightman came backstage singing Karla's praises. Michael Eisner echoed their enthusiasm: "It would cost me a million dollars to put on a show of this quality at Disney World."

Despite events such as this which brought positive national attention to the University, there was growing resentment toward the perceived 'extravagances' of Dr. Holderman.

When a reporter ambushed me with a phone call during dinner asking what I thought about Dr. Holderman, and I praised his accomplishments, the headline the next day read: "Benson Supports Spending." (This on the day President Bush arrived in Columbia to receive his honorary degree.) The newspaper had piled me into some of the scandalous problems with the University. We received hundreds of letters of support from the community we had grown to love— and a death threat.

But on the day our *home* became front page news, when they went so far as to show a picture of where we lived— address and all— I felt *The State* Newspaper put my wife and our child in physical danger. I called a moving company and said, "We're moving today. You want the job?"

We departed South Carolina faster than you can say, 'I went for a hike on the Appalachian Trail.'

If not for the timing of the move, I would never have been able to respond to the phone call: "Robby, do you want to audition for the part of Beast in Disney's *Beauty and the Beast*?"

"Give me a second to think about it."

A half second later: "YES!"

Who Stole The Funny?

WE LEFT SOUTH CAROLINA SO QUICKLY that when we arrived in Los Angeles, the moving company had packed our garbage cans— with all of our garbage still in them.

I was just in time to audition for 'Beast' in *Beauty and the Beast*. The audition was almost a set-up for me. I read the pages of dialogue and my immediate take on Beast was to treat him as a three-dimensional character, not a cartoon character. To me, Beast was as real as any part I had played in a live action film or a Broadway show.

My first audition was recorded on, of all things, a Sony Walkman. As a musician, I had branched out into recording engineer and loved to play with sound. When I saw the Sony Walkman I knew it had a little condenser microphone in it, and if I were to get too loud, the automatic compressor and built-in limiter would 'squash' the voice— and there would be very little dynamic range to the performance. I did a quick assessment and wondered how many people who had come in to audition for the part were making that error: playing the Beast with overwhelming decibels, compressing the vocal waveforms. I decided to give the Beast 'range.' Because of my microphone technique, and an understanding of who I wanted Beast to be, they kept asking me to come back and read different dialogue. After my fifth audition, Jeffrey Katzenberg said the part was mine.

Beauty and the Beast was so refreshingly fun and inventively creative to work on that I couldn't wait to try new approaches to every line of dialogue. Don Hahn is one of the best creative producers I have ever worked with. The two young directors, Kirk Wise and Gary Trousdale, were fantastic and their enthusiasm was contagious. I not only was allowed to improvise, but they encouraged it. It never entered my mind that I was playing an animated creature. I understood the torment that Beast was going through: he felt ugly; had a horrible opinion of himself, and had a trigger-temper. Those are things that, if done right, are the perfect ingredients for comedy. Painful and pathetic comedy— but honest. The kind of comedy I understood.

In the *feature* world of Disney animation, the actors always recorded their dialogue alone in a big studio, with only a microphone and the faint images of the producers, writers, directors and engineer through a double-paned set of acoustic glass. Paige O'Hara and I became good friends; it was her idea that for certain very intimate scenes, such as when Beast is dying, we record *together*. We were able to play these scenes with an honest conviction that is often absent in the voice-over world.

What a voice! Even my Broadway/rock goddess wife was thrilled to hear the breathtaking sound of Belle come from the heart and soul of Paige O'Hara. It was because of Paige that Beast sang in "Something There." She explained to Ashman and Menken that I had made records and sang in Broadway musicals.

We were all sent to New York, and just like every Broadway show, each song was recorded live with the orchestra. We sang our song(s) once— twice at most. Paige and I were standing side-by-side when Angela Lansbury sang "Beauty and the Beast." It was a moment in time I will never forget. Something very 'Disney-esque' happened: it was *magical*.

The success of this film was the culmination of a team effort but I must say, the honors go to the animators— and for me (Beast), that's Glen Keane— and to Howard Ashman and Alan Menken. This was the perfect example of a crew who 'cared'. And the final results (every frame) of the film represent that sentiment.

During my time promoting *Beauty and the Beast*, I finally got the chance to show off the lower end of my voice. I have a freaky range as a singer and I can easily sing the lowest male part in any opera— but I can also sing along with Freddy Mercury (if only I could *sound* like Freddy Mercury). Because my singing voice was so low I developed a falsetto to reach the high notes. It amused me that some journalists questioned my soft-spoken voice and kept pushing me about 'voice enhancement'— I'd just wait for the perfect moment and then go 'Beast' on them! It was fun to roar (without compression) during the interviews and see their expressions change, along with their opinions, so quickly!

Karla, Lyric and I were flown down to Disney World where I would do press. At the time, Karla was pregnant with Zephyr, so when we signed our names in the cement, we also wrote: 'Baby on the way' in the lower right hand corner.

What a cool thing it was to revisit that spot years later, for another publicity tour, and bring 'the baby on the way' (Zephyr) with us. And Lyric, too.

When *Beauty and the Beast* won the Golden Globe Award for Best Film (Comedy or Musical) and received six Academy Award nominations in 1992, I was again asked to be a presenter.

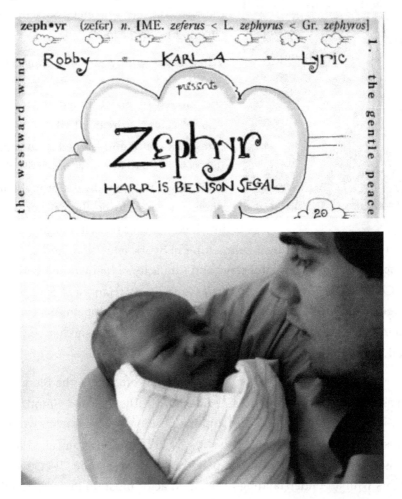

Just days after Zephyr was born, I chose to stay home cuddled up with Karla and watch it on TV like the rest of the world. I still got to do the honors— without putting on the dreaded tuxedo: Paige O'Hara and I prerecorded Beast and Belle, and the great Disney team animated our presentation.

I BEGAN TO WRITE LIKE A FIEND (*Betrayal of the Dove* and many more), direct anything (*Kids Incorporated* and other 'boot camp' TV directing jobs), and do more voice work (*Prince Valiant*, *Exo-Squad*, etc.).

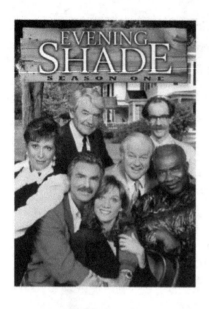

Then late in 1992, Burt Reynolds called. Burt liked the way I directed him in *Modern Love*, so he asked me if I'd be interested in directing an episode of his hit sitcom, **Evening Shade**.

When I was young and in a musical, my dream job was to be the conductor, surrounded by all of the gorgeous music. As an actor, I dreamed about being a camera operator and learned from some of the best. When I was a baseball player, even though I was always brought in to pitch, I wanted to be the catcher and be involved in every pitch in the game. Now I had an opportunity to direct prime-time network television, and an all-star cast including three wonderful stage and film actors I had worked with in the past: Charles Durning *(Die Laughing)*, Ossie Davis *(Harry and Son)* and Hal Holbrook *(Our Town)*. Working with these actors and Elizabeth Ashley, Marilu Henner and Michael Jeter was a dream. We respected one another because we all had been working in the business for decades.

Burt had a reputation with his executive producers, the Bloodworth-Thomasons, and show runners as being hard to handle and 'impossible to direct.' But if you understood Burt and the position he was in, you would see that his occasional 'outrageous' behavior wasn't necessarily uncalled for. The truth is, Burt Reynolds was a complete pro as long as you discussed your thoughts with an understanding of what an actor must do in order to follow the directions given. So for me, the job was a perfect fit. I was always honest with Burt and he respected me for it.

Burt Reynolds is one of the all-time great men in our business. I love him. He is as kind and giving and loyal as anyone I've ever met. And because of Burt, I have number one shows on my resume.

DIRECTING TELEVISION BECAME A DREAM JOB. I had overcome open-heart surgery and proved to my community, but more importantly, to myself, that life can move forward in a glorious way after such a life altering operation.

As a matter of fact, this was a high point in my life. I was able to be creative but because it was TV, I was able to have a home life. I wasn't on the road with a film working horrendous hours; I could have breakfast with my family, go to work, Karla could stop by for lunch, and then I would go home in time to watch the sunset with Karla, Lyric and Zephyr. It was a gift from the Entertainment Gods.

I was still passionate about teaching, not only because I loved it, but because of the stability factor for my family. In the fall of 1993, the former provost at the University of South Carolina, Arthur K. Smith, who was now the first non-Mormon President at the University of Utah, contacted me. He wanted to beef up the arts and asked me if I would be interested in teaching at The University of Utah. The

answer was a quick 'Yes.'

Salt Lake City, from my first glimpse at a map, was a 90-minute flight from L.A. in case I needed to get some work done and then fly home. We found a dream home 35 minutes up the mountain from the airport in Park City where hot air balloons took off in the back yard. It was magical; whimsical. Should we buy it? I could commute... I wasn't working every week as a TV director, and we could all live in this fairy-tale of a place— and learn how to ski, too! It was tempting. Karla and I had giddy conversations about our next adventure. (Everything to us was an adventure.)

But then, like everyone in L.A., on January 17, 1994 we were suddenly awakened at 4:30 a.m. Our home in Tarzana was only six miles from the epicenter of the Northridge Earthquake. The most violent shocks were measured less than a mile away from our house. Guess what? It was time for a new friggin' adventure. That was a mean earthquake. It had a personality; a bad one.

Off we went to our dream house. Karla and I talked about uprooting the family but we didn't discuss any medical concerns. It had been more than nine years since my heart surgery, and my bovine valve had lasted a long time— when would it need to be replaced? I had no symptoms, and I seemed to have plenty of energy, whatever the altitude. Life was good. Oh, so good.

We settled in Park City, I taught at the University of Utah and did a few directing jobs in Los Angeles.

What a perfect situation, I thought. Little did I know that because Burt Reynolds took a chance on me, I would soon be flying back and forth from Burbank to Salt Lake City as much as a pilot for Southwest Airlines.

I WAS HIRED BY THE TALENTED PEOPLE at Wind Dancer Productions. They made working on the sitcom **Thunder Alley** (starring Ed Asner and Haley Joel Osment) a great experience. Matt Williams, Carmen Finestra and David McFadzean were the producer-writing dream-team in my TV career. They are magnificent men with extraordinary talent and very secure in their own skin. I directed a complete season for them.

Karla and I were still living in Park City because of my affiliation with the University of Utah. The consequence and irony of (success) my directing career taking over our lives and schedules, yet fitting teaching and directing into the same equation had become... difficult, but doable. Yes; I still made/forced it all to work.

It was great for my students (that fact being so very important to me) because not only was their professor up-to-date with what was happening on sets in L.A., but I could get students at the U. of U. to visit Hollywood sets, take tours of Panavision, and get them into places and see things they normally would not be allowed to soak up back in Salt Lake City. (I owe a lifetime of thanks to the good people at Panavision, especially going back to the Robert Gottschalk era when I was allowed to learn and 'play' with every new and old piece of equipment on a weekly basis at the 'Old Panavision' in Tarzana.)

My directing career skyrocketed in the 90s— I became one of the most sought after TV directors in the business. From the top 20 to the number one rated show on the air, if it was funny, I directed it. I never had a day off. Even on weekends I would be prepping for the next week's show, which is professional— which is why I kept getting more and more work. Funny is serious business.

'The Funny' means everything to me. Without 'the funny' life is... tough. I don't expect people to live like me, but through the hardest times, when I see 'the funny'— I survive. I also think 'the funny' is what keeps Karla and me so in tune with one another. If I take something too seriously, all Karla has to do is make fun of me and suddenly I see what a jerk I'm being— and abruptly, everything is funny and I stop being an ass. The pressure valve is released and the laughs are contagious. Comedy: what a great elixir for an open-heart patient.

But with every medicine comes a side effect.

Because I was good at my job, I began directing 24/7. I was very 'old school.' In other words, I believed a show had to be worthy of being broadcast to millions of people. It was not my job just to get a show in the can, or to merely shoot the show. I had to find every bit of funny available and exploit it honestly. To me, my job description was the same as the men and women who taught me my craft: it must be your best effort— *or don't do it*. I loved the process of finding funny bits that weren't on the page. I adored taking care of the actors, and at the same time, because I was a writer and the son of a writer, nothing was ever at the expense of the writer or the script.

WHEN THE OFFER CAME TO DIRECT the complete 1995-96 season of **Ellen** (25 episodes), Karla and I knew we had no choice but to.move back to L.A. We kept our home in Park City for family getaways and rented a house in Burbank near the Disney studios. Again, our priorities never shifted— it was always love and family first. It always will be…

I was devoted to *Ellen* and to Ellen DeGeneres, one of the hardest-working and funniest comedians in the business. Despite the show's success, she was never satisfied and never stopped trying to make it better— my type of actor.

Ellen was also struggling with the question of 'coming out' (which happened the following season), at a time when the outcome was far from certain. We had many deep private conversations after everyone else had left the set, and I always went to bat for her.

Knowing that ageism is endemic in the business, I tried to deflect problems from being blamed on an older producer, thinking of him as I would my father. Then, in an 'executive meeting' held in the Disney Studios cafeteria (to prevent us from losing our temper in public), I found out he had been lying to both me and the show runners— creating huge problems between us that 'only he could fix.' It was the classic syndrome of making yourself invaluable and irreplaceable when in truth, you added no value to the process to begin with. (I had seen this behavior many times before in the film industry; when managers took over the role of what agents used to do, managers became necessary. The same with publicists.) After directing twenty-four shows in a row I was truly blindsided by a guy I had tried to protect. Talk about *heart*-breaking.

Ellen and the beautiful Joely Fisher were an amazing comedy team— Lucy and Ethel for a new generation. (Joely has remained our true family friend, not a 'Hollywood' friend, ever since.) We also had some memorable guests, including Mary Tyler Moore, Martha Stewart and Kathy Griffin. I adored the entire cast— Jeremy Piven, Clea Lewis, and Dave Higgins. We all worked our asses off, and shooting the third season of *Ellen* was a high point in my TV career.

MARTA KAUFFMAN, DAVID CRANE AND KEVIN BRIGHT became one of the best creative, writing/producing teams in television. They gave me a shot early on, in 1993, when I directed Peter Scolari in their first network series, *Family Album*. I worked for them again in 1995 on the cutting edge HBO comedy series *Dream On*— and got a Cable Ace nomination for the episode: "Try Not To Remember," starring Brian Benben, which featured our friend Cliff Bemis, and Louise Fletcher.

When Bright/Kauffman/Crane was casting a show about a group of twenty-somethings in New York, I was happy to recommend two talented actors I had directed: Jennifer Aniston, in *Muddling Through;* and David Schwimmer, in the Henry Winkler series, *Monty.*

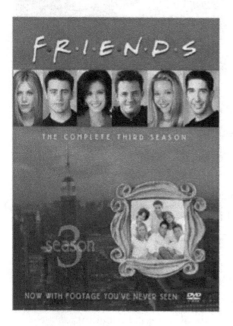

After a frantic call from Kevin Bright, I went so far as to page Schwimmer— who was at the airport planning to leave after his audition— and convince him to stay on.

I enjoyed directing an episode of **Friends** in 1995. A year and a half later, when the show had become a smash, I returned.

There was a lot of talent on that show, and I have great admiration for talent. We did some good work together. But with talent comes responsibility, and when I found it wasn't the place for discipline, it wasn't for me.

I SHOT SO MANY EPISODES OF TELEVISION, it's hard for me to remember when it happened or which show— but one night in front of a live audience, an actor

kicked a writer in the ass. Not 'kicked his ass'— kicked him in the ass. (I never understood the phrase 'I'm gonna kick your ass' until that night.) All hell broke loose, but I made them 'take it outside' while I finished the show, and the audience had no clue what was going on. Television was becoming... insane!

As every new sitcom week was shot and aired, the actor in me could hide my frustrations, but how could I allow a baby-producer/writer/egomaniac to fire a man named Joe Marquette on the 'A' Camera?

Joe Marquette was the camera operator on *Raging Bull!* He even has a credit as the Camera Operator in the opening title sequence. That is unheard of in today's world. Now, in all of the multiplexes, it seems like everyone has left the movie theater before the credits roll for all of the talented crew members who really make the film. It's pitiful. Sad. To see the empty movie theater as all of the hard working, skilled crew members get their credit and the movie theater is empty. But Martin Scorsese understood Joe's talent (and the D.P. Michael Chapman) and gave him his deserved credit.

Yet one day, on a sitcom not to be mentioned, some little punk who didn't understand framing (or film) was about to fire a man who had decades of experience and more skill and talent than anyone in the writer's room. I told him and the studio and the network that if they fired Joe, they could find

themselves another director. Luckily, this happened when I still had 'cache.' So, defending my crew, my actors— that suddenly took me from 'savior director-guy' (in the eyes of executives and the networks) to the new title of 'trouble-maker director-guy.'

BECAUSE OF KARLA AND THE KIDS, I still had perspective and managed to take work in stride. Lyric and Zephyr were a delight to me and there wasn't anything I wouldn't do for them.

An example with a funny twist: Zephyr wanted to 'be like Mike'— and he wanted to look like Michael Jordan too. He had been asking Karla for months if he could get his head shaved, "just like Michael Jordan." Finally Karla said, "Go ask your dad."

And of course, when that little face asked me if I would shave his head to look like Michael Jordan, I immediately said, "Sure. Why not."

"Now, Daddy?"

"Now? Well, um— okay— but is it cool with you that I do it? If you're gonna have your head shaved like Michael Jordan, I think I can do it as well as any barber— or... whatever they call barbers— hairstylists... for kids."

"Sure Daddy. Let's do it. I just wanna look like Michael Jordan." And to think that some athletes don't believe they are 'role models.'

"Sure big guy. Let's do it!"

I got all of the 'tools' ready and put the barber cape around him and we laughed and laughed and told Karla she couldn't come in until we called her. It was too cool.

"Um... hold real still, okay?"

"Do you like it?" "Yeah!"

Then he looked up at me and in the most adorable way said, "Now it's your turn, Daddy!"

"Um… my turn? Well, I didn't…"

"Don't you want to look like Michael Jordan, too?"

"Well, seriously, I think I might look more like a white supremacist."

"What's that?"

"Well…"

"Please, Daddy."

Wow, it's hard to resist a pure young mind that hasn't been polluted with hate… yet.

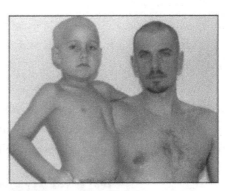

"Let's do it!" And we did.

Even though Zephyr thought we looked like Michael Jordan, in real life, I looked like someone who would want to *harm* Michael Jordan; we looked like extras in *American History X.*

It didn't go over well on all the TV shows I was directing at the time, either. But it worked wonders on the L.A. freeways. Every time someone cut me off or was about to give me the finger, one look at my skinhead and they'd slink away.

EACH AND EVERY TELEVISION EPISODE brought a great deal of excessive stress; it came from the writer/producers, the network and studio executives— and sometimes the actors. I had a guest star tell me she didn't want to be shot on the left side of her face— "Only shoot my right side." Even after I explained the mathematics of shooting simultaneously with four cameras, that it was physically impossible, she didn't waver— "Only shoot my good side!" The stress had a profound affect upon my heart. I felt like someone had my heart in their hand and was just squeezing it like Play-Doh.

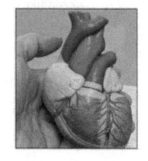

In 1997 I was working with Tea Leoni, a tremendous talent, on **The Naked Truth**. I was also lucky enough to work with a comic genius who did a guest spot on the show: Jon Lovitz. No matter what the problem, we couldn't stop making up bits and laughing until we cried.

Tea Leoni can do drama and comedy. I believe that as good as she is, she still hasn't even come close to her potential as an actor. But on *The Naked Truth*, it didn't feel like anyone was writing to her strengths— and she was highly aware of this (she is scary smart. *Mensa* smart). As director, I knew I was doing the right thing, fighting for *everyone* on *every* show who needed defending, but it was just too much. I would come home dragging, with no energy to eat, let alone talk about the day and be a good husband and father. All I could do was collapse in a chair and fall asleep.

There was a new breed in Hollywood and they were ruining... err, running the show. It was impossible to get through a day without dealing with absurdities and wild power trips: "I think the marshmallow is too small for the joke to work."

"The marshmallow joke was cut from the script on Tuesday. By *you*."

"Really? Oh. Let's put it back."

"We're in front of a live audience and it hasn't been rehearsed."

"Maybe the actor will screw up and *that* will be funny."

It wasn't so funny anymore. Anxiety, pain, heartache, fears— all of these can actually be harnessed and put to good use— but now it was killing me. Suddenly stress didn't seem like pop culture bullshit. It felt like my heart was going to explode inside my rib cage. It was so very important to me to take care of my cast and crew. But I took on responsibility the way a glutton would take on a feast. I guess I was a fool, but I wouldn't do it differently today. I only know how to do the best job I can possibly do— and if others aren't 'on-board' it's my job to *get* them on-board.

'MAN IS STUPID'— okay, let me *personalize* this so I don't offend a lot of smart men— *I am stupid* because this next, moronic story places me on the all-time list of: *The Stupidest Things A Man Can Do, Knowingly.* I cannot blame anyone else. This one falls flat on me.

It had been 13 years since my bovine valve was put into my chest,

sewn onto my heart in the aortic position. Since that time, I had been containing a lot of powerful emotions while working non-stop with practically no sleep (I would dream of better edits, better blocking, better performances, better camera positions… everything— as long as it made a show *funnier*) on shows that are supposed to make people laugh.

One day we were skiing in Park City, Utah. It was during spring break. Little Zephyr, our amazing son, was learning how to ski. I told him— I promised him— "After your lesson I will take you up on the bunny hill."

While he was learning, I was skiing my favorite Black Diamond. As I skied, I felt something... *something odd in my chest...* it felt like... maybe my

valve...*ripped.*

I blacked out.

When I came to, I was still skiing— halfway down the treacherous Black Diamond hill. (And I was skiing better than I had ever skied before— because I was completely relaxed, 'out on my feet.') By the time I got to the bottom of the hill, I couldn't breathe. At all.

I recognized the feeling immediately. I knew: something was terribly wrong. But I had promised my son I would take him up to the bunny hill and ski with him. Is this being a good dad, or a really bad, stupid dad? Or, let me put it in more honest terms: Is this insane? Yes. Is it reasonable for someone who directs for a living? Here is the rub: a director is nothing more than a creative control freak. (Everything that happens in my world, happens in an aspect ratio. For my entire life— since I can remember— I would close my one eye and I'd see the world in my own aspect ratio, and that is my reality.) I control that reality.

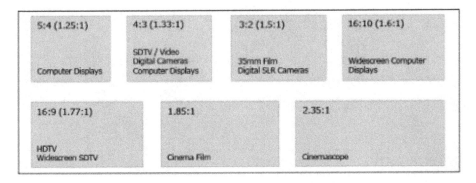

5:4 (1.25:1)	4:3 (1.33:1)	3:2 (1.5:1)	16:10 (1.6:1)
Computer Displays	SDTV / Video Digital Cameras Computer Displays	35mm Film Digital SLR Cameras	Widescreen Computer Displays

16:9 (1.77:1)	1.85:1	2.35:1
HDTV Widescreen SDTV	Cinema Film	Cinemascope

A bit twisted, but as a director, things happen when you say they will happen. And your word should stand for something. I *said* I would take my son to the bunny hill and then ski down with him. Even if I was putting my life at risk (because to others, that is exactly what I was doing) I still had to accomplish what I *said* I was going to do. I could still control that promise. Here was my 'aspect ratio': Who could say 'No' to him? (He's an amazing young man.)

So, as I skied with my son down the bunny hill, I found myself internally scheduling my operation and recovery time in my head.

I had been hired to shoot a pilot for a lot of money that started the following week. I would work on the pilot for two straight weeks and then (on the schedule in my *Man-is-Stupid* head) after we finished shooting, I'd have open-heart surgery to repair my torn valve. Then back to work, asap. In the meantime, if anyone had learned how to hide symptoms, especially shortness of breath, it was I. Again, my best acting was always off-screen.

But what makes this worse (more stupid; outrageously 'human') is what I did next.

The Experiment

WHEN WE RETURNED FROM SKIING in Park City and came back to Los Angeles, physically, I knew I was in trouble. But in one of the most boneheaded moves I have ever made in my life, I wasn't going to do anything about it... yet. I had a plan. And if this bonehead plan were to work, I had to be smart with my stupidity.

By sheer coincidence, I had a scheduled appointment for my yearly cardiac checkup as soon as I got home. I had changed doctors when we moved back to LA. I was told this new doctor was the 'best cardiologist west of the Rockies' which also made him the busiest in Hollywood. (Like most doctors in the United States, he is paid *by the volume of patients he sees*. This is *not* the case at The Cleveland Clinic. More on them later.) Those in the know called him the 'cardiologist to the stars' which in Hollywood meant not only bankable stars and minor luminaries, but also the star agents, studio moguls, etc., so his schedule was jammed. He had a great sense of humor and his entertaining repartee down cold. He should've been the actor and I should've been the cardiologist.

When he finally came into the examining room on the day of my check-up, to listen to my heart, I launched into a performance with a scenario that got his attention.

ROBBY (With feeling:)

"If someone had a bovine valve in their heart and let's say it ripped, but because it's not stenosis— it's leaking, not tightening— that person could continue to live with a torn valve for how long? Would you say... a month? Weeks?"

The cardiologist looked at me and began to scold (on cue).

Cardiologist To The Stars (Barely paying attention:)

"I don't know. I suppose as long as it's not constricted there would be some time because it's not a cardiac emergency, per se. But it is truly dangerous. (Suddenly faux compassion:) Hey, if you are *ever* in a situation like that, you'd better not try any funny stuff. You'd be playing Russian roulette. Understand, Robby?"

Again— my best work was off-screen. I nodded my head, said thanks, and *began to put on my shirt back on* (sound familiar?)— knowing he was so busy that he might forget that he didn't give me a check-up or even listen to my heart. And you know what? *It worked.* I could go to work.

Control Freak

Control freak behavior comes in all varieties and flavors and one doesn't have to be a director to behave like one. Why do we do this? (Why did I?) In my case it ranged from ignorance, to fear, to denial, to wanting to make a big payday by directing a pilot.

It was the first time in my career where I was making real money. When I was starring in films, young actors were poorly paid— before the 'Brat Pack' came along. The moment Karla got pregnant with Lyric we started a college fund rather than buy furniture. Same with Zephyr. So I wasn't going to turn down that payday if deep inside of me I truly believed I could live through the pilot, then have the operation— and all would be fine.

This particular motive was driven by my ego: thinking I knew better than God/fate/whatever you believe in/ all of the above— or Stephen Hawking. If something happened to me during this next surgery, at least I had peace of mind knowing I had banked an extra financial cushion for my family. Who says a control freak can't be well meaning? That was my one purpose in life: to take care of my family. We don't live in The United States of Utopia. I never had job security. To me, it made sense. It shouldn't have. But ever since I knew I had a serious heart problem as an adult, every choice I made was motivated by love— and the fact that I could drop dead at any second.

My understanding about how fragile life is and how *all of us* are living on borrowed time may seem like a lame excuse— but it wasn't to me because I confronted death when I was 28 and death had become my shadow ever since. So my thought process wasn't as screwed up as it sounds. Immature? Juvenile, yes. But I was passionate with a resilient spine (and body) that conveniently wore blinkers, which made all of these decisions so dangerous— even though I could perceive and present the *concept* as noble. The reality is ludicrous, inane (very selfish and indulgent) and irresponsible.

And that explanation makes me even more of a misguided imbecile because it's also so hypocritical: if someone told me that was how they were going to deal with a similar situation, I'd take them hostage and personally strap them into an ambulance. But for me, playing under my rules, I had to be sure that my family *always* had a roof over their heads. My accountant Ed Lieberman, a great guy and one of my oldest friends who still handles our finances, always knew to never put our money in medium or high risk areas of the stock market. I worked too hard for my money. No gambling. Ever. I'd gamble with my own body parts because I knew I'd win that gamble. My motto was: 'If you're going to bet, bet on yourself.' There was only one problem with this bet: I still didn't realize that being there for my wife and kids was more important than any roof over our heads.

I SOON REALIZED BECAUSE OF MY CONDITION I couldn't put up with the the usual crap that comes with shooting a pilot. This includes the studio sitting in the corner on every shot, whispering how the show wasn't funny and that I might be the one to blame (in TV, *there always must be someone to blame*).

Because the script was not working, the powers that be decided to fire the lead and recast. I had begged them to hire another actor earlier in the process, but they said no. They couldn't live without him, and now they wanted to fire him. While they were auditioning other actors in the bungalow next to the sound stage, they wanted me to keep rehearsing with this poor kid (in his early 20s). They wanted me to pretend all was well so we wouldn't lose rehearsal time with the rest of the cast. This would fall into the realm of the 'crap I couldn't handle' category, even if my heart was perfect. I refused and took the kid aside. I told him the truth.

I said, "Look, this really sucks but you are being fired. They want you to stick around so we don't lose rehearsal time. And just for the record, your manager is in the office with them at this very moment, negotiating for another actor— *her client as well*. I'd think about firing her if I were you. And, if it were me, I'd walk right now. If you do, you have my respect and I'll stick up for you. It's bad enough to get fired. It's worse when you're being fired and manipulated."

The actor needed to sit— immediately. I got him something to drink. I walked him out to his car and told him to not look back, and if anyone challenged this move, "I want you to tell them I'm the one who told you to leave. That way, you can't get sued. I'll take the hit— don't worry. Go."

As I was talking to him, I began to feel a horrible pain in my chest worsen with every word. Was it my heart, or was this project giving me these pains? Maybe one of my well-intentioned plans would finally fail me and I'd lose the gamble.

When I finished directing the pilot, I came clean to Karla and she called my cardiologist. I had a lot of loved ones very upset with me (rightfully so). I had done it before: 'It just hurts a little. Why call 9-1-1? It'll get better. I'll be fine, you'll see. I can *control* this.' I now understand the people we love don't deserve to be manipulated the way I manipulated my family, just to shoot a lousy (okay— even if it were great) TV pilot. It was grossly unfair to my wife and children. I know *everyone* pays a price in the long run. Trying to make money this way is much more expensive to the soul, let alone the heart.

My cow valve (bovine as opposed to porcine or mechanical) was supposed to last eight to twelve years. It was now 13 and a half years old. The thought of its demise never dominated our existence, but about nine years in, the 800 pound gorilla in the room had both Karla and me silently looking over our shoulders wondering exactly when and how *it* would happen: Would it be a slow progression? Would it be a dramatic 911 call straight into emergency open-heart surgery? Would it be like a horror movie and my chest would explode and my heart would get a close-up as it was beating inside my rib cage? (Cool…) Would I be one of the small percentages who, even in the most perfect situation, happens to die on the table? (The house and the proverbial roof would be fine. What an ass!)

I had gone through yearly cardiac check-ups with stress echoes. A couple of times over the years I had to be wired with a **Holter Monitor** hidden under my bulky sweatshirt to work, trying to catch the 'on switch' of tachycardia arrhythmia on tape (without scaring my children or my actors), and many other heart tests, including my least favorite— the Transesophogeal Echo (TEE).

More important than keeping that movie star smile, heart patients must take care of their teeth and gums because there is a direct link from bacteria leaked into the bloodstream from dental work to bacterial growth in the heart, especially on repaired valves. Back in the 80s and early 90s, the protocol for a heart patient with an artificial valve was every trip to the dentist meant going to my cardiologist first, having several shots of penicillin in the muscles near my hip, and then taking large doses of oral antibiotics after the dental procedure. Not fun for the 'good guy-bacteria' in your lower digestive track. (Karla had me taking acidophilus long before any mainstream media talked about needing it with antibiotic therapy. She's always been ahead of the curve when it comes to health— and other very cool things that I can't put in the book.)

Any time I was sick with a fever for too long they would do many blood tests; if my kids had strep throat I had to take antibiotics to make sure strep didn't attack my valve.

Once I passed a kidney stone in my parent's bathroom. Because I didn't want them to worry, I had to chew on a towel while I was in the long process of passing the stone. (It probably sounded like I was making love to Karla when I tried to keep my painful screams down a few notches and they came out as moans. But Karla wasn't there. Lord knows what my parents thought I was doing in the bathroom. I looked like the old coach Jerry Tarkanian from the UNLV Running Rebels, always chewing on a towel during the game like a homicidal, rabies-infected psychopath. It's a good look.) I passed the kidney stone and came out and watched more football with my father, but tears from the pain kept coming down my cheeks. I said my contact lenses were bugging me. (Don't ask. Don't tell. I am such a moron. Don't be a moron!) I guess karma or whatever you believe in struck back— the kidney stone caused a bladder infection, and they kept me in the hospital for 36 hours on an antibiotic IV to protect my valve and heart. (The man on call, my doctor du jour, a brilliant doctor who took wonderful care of me, is infectious disease specialist Jeffrey Galpin. Jeff is a sage; a profoundly intelligent doctor who is also a compassionate man. He is one of the finest men I have ever met.)

BACK TO THE PLAN, or the manifestation of Karla's theory: 'Man Is Stupid.'

I was at my cardiologists taking every out-patient test possible short of an angiogram to find out what exactly was going on with my heart.

An echocardiogram is a breeze, but a **Transesophageal Echo (TEE)** on the other hand, is an experience I wouldn't wish on anyone. Even Mel Gibson. The next thing I knew, I was given a drug called Versed. (I never took recreational drugs— remember, I'm soft. But if I was suddenly 'Hollywood edgy,' Versed would be the substance to land me in the tabloids. Wow— I had never been so happy to feel so lousy.)

I was told Versed would make me feel woozy, but more importantly, it would act as an amnesiac so I wouldn't remember what happened next. Well, here is exactly what happened next: they sprayed a wickedly bitter topical anesthetic in my mouth and aimed it at the back of my throat and told me to swallow. Then they made me gargle with a disgusting pink liquid anesthetic for two minutes and told me to swallow. When my gag reflex was finally subdued, some 'dude' told me he was going to put an ultrasound camera, tethered to a thick black cord, "...down your throat, dude," and they would take ultrasound pictures from inside my stomach of the back side of my heart, which is not visible using a regular echocardiogram. "Open wide, dude," and I *swallowed* the echo transducer and at least a foot of endoscope.

Times have changed— this camera and the tethering wires are much smaller than the first time I had to take this test in the early 90s. (And the surfer technician dude was eaten by a shark. Really.)

Later, I told our best friend, who happens to be gay, about the TEE test. I was re-enacting and full of wonder and energy.

"I had to swallow this big thing that was at least a foot long!"

"Yeah, so?"

"Well," I continued, pissed that he wasn't even slightly alarmed or sympathetic, "it was connected to this ultrasound camera and I wasn't allowed to gag! And it was like this long!" I held out my arms as far as they could go for effect.

"Yeah, so?"

Nothing. As a matter of fact, nothing about this test seemed to faze him.

Let me clarify: many of my friends are gay. I once got into a fight because a homophobic ass on one of my sets said, "Where do all the gay Santas go for vacation? Santa *Fey.*" (Whack!) I can discuss things other than sports with these men and almost down to every gay friend, man or woman, they are caring and kind. I think it's because of all the shit they have to put up with their entire lives, and people who have been persecuted for their sexual orientation seem to understand ardently acute personal pain— and that gives them a sense of compassion for others. At least, that's what I've noticed. As a matter of fact, if I had to go to war, I'd be glad to fight side-by-side with my gay friends. And for heavens sake, let them marry if they love each other— like the rest of us. (Jumpin' off my soap box...)

The results of my TEE had my doctor worried. They weren't certain, but thought they saw a shadowy 'vegetation' on my aortic bovine valve. Vegetation means some kind of bacterial growth that can lead to many things worse than valve replacement— like heart replacement. Not good. Whatever was going on with my valve, I was on a fast track for open-heart surgery.

There was no time for 'what ifs'— I needed open-heart surgery stat. If there had been the luxury of time, we would have gotten a second opinion from Dr. Laks at UCLA.

The 'cardiologist to the stars' worked out of Cedars Sinai Medical Center— not UCLA. We had never discussed it, but because Karla's mom Vivienne had died at UCLA, I wasn't about to put the love of my life in a place where every hallway, color, odor, would be a reminder of that tragic day. So Cedars it was. ASAP.

Our cardiologist presented what he thought was a good choice for my second valve surgery: the Ross Procedure. (Karla knew about it from scouring the internet for information about non-mechanical valve possibilities. She knew the last thing I wanted was to be on Coumadin for the rest of my life.) The cardiologist said,"the statistics show the Ross Procedure lasting twenty years or more," and like the bovine valve, the only med I'd have to take was one aspirin a day. And this is where my gamble failed. Because of my arrogant, control-freak need to get this over with immediately, there was no time to get a second opinion; no time to discuss the pros and cons or concerns regarding the Ross Procedure. There was no time to meet with the new surgeon beforehand.

He handed Karla pages of xeroxed information about it that he had just downloaded from the internet. (That alone should have given us a hint that the Ross Procedure had not been done very often at this hospital, but we did not ask that all important question: How many successful Ross Procedures had the surgeon done here?) Karla was encouraged by the possibility of twenty years or more without me having another open-heart surgery for valve replacement. Twenty years is a lot of time for new techniques to be developed. If it lasted until 2018 maybe something new would be invented.

The Ross Procedure

I see a mouth saying this phrase in super-slow motion every time I think about it. Probably 120 frames per second if we were shooting 35-mm film. And yes, just like on Sesame Street, a new phrase entered my life: **The Ross Procedure**.

Basically, the Ross Procedure is a technique that consists of the surgeon taking the patient's pulmonary valve off of the pulmonary position and placing it onto the aortic valve position and then placing a cadaver valve (okay, a pulmonary homograph) on the pulmonary position.

Twenty years or not, here is where my logic chimes in: If there is *one* valve that is giving the patient problems, why on earth would we want to start cutting into *two* valves? As a director, or anyone who juggles tons of satellite issues at once, this question should come to mind: 'Why create *variables?*' When solving problems, we want to diminish the variables, not expand upon them. I never spoke up. (I'm sure any of the producers I've worked with can't even imagine that: me 'not speaking up…')

Unlike my first surgery, where we had spent an hour with Dr. Laks in his office, Karla and the kids, my parents, my sister Shelli, brother in law Moshe, and our best friend Cliff were all crowded in my hospital room the night before my surgery when my surgeon finally met me to speak about his plan for the next morning. I didn't ask anyone to leave. He talked to us as if we were in high school:

THE SURGEON

"The aortic valve does most of the heavy lifting in the heart. That's why the bovine and porcine valves wear out in that position. Replacing the pulmonary valve with a homograph or even a porcine tissue valve isn't such a big deal because the pulmonary position doesn't take the same kind of pressure, and whatever we put in there will last. Research has shown placing your own living tissue valve in the aortic position— the place that gets the most wear and tear— will potentially last the longest."

ROBBY (Dumbfounded:)

"Uh, okay."

The surgeon was careful to mention if the pulmonary valve-size didn't match perfectly, he would most likely use another bovine valve on my aorta. I had been told, off-the-record, this had been the problem with Arnold Schwarzenegger who had the Ross Procedure recently at another hospital— and it failed while he was in the ICU. They had to take him back into emergency surgery, reopen him up and change the valve to save his life.

I'm not a doctor and I never played one on TV, but the question occurred to me again: why would anyone mess with *two* parts of the human heart when only *one* part is in need of help? (There are many, many good answers to this question and the people at The Cleveland Clinic answered them beautifully for us recently and even came to the defense of the procedure, which can be right for *some patients*.)

The meeting with my surgeon, the man who was going to saw me open again and put his hands on my heart, lasted less than ten minutes. (I've spent more time with a used car salesman.)

He was very specific and convincing. ('And this Volvo only has 20,000 miles on it.')

My cardiologist told me my surgeon's father, who lived outside the country, was tragically dying, and believe it or not, my surgeon was going to stay one extra day in the States before flying to his father's side, just to operate on me. That alone was extremely persuasive.

That sacrifice hit me hard on a human level, even though I kept thinking, 'Why would we want to deal with the variables? It makes no sense.' But after all: I was the guy who knew his valve ripped and directed a pilot, putting off my surgery. Was a guy with Greed and Stupidity tattooed on his forehead allowed to question a world-famous surgeon?

Because of my plan, we had to trust my doctors because 'doctors know everything and they would never experiment on me.' Karla and I exchanged looks and with one small smile, it was a done deal. If it fit, the Ross Procedure it would be.

So... I pretended to take a deep breath and said, "Let's do it!"

The next morning, 'they did it.'

Cedars Sinai Hospital knew how to take care of the families in the waiting room. A representative would update Karla as to where they were in the surgery and how I was doing and she would share it with my family and friends.

The representative came out and told her I was doing well and the surgeon had finished the hardest part—harvesting my pulmonary valve and successfully sewing it onto the aortic position. Karla recalls him saying she would not be speaking with my surgeon as he was leaving for the airport.

These words would hold great meaning six and a half years later: "Another surgeon is finishing up the easier part of your husband's surgery..."

WHAT MAKES OPEN HEART SURGERY SO BRUTAL? It is a Kafkaesque experience that is really a continual enigma of *uber* horrors from surgery to surgery. Its impact varies depending on the patient's age, spirit going into the surgery and health prior to the surgery. But, *break no chest bones about it*, the surgery begins with a 10 - 11 inch-long incision right down the middle of your chest. This, of course, after you are under general anesthesia— so you feel no pain.

I don't want to upset anyone so I'll keep this as simple as possible, because even as I type, I can imagine the fear in a first-time patient or loved one reading this. Even though it is a defenseless massacre that takes place upon the entire body— and the patient's future mental condition (in a second...)— you should know what happens when the patient is in the O.R.

The next thing to be assaulted is the patient's breast bone which is separated so that the medical team and the brilliant surgeon (hopefully) can see the heart, and in my case my aortic valve. The aorta itself is the main thoroughfare that sends blood from your heart and then to the freeways that make up the transportation in the rest of the patient's body.

The apposite next step is the life-saving, yet life-changing connection to the heart-lung machine. It is basically a mechanical heart in the sense that the patient's heart is stopped, but the rest of the body still needs to receive appropriate and very necessary oxygen-rich blood.

Why do I believe it is life-changing? There have been studies regarding what the heart-lung machine does to a patient's mental abilities once the patient is out of surgery. Its afterlife effects have been noticeably affected by *moi*. See? I'm not as funny and it's the only French word I remember after eight years of French in school.

I've been told, I forget by whom, that the heart-lung machine can affect memory. I can't remember if that's true. I've also been told that the heart-lung machine can induce a sense of fogginess and this is exponential with each passing, let's say, hour a patient is on the machine. I can't tell you who told me this because I'm a bit foggy so I don't know if it's true.

Where was I? (This memory abuse is so true that in my teaching career, I ask the student in my classes who I believe to be the most alert to always help me stay on track when I go off on a tangent and then completely forget where or why I even went on that tangent.)

I'll also admit, even though it's early in the book, that I have had four open-heart surgeries so my fogginess is like that of the Blue Ridge Mountains (sometimes I have brain games to keep my mind alert— like I learn new musical computer software and always keep my brain exercising, the same way I keep exercising my body. I refuse to give up or give in), and a one time open-heart patient's fogginess could be like the need to wipe down their computer screen every few months.

So... Where was I? Yes! The need for sex. No— that wasn't it. Ah— love. The need for... **Breastbone** cut, chest opened and many hands and instruments are inside your torso while a machine breathes for you. That's where I was. I'll still go with sex for 200, Alex. But only with Karla, Alex! Me. Not you, Alex. See? I am demonstrating what I fight when I write this book or even hold a conversation. I can begin to look like Charlie Sheen driven by his megalomaniac producer to that stage of 'winning,' but I don't get Tiger Blood or conquer trolls— I get a new lease on life. I think I'm actually, 'Winning!' See? This is really *serious* comedy.

In my case, the next thing to be done was to put the bovine valve in the position of the aortic valve, sew it into place with the delicate hands of a Mom picking up tiny pieces of glass so her baby will never be cut as the baby is learning to walk, yet these are the hands of a grown man or woman surgeon (I need a larger fret guitar to play music, so I admire someone who doesn't poke themselves in the eye when trying to pick their nose. Again, I apologize but am demonstrating the affects of that damn heart-lung machine that has saved my life). Love-hate.

Once the 3 leaflet valve (tricuspid) is working properly, the surgeon will then go for a smoke and a first year medical student will 'close the heart' and take the patient off the bypass pump (heart-lung machine), put tubes inside your body, near the heart to help drain the unwanted fluids that will accumulate because of the surgery. The body needs a way to drain all of the fluid build-up— which means these drainage tubes are in and out of your chest. They slit holes in your skin so they can drain into a plastic bag and they keep an eye on how much is draining and for how long, so they know when to pull the drainage tubes later in the week. Then they pull the breast bone back in place and keep it there by using stainless steel wire that they may have purchased at Home Depot for a dollar a foot, but your insurance (or you) will pay hundreds per inch, and your breastbone is now held together (hopefully) for the rest of your life by these wires.

The length of the surgery varies. It can be as quick as a dog race (okay, about 3 hours), or a bad year at the Belmont mile and a half— in other words, Secretariat would be ashamed with the seven hour version.

I don't believe I scared anyone with my explanation of the surgery and that is not the intention of the book. The point is to help you get through the aftermath of this military strike on the only mind and body we have (in this lifetime— you may believe in the next lifetime, and if you do, come back as a human because the techniques are getting better every day!)

THE MOMENT I AWOKE IN THE ICU I WAS CRAZED. Every alarm went off in my mind and body. *Something was terribly wrong.*

I couldn't breathe!

This was *not* how I felt after my first open-heart surgery. I could not... breathe— not even a little. I was suffocating. And the pain!

The pain was tremendous!

I managed to look up and without my contact lenses, I could barely make out Karla's face looking down at me. Everything was a blur. Because I had the huge breathing tube down my throat (and every other possible place a tube can go, and then pick a few more) I tried to tell her, "Something's wrong!" That's when I realized a very frightening detail: *my hands were tied*

down!

I tried to do my best Houdini and when that didn't work, I tried to pull frantically and see if I could loosen the restraints. No. I was a prisoner. I tried to move my eyes back and forth so Karla might notice my hands were tied down— but my hands were neatly tucked under the white blanket. I started to freak even more (which was a side of me no one had really seen before— including me). I kept thinking, 'You're not very good at panicking. No one seems to care.' No one could tell because I looked as if I had a bad 'trip' as I was coming out of anesthesia— I was helpless. In my mind I was screaming: something is *wrong*. I CAN NOT BREATHE!

The nurse made Karla leave, saying I needed quiet. Suddenly I felt like I was in a Stephen King novel. I did everything I could to calm myself down. Lots of shallow breathing. I needed to get some oxygen into my system.

An hour later when Karla was allowed to come back for a ten minute visit in the ICU, she reached to hold my hand and saw my hands were bound flat to the bed under the blanket. Karla saw in my eyes how it was distressing me (it's that look in a horse's eyes right before they rear up in the air— there's more white in the eye than eye-ball), and told the ICU nurse I wanted my hands untied. The nurse snapped back, "He's not The Director in here. I'm The Director here!"

This experience, along with the next 12 hours with this nurse, inspired a scene I wrote in my musical, *Open Heart*. The nurse was so sadistic and relished her cruelty so much that it made for great comedy. Even as I panicked I kept thinking how funny this was. Finally, when my hands were untied and my breathing tubes were removed from my throat, I managed to tell the nurse I was in pain, to which she responded, "What pain medication you take at home?"

"Excedrin."

"I can't give you Excedrin. You just had open heart s-u-u-urgery."

"I need to see a doctor!"

"That's why you in hospital. Doctors are everywhere. You'll see one."

"I need to see one now! I think I'm having a panic attack!"

"You ever have panic attack before?"

"No..."

"Then how you know it's panic attack?"

This went on and on and on. She finally told me that I'd be very sorry when I left the ICU because there would be no one else to take care of me like she did.

A doctor finally made his way to my bed and I managed to say, "I...can't breathe...I think...I'm having a panic attack."

"Yes. It seems like you are having a panic attack." (This *is* a Stephen King novel, I thought. I must not have awakened yet— this is too weird.) It got weirder when he told the nurse to get me a sedative and it took the nurse over an hour to return with 5 milligrams of valium.

"Gee, I feel so much BBBEEEETTTTTERRRR! I STILL CAN'T BREATHE AND IT HURTS MORE THAN ANYTHING I COULD EVER IMAGINE!"

"That's because you just had OPEN HEART S-U-U-URGERY!" the nurse yelled, and I smelled the garlic on her breath.

'I think I'm dying,' was all I kept saying in my head, over and over like an old vinyl record caught in a groove.

THE LESSON I LEARNED FROM MY SECOND TRIP into the ICU after open-heart surgery was that they *tied my hands down*. No one told me *prior* to surgery that when I awoke from anesthesia, my hands would be tied down. It may not seem like much, but I was already a 'prisoner' because my chest had just been sawed open, so really, where was I going to go? Who am I going to assault or strangle? When you are in the ICU, you might not even have the strength to lift your arms. So why do they tie your hands down? To protect you from pulling out the tubes that are stuck down your throat. But, as I would later learn from the good people at the Cleveland Clinic, if a nurse is with you when you arrive in the ICU and he or she sees that you are beginning to come out of the anesthesia, they should check to see if you can breathe without the breathing tubes. If the answer is 'Yes,' you may never know that your hands had been tied down.

My suggestion to anyone having any kind of surgery is to ask what is expected from you after the surgery, so you can understand what you must accomplish in order to get out of the ICU. You will have to prove you can sit up, talk, breathe and clear your lungs with the 'breathing toy.' Each hospital may have its own protocol, so it's necessary to ask ahead of time. It's very simple. What may seem like a no-brainer suddenly becomes torture because you cannot speak with tubes down your throat and if your hands are tied down, you have absolutely *no way to communicate* with anyone.

Because I had been through it before, I knew something was wrong with the outcome of this surgery from the moment I awoke and could not breathe. I wanted to tell someone in charge. A doctor. Anyone who would listen.

By the time I had a chance to tell my cardiologist the surgery must not have gone as planned because I could not breathe, he patted me and condescendingly said, "Your surgery was a success. What do you expect, Robby? You've had two open-heart surgeries. This is your life. Get used to it."

Nothing about this particular stay in this particular hospital went well for me. This is not to condemn this hospital; it's just a fact. But leaving the hospital was a triumphant day. Again, I was ready to prove that I could have open-heart surgery and get back to a wonderful and productive life. So even though I couldn't breathe, I thought, 'Well, if this is what it's like, so be it. I'll make the best of it.'

I got up very early the morning I was to be released, so excited to get out of the hospital that I began walking the hallways. When I came to a window I looked outside, down below— at the back entrance to the hospital.

'Hmmm. There's a lot of press down there. I wonder who died.' I quickly pinched myself. Okay— it wasn't me.

A very nice gentleman was mopping the floor and I turned to him and asked, "Who died?" (I don't know why I went straight to 'death'— it could've been anything, but for some reason, maybe the size of the press corps down below us— and it was a hospital— death seemed logical.)

"Frank Sinatra."

"You're kidding? Frank Sinatra died?"

"Yup."

"He's here? Now?"

"His body is."

We both looked at each other. Of course his body was here— but it seemed like a perfectly good question until you hear the answer. I was also still on pain medication so I lost track of boundaries, good taste, and was not the least bit self-conscious. I was stoned out of my mind, actually.

I began singing a medley of Frank Sinatra songs. I went back to my room and was given permission to shower. Showering for the first time after an operation can be like sex. Feeling the warm water on your body, shampooing your hair, it's all orgasmic. And the acoustics in the shower were tremendous. I started to croon, louder and louder:

"Start Spreading The Jews. I'm Leaving Today! You Can Stick A Fork In Him, New York, New York. I Want To Wake Up Some Place Where I Can Actually Sleep. I'm Gonna Sing For My Pills, Speaking Of Pills, I Wanna Hill Of 'Em, I'd Even Kill For 'Em—"

"Robby!" Karla stuck her head in. She was early.

"Hi, honey. I'm taking a shower!"

"I know. I'm looking right at you."

"See anything you like? Wanna get some?"

"Robby... you've got to keep your voice down. It must be going through the vents or something but I heard you all the way in the elevator and Frank Sinatra just died!"

"I know! Modulate: 'That Greg LeMond cruise! Is leaving today!I wanna hear the roar of it: U.S. of A!"

"Robby— shhh!"

"Okay doll."

Ah, victory! Leaving the hospital. Upright. Alive! My Tour de France.

Raising The Stakes

WHEN I GOT HOME FROM THE HOSPITAL after my second surgery, I found that my old recliner in our bedroom was the only place I wanted to be. I was home in record time, but why was I feeling so awful? Was this the way it was supposed to be? There was no one who had been through it for me to talk to— no one to ask.

My gifts from the surgery were being home and hearing my children Lyric, (now 14) and Zephyr (now 6) playing with their friends and laughing and having fun. Our children's lives seemed to be changing so quickly: the kind of jokes they laughed at; the sound of their voices when they laughed. I felt so ashamed that I was making the recliner my new home. I was ashamed that the children had to see me like this. I tried every trick I knew to not look sick or uncomfortable. I found that I would have to position my body in an awkward way every single time I needed a good gasp of air. I tried shallow breathing when my children were in the room.

Karla called the 'cardiologist to the stars' because this shortness of breath and the pain in my chest were like nothing I had experienced after my first open heart surgery. We knew I had perfectly clear arteries and low blood pressure; no worries there. Prescribed post op beta-blockers made me feel awful; comatose. I was given Digoxin short term. I was told to take pain medication short term— but nothing offered any relief. I got off the pain meds because they made me feel awful, too. (I ended up having acute surgical recovery pain for two and a half years without my doctors taking any notice or concern. It was as if when I spoke to them they hit the 'Mute' button.) My body knew something was wrong, but the doctors all told me it was '... natural to feel like this,' *always ending with the sentence:*

'What do you expect—
you've had two open-heart surgeries.'

Was this the way it was going to be for the rest of my life? No. I won't allow it!

I checked out local cardiac rehab— thirteen and a half years later, it still was not for me. I had to do something. So I designed my own again at home— not the same as first post op because I still couldn't breathe, but I had a new idea: I began running in place in the deep end of the swimming pool and I'd move my arms in different directions to gain upper body strength. It helped my chronically bad back and opened up my chest muscles, still tight from surgery. I had seen other cardio rehab programs where people ran in place in the shallow end of the pool, but in the deep end, the exercise was significantly more difficult and I also felt like it was straightening out my spine. I continued to roll on my basketball (something I did since I was a teenager, before the Swedish Balls came along) to lengthen my spine, and that helped too. If the deep end of the pool was good physical therapy for million dollar racehorses, it was certainly good enough for me. This routine was absolutely low-impact and still a tough cardio work-out. Eventually I did this for 60-to-90 minutes a day. I tested myself every day— my breathing did not get better, but it never got worse.

Exercise always helped. Whenever I was...blue, I would exercise. As a former jock, I knew my body. At least, I thought I did. The only way I knew to fix something was to exercise. It minimized my pain short term, I felt refreshed, and I felt like I was 'trying' to get better. At least I was trying. Out of that damn recliner.

I always had to try.

It was close to three weeks post-op when the phone rang (oh, I do love the phone when it comes to show business). It was my directing agent Rob Rothman saying my old friends— *Friends* producers Kevin Bright, Marta Kaufman and David Crane— wanted me to direct twelve episodes in a row of their new series **Jesse** starring Christina Applegate. Rob Rothman had become almost like a brother to me, and in all my years in Hollywood, I had only a few close friends.

Karla immediately voted 'No.' We had just discussed how an acquaintance who had recovered from a traumatic surgery advised me to take off a full year to heal. He hadn't, and he felt it set him back immeasurably in the healing process. I pretended to understand but *a full year?* No way. When my best friend and wife, partner for life and goddess of everything tells me 'No,' *I listen.* And then I do whatever I think is right. So, like an ass who didn't learn a single thing, *I took the job.*

It seemed impossible to change a life long work ethic and *raison d'etre.* It also seemed impossible to ignore pain and ignore my inability to breathe. I should've been home healing? Sitting home wallowing in my physical hell wasn't a good answer. My chest wound was still seepy, but I convinced everyone I was "A-Okay," because I felt my stamped expiration date for being a 'victim' had passed.

Karla understands the yin and yang of being me better than anyone. She knew I was worried the phone would never ring again. I promised her I'd 'take it easy.' Going to work meant feeling useful and having purpose. It also helped me take my mind off of my breathing problems, but I could see from day one that because I would lose air at the end of each sentence and then gasp to finish the sentence, my actors were a bit worried. I explained, "It's just the way things are. I'm over it. Not a problem."

When I worked, I loved having Karla stop by the set. The show was being shot on the Warner's lot in Burbank, just five minutes from our home in Toluca Lake. What could go wrong?

CUT TO: Karla walks onto the soundstage of *Jesse*, she hears my voice, looks up and realizes her husband, barely 6 weeks out of the hospital, is on top of a 20 foot ladder showing Christina Applegate how to do a comic fall through a window without hurting herself. Karla is witness to me balancing on the window ledge, placing my entire body weight on my wound.

I didn't break anything, and it hurt like hell later, but it didn't matter. I was completely focused on what did matter to me— that the stunt be safe for Christina and look good on camera. I never allowed any actor to perform a 'bit' that I didn't do first to make sure that it was absolutely safe. Christina is athletic, extremely talented and a hard working, seasoned pro; I found out it was safe for her. Not so safe for director-guy falling on his freshly wired sternum who was just cleared to drive a car post op, but cool for Christina.

DISSOLVE TO: Karla lecturing me outside of the studio and me having to realize that what I did was really...dumb. Crap. She was right and I knew it.

CUT TO: Eight grueling episodes in a row later. Good or bad, it's always grueling for a director if they're worth their salt. I know it's not digging ditches, but I would have welcomed the simplicity of digging ditches at this point. Shovel. Ground. Dig. Hole. (Jump in?)

One day, after dealing with an arrogant Executive Producer who did not know the difference between a Gaffer and a Best Boy, (Arrogance plus Ignorance equals very bad creative math.) I could no longer take it. I had to call Karla. That's all I kept thinking. I must call Karla!

I made it back to my little office/trailer and was barely able to dial the phone— I was shaking and frozen simultaneously. Tears were running down my face. I think it was the first time I realized I was... not a machine.

"H--e---l-l-o Karla? I need you. Please come now."

Minutes later she found me curled up in a fetal position on the floor of my private office/trailer. I could hardly speak but muttered something I have never said in my entire life— about anything: "I can't do this. Call Rob and get me replaced."

The advice my agent gave me was, "Just give 50 percent. Your 50 percent is like everyone else's 100 percent." I thought, what a horrible thing to say about my fellow directors. My problem is I simply can't do anything half way (not even wash the dishes). I was taught to do everything to the best of my abilities or why do it? That's still my M.O. I can't be a traffic cop/hack director just to get a paycheck. I can't *not care*. (The use of a double negative is my way of showing the DOUBLE NEGATIVE!)

People may hear that you have had open-heart surgery, but there is no way for the uninitiated to understand what that means. They expect you to quickly heal and forget about it, like it was a broken leg or an appendectomy. (Or in Hollywood, a face-lift and a tummy-tuck.) This mindset is hard to defeat. Open-heart surgery is in a category of its own. And when the results are not good, you can't 'just pull yourself up by your bootstraps.'

I was told Christina was upset with me and felt like I had abandoned her and her show, but how could I explain to her what even I didn't completely comprehend? Our friend was right— I needed a much longer time to heal properly.

I NOW HAD TIME TO REFLECT. I tried to replay all that had happened to me and what was making me feel the way I was feeling (inadequate; ashamed. Why?).

I remembered the day when Karla and I were sitting forever (it was only two hours but it really seemed endless) in my surgeon's waiting room for my post open-heart appointment just after the Ross Procedure. While we waited, the line of appointments to see the surgeon was backing up and many patients ended up crowded in the room staring silently at one another.

First, someone responded to small talk, "It's funny you should mention that. My scar hurts more than the doctors told me it was going to hurt."

"Really?" another patient perked up. "So does mine."

I couldn't help myself. "My scar hurts me too. Much more than with my first operation." We all nodded and went back to *Field & Stream, Sports Illustrated* and *Time Magazine*.

Then some brave soul blurted out, "I've been feeling a bit... blue. You know... sad." So there are other people who don't want the "D" word in their cranial lexicon, I thought. Hmmm.

"Me, too," a grown man said. I looked at him. He was rugged. His hands looked callous from doing real work, not 'show biz' work, like my hands. My hands were pink and soft. 'Damn,' I thought, 'I'm such a wuss.' This was a man— through and through— this was one tough guy.

"Yeah... I've been feeling really depressed lately." He stated, without a hint of embarrassment.

He said it! I can't believe it! The *man's man* said it! He used the "D" word!

"I've been feeling like crap, too," I blurted out and all heads turned to me. Why did I open my mouth? How come 'crap' came out instead of 'depressed?'

"Me, too," uttered an elderly lady who has lived a lot of life and just oozed wisdom. "They definitely don't prepare us for that. They give us pain pills or they tell us where to go for cardiac rehab and how to stretch and when we're allowed to drive a car, but no one even mentions that we might be feeling a bit *depressed,*" she softly continued.

"A *bit*?" an older man with his wife holding his hand extra tightly, said. "A *bit*? I think of suicide every single day."

"Whoa," I heard myself say. "Are you seeing a psychiatrist?"

"It doesn't help. They want me to talk about problems I had with my father and mother. I'm 73 years old. I stopped blaming my parents 30 years ago." Everyone laughed. We needed to laugh. In just a few minutes of honesty, we all felt like family. Fascinating feeling...

Finally, the surgeon returned from emergency surgery. When Karla and I got in his office he asked me how I was doing and I spoke honestly of my shortness of breath and my chest pain. He looked at my records and said my post op aortic echocardiogram looked great— this was all part of the second surgery healing process. I knew he was busy, but we were in and out of his office in less than five minutes.

That was that.

I still felt guilty that he stayed for my surgery, when he could've been with his dying father— but now... I also found that I couldn't ask (but wondered) if he got to his dad before his father passed away.

As we left the surgeon's office I said goodbye to my new 'friends for life,' even though I knew I'd never see them again. We came looking for answers and the best ones I received were from my older open-heart compatriots in the waiting room.

I BEGAN TO TRY AND MAKE LIFE BETTER with just an attitude adjustment. I had very simple pleasures: hearing my children's voices; Karla in any shape or form; holding very still in my chair watching *Jeopardy*; watching my favorite old *Three Stooges* episodes with Zephyr for the first time. Hearing his honest little laugh gave me the most pleasure imaginable. And, I loved to write. I could write. Nobody said I had to breathe perfectly in order to be a

writer. So I wrote, I composed music, I exercised— and of all things, I loved building playhouses for my children.

One for Lyric after my first surgery— when I was feeling great...

and one for Zephyr after my second surgery (when I wasn't).

People were still interested in my ideas in the compost heap that was becoming TV, so I kept writing. I wrote one pilot script - a work place comedy about actors who do voiceovers for animated series (something I know a lot about...). One of the stars of the show would be a paraplegic whose character would be the voice of a superhero. The other lead, a large muscular young man would voice the wimpy sidekick The show was about their lives *behind* the microphone and how that switched immediately once *away* from the microphone. Since she has a great comic mind and experience working on cartoon series, I asked Karla to help me create the show... We called it *Anim8ed*. The 'Must See TV' network bought the show from my pitch in the room, but my agent and the network wanted us to use a TV writer they both had a deal with to write the pilot. (Standard, but someone at the networks ought to think this process through if they like the soul of the show...) This man took over the script, wouldn't listen to the head of network comedy's notes, let alone ours, and he destroyed it. That simple.

As I was writing very, very late one night for a pitch at another network the following day, little Zephyr came into my office. Usually, when I was writing, nobody disturbed me in my ...'west wing.' But little Zephyr wandered in and asked me what I was doing.

"I'm writing an outline for a show for a television series, sweetheart. Shouldn't you be in bed?"

"I know something you can write, Daddy."

"That's nice. We can talk about it tomorrow. You need to go to bed and I need to write."

"But Daddy, it would be a great show."

"I'm sure it would. Now, please— let Daddy write and go to bed."

"It would be like *The Three Stooges*."

"Well, there's already been a show called *The Three Stooges* so who would want another one? Aren't you feeling sleepy? Karla!"

"But Dad— you should make it for women."

"Zephyr, demographics show that women don't like *The Three Stooges*." I couldn't believe I was talking demographics to a 6 year-old.

"And you could call it, 'The She-Stooges.'"

I froze. Did he just say, 'The She Stooges?' All of the brilliant female comic talent out there not getting a chance to do physical comedy unless it's a brief skit on *Saturday Night Live* or other sketch shows was a brilliant idea. And the title? Whoa.

"Did you just say '**The She Stooges**?'"

"Yes, Daddy. It would be so cool. We could watch it together."

"Zephyr. I want you to know two things: one, I love your idea; two, you need to go to sleep— but if you ever have any more ideas, I want you to come tell Daddy. Promise?"

"Promise!"

"Good boy. Now go to bed. And when you sleep, know your idea was really wonderful."

"I did good?"

"You did better than good."

Zephyr ran out of the room clutching his stuffed animal yelling to Karla, "Mommy, Daddy said I did good!"

The next day I did not bring my work with me to the meeting at the network. I only brought a title. 'The She Stooges.'

"Did you say 'The She Stooges?'" the head of comedy asked me.

"The She Stooges," I repeated, slowly.

"I love it!" he said.

'The She Stooges' got a green-light in the room (sounds like it happens all the time— it doesn't) to be a pilot script.

"I just want you to know, it wasn't my idea. You'll need an extra credit for the creator."

The head of comedy for the network looked at me as if I might have stolen the idea. "What do you mean?" he asked.

"It was my son's idea. Created by Zephyr Benson. Oh— he's 6 years-old."

IN 2000, I WOULD HAVE MANY 'EVENTS' OF TACHYCARDIA. My normal, standing heart rate was still about 50 beats per minute. But, like a light switch, suddenly my heart would race at 180 beats per minute and now, no matter what I would do (put my hand to my veins on my neck and grunt, like I was taught years earlier), nothing would stop these bouts of tachycardia— they would end when my heart decided they would end. On days when my heart rate would stay at 180 beats per minute for hours, by the time my the heart rate plummeted back to normal, I'd feel completely exhausted— as if I had just run a marathon.

Finally, I had what is called an **ablation**. From my point of view, it's similar to a heart catheterization. To quote the Cleveland Clinic experts: "During ablation, a doctor inserts a catheter (thin, flexible tube) into the heart. A special machine delivers energy through the catheter to tiny areas of the heart muscle that cause the abnormal heart rhythm. This energy 'disconnects' the pathway of the abnormal rhythm."

A successful ablation was performed at Cedars Sinai Hospital by Dr. Eli Gang. It fixed the tachycardia, but that's all it fixed. I still couldn't breathe.

I could fake it beautifully on set. No one had a clue. But sometimes I found myself in the most absurd situations. One evening after everyone left and I was on the set trying to figure out how to change a scene from a train station to an airport (physically!)— a scene we were shooting the following morning, in less than 12 hours. I saw one of the producers of the show going to his car, which was about a quarter of a mile away, in a parking structure (he was late coming onto the show, so he didn't have the prize possession of having a parking space with his name on it in front of the stage, like all the other producers).

I asked him if he understood what this change would do to our day and if he had a way to get in touch with the scenic designer because a train station was not going to change into an airport by itself. The dialogue could change, but the actors would be talking about airplanes at a train station.

His infamous words, the words I never want to hear, the words of someone who is not invested in the 'whole'— the words that to me are a *sin* were: "I don't care" he said flatly and kept walking toward his car. *Indifference!*

"You don't care?" I laughed, surely thinking he was kidding. If there is one thing that should bond all of us, it's our passion to make the best show possible, even if our personalities were like oil and water. And— I fought depression, err, ennuis, by *caring.*

"I said, I don't care," he repeated.

"Of course *you care*," I said like an idiot savant, following him to his car. Yet, with each stride, I became more of the idiot and 'savant' was deleted from this conversation's dictionary.

"I-do-not-care!" he said, again.

This absurd dialogue between the two of us continued for a quarter of a mile until it finally got through my thick idiot-skull that he did not care! How could that be? If he didn't care, why was I still on the lot and not at home with my family? Wait, I thought— where was everyone else who should be here to make this set-change work? Were they home with their families? I started to do my own private investigation into the 'I Don't Care' contagion. Was my passion the remedy? Actually, many who made more than a million dollars a season had the 'I Don't Care' syndrome. Pharmaceutical Companies could be making a fortune with Restless I Don't Care Disorder: R-I-D-C-D. Symptom: 'If you have **indifference** lasting more than three hours, please see Robby Benson and he'll smack you upside the head.'

I once told a young writer/producer who I felt badly for (because the star of the show hated him and made it very public), "I wouldn't have your job for a million dollars!"

He laughed and said, "A million? Ha! Neither would I!" He made $3 million bucks a year— and he didn't care, either!

It was an epidemic and I looked like a fool for 'giving too much effort' while all the other shows in town were barely rehearsing. I would still approach the work as if I were Sisyphus with a lobotomy— why do anything unless you're going to do it the best you can?

"Robby must need more time because he sucks." I need more time, because nothing is funny and we're supposed to make people laugh! Where is my echo chamber plug-in, under the heading of: REVERB Grand Canyon?

All of the passion that went into every decision I made— all of the compassion I had for every worker on every show, in front and behind the camera— was being mocked by the 'I Don't Care' people. The 'I Don't Care' Syndrome was finally identified as a condition, not a disease. It was a cult, and for the life of me, I must have burned my secret 'I Don't Care' draft card when I took a job.

I had a 'passion valve' that could not be turned off— it was connected to another set of valves that were impossible for me to calibrate. Those 'valves' were set to nuclear when I believed that people just didn't give a damn— they just wanted their paychecks. How could we not care? Being given the opportunity to speak to millions of viewers during a 22-minute sitcom was a gift. In the show business I had been schooled in, *indifference* (along with petty and clever cynicism) is a foe that I no longer had the energy to conquer.

I WENT BACK TO MY 'CARDIOLOGIST TO THE STARS' and explained to him that I was in trouble because *I just couldn't breathe,* and it was so bad that I couldn't work! That had to mean something because it meant everything to me! I stood there and begged him for answers as to why I could not breathe. He looked at me, shrugged his shoulders and then ordered a *ton* of tests. Like it was his way of proving me wrong, the tests were endless.

When we hadn't heard anything for weeks, Karla called and asked for a follow-up appointment. We drove back to his posh Beverly Hills' office. When I was told to go to a room, I went, sat there and waited.

The 'cardiologist to the stars' came in smiling and immediately the phone rang. There was a medical emergency in a plastic surgeons office upstairs— in the same building. A patient up a few flight of stairs, had gone into *cardiac arrest*. My doctor did not go upstairs. My doctor did not send other doctors on his staff to go upstairs; my doctor even took his time with the phone call— there was no urgency from my doctor whatsoever; I was... absolutely mortified by my doctor's behavior. There was a human being in cardiac arrest just a few flights above the office we were in. There was even an emergency crash cart in the office we were in!

My cardiologist (to the stars) dispassionately told the frantic nurse on the other end of the phone, "*Call 9-1-1.*" He hung up and sat down next to me, placing his hand on my knee.

"Robby," he said, patting my knee as he spoke, "I know what it must be like to be in your *position* in show business."

"Um... why aren't you going upstairs to help the person in cardiac arrest?" I asked bluntly and sincerely.

"I know it looks bad, but if I even 'make an appearance' on that floor — if the elevator takes me there accidentally, I could be liable in a law suit. I can't deal with that. It could be a very expensive elevator ride."

(To this day, as I am typing this book, I cannot help but wonder, what happened to the person who went into cardiac arrest and my doctor refused to get in an elevator because of the fear of malpractice.)

Then, he continued with me, as I was sitting next to him, my mouth wide open, like I was in an oral fly-catching contest.

"The stress. The constant stress. I see this every single day with celebrities and executives in your business. So a part of me understands why someone like you might turn to drugs and alcohol."

"What?" I was flabbergasted... Is it possible to be even *more* flabbergasted? Yes. If flabber were a flammable gas, I was pure Hindenburg-gasted! Oh, the humanity! Karla fell off her chair. Maybe the chair fell off Karla. This was a *Twilight Zone* moment for the two of us.

Okay, calm down, I thought. Listen to the expert who is allowing someone to die a few floors above us.

He patted me on the leg again and I looked at my file that he was holding, which looked like an over-sized encyclopedia because of my 2 open-heart surgeries and all of the recent test results he had ordered. But he never opened my file.

"'Drug use causes symptoms," he said, seriously. *"These people* shouldn't kill themselves, Robby. *These people* should save themselves."

I tried to speak clearly but it was hard to get enough of a breath to say: I'm not 'these people.' I have had two open-heart surgeries and I really can't breathe. I may be a weirdo to you, but I don't do drugs— never did drugs and will never do drugs. And if I were you doctor, instead of accusing me of recreational drug use, I'd get my ass upstairs and help the person who went into cardiac arrest."

"Calm down, Robby. You are far too self-righteous. Get your 'problems' under control and come see me in a year. Let's see how your 'shortness of breath' is doing then."

We left his office stunned; morally disoriented. (A very L.A. feeling.)

I FELT SHAME, A SENSE OF HOPELESSNESS, and I completely lacked a sense of joy. Why?

It's easy now to sit back and speculate but these were very trying times... (easy for me to write about now, but then— then I was a lost soul).

In my own stuttering way, I finally admitted to Karla, "I'm feeling a bit... blue."

"Depressed?" Karla asked.

"I wouldn't say the "D" word. I'd just say that I'm filled with... ennui."

"Ennui? All the time?" she sweetly inquired.

"Yeah. Pretty much," I answered. I always told Karla everything. Eventually.

"Well," Karla said, "how bad is your ...ennui?"

"Pretty bad ennui," I admitted. "As ennuis go, yup, pretty bad. Yup, ennui's bad."

"Bad enough to say that you're depressed?"

"Me? Depressed? Absolutely not."

"Robby— do you ever think of... hurting yourself?" Karla could not have been more thoughtful, more compassionate and gentle.

"Um... yeah. I can say I've thought about hurting myself... a few times."

"What do you mean by a few times?"

"You know... like every day." I looked down. I was so ashamed; I couldn't look her in the eyes. "Sometimes when I go to bed, I hope I don't wake up..."

"So, Robby— you're depressed."

"No, I wouldn't exactly use that word."

"Well," she said, "if I called it 'feeling like crap' instead of using the word 'depressed' would you say you 'felt like crap?'"

"Oh, definitely. I feel like crap, big time crap. I'm just *not* depressed."

During my first open-heart surgery, I mentioned that Joan Rivers was there because her husband had heart surgery. Later, her dear husband committed suicide. I heard he was depressed.

I never understood (then) how someone could suffer from depression after a team of doctors, surgeons and nurses who trained their entire lives to fix our hearts, gave us a new lease on life. Elation, I understood. Depression, no. Suicide? Never.

Until that day. The day I confessed to Karla how I... how *dark* I was feeling. (It's a "D" word...)

Karla began her own quest for someone to help me. She called my 'cardiologist to the stars' and mentioned that she had heard about 'Cardiac Depression' and it possibly being an effect of time on the heart-lung machine. Knowing how result-oriented I am she didn't want to waste my time (Woody Allen's 50 plus years in therapy came to mind) with just any psychiatrist and wondered if he could recommend someone who specialized in Cardiac Depression. He said he had 'no idea whatsoever,' and that 'you should call your family physician for a referral.' Thank you, 'cardiologist to the stars.'

Cardiac Depression

Cardiac Depression can strike patients for many reasons but some people think it may have something to do with the heart-lung machine and how long a patient is on it. Others believe it has something to do with the fact that your chest is sawed open and some stranger holds your heart in his or her hands. There are doctors at the Cleveland Clinic who deal specifically with cardiac depression.. I met one of the doctors, Leo Pozuelo, M.D. and he helped Karla and me immensely. He pursues answers aggressively— all for the good of the patient and the patient's family.

Cardiac depression can be more of a hurdle than healing physically from open-heart surgery. One of the more obvious reasons that I believe I suffered from cardiac depression was because I was young and athletic. For my first surgery, the healing and my energy to bounce back was turned into an Olympic event (by me). But for the second open-heart surgery, a surgery that didn't seem to be working (I just *could not* breathe), I suddenly felt as if I were less of a man. I could not do all of the things I thought I'd still be able to do. What kind of *husband* was I? Karla certainly didn't sign up for this. What kind of *father* was I? 'Come on, Daddy, let's do something.' 'I'm sorry son, but I feel too tired to even get up, let alone play catch.' (I felt such *shame*. Shame, shame, shame...)

I don't believe in ever being 'the victim.' But creatively, as far as my jobs went, I suddenly found myself in situations where I would be tiring when normally I'd be the only one with energy who could continue to work. Not anymore. That too caused serious self-doubt, which lead to depression. I found myself in bed on weekends instead of studying my scripts, I was holding a pillow to my chest, weeping for no reason. And I was humiliated that Karla and my children might see me like this. They made sure the house was quiet so 'Daddy could rest.' Unbelievable. They were so understanding.

Confronting depression may help others in your family; friends and people who love you. The spouses, partners, family members and dear friends, go through hell, trying to 'be there for you.' I found that discussing

my emotions (whatever they may be) with Karla was and is not only good for me (the patient) but it is extremely helpful to the people who love me. Trying to be the strong, heroic, silent type is cruel to them. I should know. It took me three surgeries to realize how hurtful it was to be silent and keep Karla (and others I love) in the dark. They are floating in the same sea of despair, yet they have no compass whatsoever— no frame of reference and they tend to think things like: 'I don't matter in his life;' 'I want to help him, but he won't allow me to help;' 'Please, let me in...'

Now there is a new equation: your psychological problems from the surgery and your loved one's psychological problems from your *silence*. It's not valiant or noble to live in silence. I thought it was. I was wrong. It is courageous to discuss your fears, no matter how absurd they feel to you, with the people you love and trust. And, if it is more than they can handle (and you as well), seek out professional psychological help— and personally, my advice is to go see these doctors with your loved one. Let them in. Make this event in your life liminal— don't allow it to consume you and your loved ones forever.

I wrote the song "Let Me In" from *Open Heart* for this very reason.

If you feel depressed, don't delay— seek professional help! If you feel a lack of joy; a lack of hope; if you feel like you don't want to wake up the next morning when you go to sleep, seek professional help immediately. Please. I was against it in my own ignorance and found true value, but of course had to find the right person to talk to.

If you or a loved one want to know more about **cardiac depression**, *which is very real*, please go to The Cleveland Clinic's website. It's a great place to start.

I NEEDED TO TALK TO A PROFESSIONAL, especially after someone close to me told me to skip the psychiatrist mumbo-jumbo and have an affair. My 'depressions' would disappear if I had an affair. An affair! I was then and I am now madly in love with Karla; the only thing right about my life was and is Karla and our children. How dare he! But he dared, and I never discussed anything more intimate than a planter's wart with him from that millisecond on...

An affair? Go fuck yourself. (Sorry...) No wonder some people are so fucked up. Excuse my language, but if there is ever a place to use it, it's in reference to me having an affair to get past my 'I can't breathe' depression.

Taking The Plunge

ONCE I TOOK THE PLUNGE into the psychiatric world, I should've taken a plunger with me.

My first psychiatrist literally creeped me out. Not a single thing that he said made any sense whatsoever. This doctor in Birkenstocks wrote me a prescription for something that would immobilize a horse and then told me that every time I felt depressed, I should "put a hard lemon candy drop in my mouth and just suck on it. But—" he continued, "if you don't have a lemon candy, use a pebble. Any *pebble* would do."

A pebble. A pebble A pebble.

As in any profession, there are people who are gifted, and there are people who really should be doing something else. I would have been better off getting advice from the guy selling Dodger Dogs in Chavez Ravine and singing "Take Me Out To The Ballgame" I thought I was nutty— whoa. So it is a process and you must be patient or else the bad shrinks may have you jumping off buildings just because of their incompetence. Now that I've said that, I must say that the ones who were good at their jobs were actually brilliant and helped me. A lot. Everyone will find the 'flavor' of shrink that will suit him or her the best. But the true test is how willing you are to keep looking...

I found that I was always drawn to people who were disabled. In Los Angeles, I met with an older woman who had polio as a child and needed crutches and a strong upper body (not to mention a strong constitution) to just get into a chair in her office. I felt at home speaking to someone who wanted to get to the bottom of a problem rather than someone who wanted me to suck on a pebble or take strange drugs that made me want to jump off an ant hill with a single bound, oh, and 'Time's up! That will cost you... A LOT!'

Exercise is a remarkably helpful tool that keeps me from disappearing into the deepest, colorless void in the haunted, agonizing blur of the amorphous, tenebrous nebulae of rotting depression. Getting my body moving (out of bed!) and into any kind of routine, especially one that is aerobic, helps me more than any medicine I've ever been prescribed.

If you know your body and mind well enough, you can find certain tricks to pull you out from under the cement ceiling caving in on you. Sometimes that can come from something as simple as comfort foods. Other times, it's sounds; music; smells... talking to someone on the phone— helping others! None of these are going to get you out of a deep depression but they can help you cope.

It's easy to blame. It's easy to blame loved ones. Go through the scenarios and realize, 'Does my mate or best friend really deserve the crap I'm shoveling at them? Is it their fault that I'm depressed?' Odds are, the answer will be 'No.' Try not to bite the hands that nurture you... easier said than done.

MY BRAIN SEARCHED FOR ANSWERS and only came up with the fact that I had been sawed open and my heart was 'under attack.' I had recurring nightmares that turned into 'daymares.' I became dyspeptic around loved ones, often weltering when thoughts about a phantom table saw made me cover my chest as if nurturing a child. The visuals became more and more real to me until I literally thought I was going insane.

Karla and I believed (with humility), what I was going through was a form of **Post Traumatic Stress Disorder** (PTSD). What happens after a traumatic event is unique to everyone; there is no doubt that my symptoms were triggered by the brutality and negative result of my second surgery. PTSD symptoms shouldn't be ignored.

There is growing research on an effective alternative method for helping heal traumatic stress. Go to the **David Lynch Foundation** to learn more.

It wasn't until years later, when our daughter Lyric introduced me to Transcendental Meditation, that I found another tool to help with depression.

After learning TM Lyric had immediate, profound results: the spine and fibromyalgia pain she endured since age 16 disappeared completely within the first two weeks of meditating. She found it to be the most scientifically researched method of meditation, with hundreds of rigorous studies showing TM's success in multiple areas of physical and mental health, including alleviating depression. Karla was on board.

My initial reaction was, "Perfect— now I'm supposed to join a cult!"

It was hard for me to consider at the time, as having an open-mind and being clinically depressed don't necessarily hang out in the same room together.

While humanity barks, chatters, babbles, explodes, resonates its greedy thunder in a world where decibels bombard us wherever we go, there must be a place to delve inward into our own silence.

When I eventually learned the simple, effortless TM technique and actually allowed myself— gave myself that 20 minutes twice a day (Okay, still working on giving myself the time to do it twice a day. Why is it so hard to make time for ourselves to do something that actually makes us feel so much better?)— I realized its value. I come out of this 20 minutes refreshed, with more focus, clarity and creativity— and it's great for your heart.

In discussing his book *Transcendence*, Dr. Norman Rosenthal, noted psychiatrist and former senior National Institutes of Health researcher, states, "If TM were a new drug, conferring this many benefits, it would be the biggest, multi-billion dollar blockbuster drug on the market."

It's not a religion, or a philosophy (or a cult!); it's a helpful tool. (Too bad I didn't learn it earlier…) Visit **TM.org** to find out more or **watch Dr. Oz**. explain the benefits of TM on YouTube.

I FOUND (AS USUAL) THE BEST THERAPY FOR ME was to be *creative*. Once I 'committed' (this phase of life gave a whole new meaning to the word…) to a project or even an idea, suddenly I felt empowered again and excited and joyful. Also, I never wanted to work on anything where Karla wasn't my collaborator. The idea of going to work and not sharing every moment I had left on Earth with Karla seemed absurd. When I found out she felt the same and I wasn't cornering her into projects and passions she wasn't interested in, I felt unstoppable. But interestingly enough, I found that my cardiac depression came and went when it wanted to— it had a schedule all its own. I could be fine walking across the room but almost like a switch, I could be deeply depressed by the time I reached the other side of the room.

I knew how to do battle with this evil shadow, but I still wanted to know why it would come and go like executives at a studio. One second I was fine, and the next second I'd be depressed and worried sick about people in another part of the world that I saw in a TV news report. So much so that I'd burst out into tears if I watched the nightly news… But then again, I thought, who wouldn't? I'm not insane. It's insane *not* to feel this way. Case in point: I used to feel the same when I watched the weather on the news channels in L.A. It would be a day where it was 90 degrees outside and the pollution level was so toxic (toxic to such an extent that people were being told to stay in their homes) it could damage the human lungs, yet the weatherman would say, "Another beautiful day here in sunny, Southern California." Really— who's insane?

People who watch the darkness that is shoved down our throats on the nightly news have probably become numb. But somehow these surgeries have tapped into my emotions and I can't watch anyone suffer. Karla helps me with this. We talk about it... and because I write, I can express myself on the subject, even if it's in the form of a letter to the editor of a newspaper.

So writing became even more cathartic, and in the process, I began writing of all things, a musical.

I CHOSE TO PURGE MY DEMONS by putting all of my passion into *Open Heart The Musical*. Even the name is funny in a dark, perverse way. And the only way I could write this musical was predicated on two very important issues to me: good music for Karla to sing. To me, her extraordinary talents were being wasted every night she wasn't on stage singing and performing; giving people a sonic experience they will never forget because she was one of the best singers I had ever heard and by far the best singer I had ever been on stage with— and people needed to see her comedy chops. The woman is a genius comically. It had to be funny. I wanted it to be poignant as well— but it had to be funny, funny, funny. Not indulgent.

Open Heart became a work in progress beginning in 1999. It was something I could do, even if I was out of breath or not feeling well. I could work in private— all through the night if inspired. And seeing, visualizing the night when we would open and Karla would be giving audiences a giant dose of her talent and gifts, I would be filled with hope. (Hope— I'll say it again and again: what an underrated emotion...)

Open Heart had its first official read through in March of 2000 with the amazing singer Stan Brown, and gifted musician Sterling Smith on keyboards. On May 31 we had another read through/sing through for invited guests in our living room. The process was working. The show was finding itself— it became a driving force in my life.

To make some money to pay for our musical, I directed a few episodes of random shows, like *Dharma & Greg*. The cast and crew were terrific. The show-runner and I began a war that continues to this day. He's laughing all the way to the bank and I'm content within my blood-bank and soul. To say we didn't see eye-to-eye is an understatement. To say he would've pulled one of my eyeballs out and eat it for a snack is more to the point. Insanity. Success. And too much money. Again, really bad math.

Open Heart The Musical was about to open its heart at The Tiffany Theater in Beverly Hills. (Talented artist Moshe Elimelech, my sister Shelli's husband, designed the poster for our show.) We had a read-through sing-through over two nights organized by our friend producer Susan Dietz who had seen the show in our living room. Peter Schneider, a producer on *Beauty and the Beast* who was leaving Disney to pursue theater, loved my music and wanted to produce and invest in a workshop of our show.

At 6:05 a.m. on September 11, the phone woke us up in Los Angeles. It was Lyric, 3,000 miles away, now a freshman at N.Y.U., saying a plane had hit the World Trade Center and she couldn't get Val on the phone.

Valerie Silver Ellis worked at Cantor Fitzgerald on the 102nd floor of One World Trade Center. Lyric had been Sam and Valerie's flower girl at age 4. We had just turned Lyric over to Sam and Val when we moved Lyric into her dorm on 14th St. She was supposed to have dinner with Val and Sam that night.

Our little girl, just eighteen, had only been at NYU for three weeks. I'll never forget the phone conversation I had with Sam (now one of my best friends) after the attack but before the buildings crumbled. He was waiting for a phone call from Val. Because of the 1993 attack on the World Trade Center, Sam knew exactly how long it would take for Val to get down the stairs and call to tell him everything was okay. The time limit was almost up. But even as he waited to hear from his wife, Sam tried to find Lyric, who was now bringing water to fire-fighters and emergency workers. Her instincts were to go *to* a problem, not *run from one*. Lyric grew up very quickly that moment in time.

After the towers collapsed, all cell phone signals were lost. It was the most frightening time in my life until the phone rang and I heard from Carleen Hussung Simone. (Karla and I introduced Carleen and Winston when I ran the New York Marathon.) Lyric was safe with Carleen's mom Alleen and they were heading up-town to Carleen and Winston's apartment.

But the phone never rang for Sam Ellis. Val didn't make it down those stairs.

Valerie Silver Ellis died in the towers on that day. We lost our dear friend, and like so many families, to say we were 'at a loss' is an understatement— we were never the same; we will never be the same.

9/11 has a history with all of us. If having heart surgery makes us appreciate every single breath we take, September 11th is another example of the existential world we live in and to... love and appreciate each moment of life.

I dove back into work and my writing. The moments in *Open Heart The Musical* which had to do with life and death had now become more personal and meaningful to me. With this momentum and purpose we sped to the next incarnation of the show, which had a run at the Falcon Theater in Toluca Lake as a musical workshop. *Open Heart* starred Karla (of course), Stan Brown (my ex-master student extraordinaire from the real USC), and me— writer-composer guy who couldn't breathe when he had to sing. That was a tough one. But we were successful and our hopes to go to New York with the show were brighter and brighter.

I CAN'T CONDEMN EVERYONE IN TV because that would be false and unfair, but the business of making TV shows became surreal, Fellini-esque. The 'I Don't Care' Syndrome was now an epidemic and that seemed to lead to a lack of quality control which in turn seemed to change the face of television and bring us 'reality TV.' In my early years as a TV director, I was always so enthusiastic that we could build comedy beginning on a Monday and shooting on a Friday. It reminded me of theater on steroids: get the show up and running in 5 days. Unfortunately— when an Executive Producer shot an entire season of a show and then walked up to me with a straight face and asked, "Have we been shooting film or video?"— the fun, creativity and fulfillment began to be bleached from my soul.

I began directing TV because it was fun, creative and fulfilling.

I stopped directing TV because it took on a personality of a rabid, demented, possessed mania that started 'at the top' and suddenly the director became a worthless traffic cop who was pushed aside by the show-runners and every DGA rule was broken as the writers, creators and show-runners refused to follow protocol and began giving direction to the actors and too much money was at stake for anyone to stop the madness. You will find many top directors who will secretly corroborate my beliefs but would never ever jeopardize their paychecks for their families by being foolish enough to yell it from the hill top (or write it in a book...)

Karla helped get me out of the self-destructive cycle I was in as a TV director; always believing that everyone should care; thinking foolishly that we were trying to make the best shows possible, rather than facing the truth: we were filling time and space in between commercials.

The Advocate

There are many ways one can be an advocate for a loved one, friend, family.... One way is merely to listen with an open mind and then take over, control the situation because 'the one in need' cannot fend for his or her self. Of course, there are 99 other ways to do it, if 100 means, "Get out of my way— it's going down like this!"

Karla and I began as "children" (mentally) when we faced my first open-heart surgery and we were like most people I know, completely under-educated and so confused that we had no idea what to ask doctors, surgeons, nurses friends, and family— we didn't know how to reach out for help because we thought we were completely taken care of by the hospital. Never, ever believe this to be the case. We are basically just numbers, bodies, flying in and out on the conveyer belt of life and the pursuit of health and insurance. We learned the hard way: by becoming experts through necessity and practice (4 open heart surgeries are rare so if at first you don't succeed, try, try again to not get suffocated in fear, paperwork, bewilderment, ignorance and the lack of mental endurance needed to run this medical marathon, whose rules change constantly.

I have already and will continue to point out that Karla became 'my' advocate because without her help, there are so many things I would never have been able to accomplish— some of those things are as simple as just getting a ride home after hearing news that is life-changing. But, then there are the obvious: questions we all forget to ask, so someone does research on Google and prepares and brings a pad of paper— and is not afraid to ask delicate and sometimes embarrassing questions. Karla also became my defender: "Robby is asleep now and we should not wake him up." As simple as that seems, it's huge. Food. Karla brought home the bacon and prepared it, too (even though it was fake bacon with no nitrates). Healthy foods. Foods to avoid. Medicines and when to take them— on an empty stomach— on a full stomach. These things seem trite but honestly, they are life-saving and are a daily requirement. Being tough at a doctor's office: "Excuse me but we've been here for over an hour..." Yes, being the bad guy, "Robby cannot walk there, please bring him a wheelchair. Do I have to say it 5 times?" The mountain of endless paperwork that can put the advocate in the hospital.

There is also the 'responsibility of the "mood-game-changer" that goes with being the advocate. I'd say that like on an athletic team, this is a character issue that is undeniably dominant in its essential significance, but it doesn't show up on a stat sheet after the game. The ability to keep things 'light'— funny— to be able to deflect the ominous and see it coming just as a cornerback sees the tight end sneaking into the middle of coverage to gain crucial yardage— the advocate plays great defense with peripheral vision and denies considerable yardage gained by negativity by seeing it coming and being the ultimate team player.

I recently had the opportunity to be an advocate for someone I love dearly after an operation in Dallas. (I'll refer to her as 'Mrs. Smith.') The operation made Mrs. Smith's legs swell with fluids post operative. I knew this to be normal but no one said a word to her that this was a possible side effect from surgery. Instead, with Mrs. Smith becoming bloated and her legs swelling to a painful size, a nurse mentioned that she might have internal bleeding from the operation, and uttered the words no patient ever wants to hear: "They may have to take you back into surgery."

This caused quite a disturbance in the room. In the meantime, the nurse was taking Mrs. Smith's vital signs. I noticed her blood pressure was not only stable, but it was better than mine. I also looked at her heart rate and it was at a steady 63 beats per minute (very good). Finally, I saw that her oxygen saturation was 100 percent. Perfect. My knowledge immediately told me that if she had an internal bleed that was causing the swelling, her vital signs would tell us a different story, rather than all being very stable.

Because of the hysteria that the nurse had caused by announcing a possible trip back into surgery, Mrs. Smith's surgeon made it into the room and in the most contemptuous and aloof tone, told her there might be internal bleeding because "sometimes things get nicked and we have to go back in and repair the bleed."

I looked at His Arrogance and muttered: "Her blood pressure is stable. Her heart rate is that of a runner's," (the patient was an avid exerciser) "and her oxygen saturation was at 100 percent. Wouldn't one of these vital stats be rising or plummeting if there was an internal bleed and the body was reacting to internal trauma? Wouldn't it be a more likely signal, based on her vital signs, that her body is reacting to the surgery itself with protective fluids ?"

He turned his up-turned nose at me and as if it were the hardest thing he ever said in his life, "Yes. You're probably... rrrrrrright."

But he refused to give up there— and honestly I was glad. He ordered Mrs. Smith to have an immediate contrast dye MRI.

We were all slightly relieved because even though my own medical history gave me reason to believe Mrs. Smith did not have an internal bleed that might warrant her return into surgery, I still wanted every precaution to be taken to make sure the Mrs. Smith was okay. And really— what could go wrong with a contrast dye M.R.I.? Oy.

So, in about a half hour, Mrs. Smith was returning from her procedure when I noticed that her bed was actually bypassing her hospital room!

I jumped to my feet and ran into the hallway and asked, "Where are you taking Mrs. Smith?"

"This is not Mrs. Smith. This is Mrs. Garcia!"

I was told this by a short volunteer who was very proud of the work she was doing and wanted to be 'super-responsible' according to her.

"I assure you— this is Mrs. Smith! This is not— NOT— Mrs. Garcia! Look at her wrist band. Look at her chart."

She grabbed her chart— and it was the chart for Mrs. Garcia.

"This," she said with great pride and assurance, "is Mrs. Garcia."

By this time, Mrs. Smith managed to say, I am not Mrs. Garcia. I'm Mrs. Smith."

"No. You are not! You are Mrs. Garcia!"

This continued like a Marx Brothers skit as it turned into a tug-of-war with Mrs. Smith's bed— with me at one end and the volunteer at the other, struggling for the control of Mrs. Smith-Garcia's destiny.

Finally the floor nurse showed up and took over and put 'Mrs. Smith' back into our— the correct— room.

But where on earth was Mrs. Garcia? (It sounded like a children's game, like Where's Waldo.) To this day, I still imagine poor Mrs. Garcia floating from procedure to procedure traveling around the hospital and never quite making it back to her room.

Being an advocate is like being a Man Friday, ready and willing to help in any and all ways. A good laugh, a sense of strength but not bravura, and always a calm voice is good math for any advocate.

Sometimes, just showing up means the world to a patient. I have a friend and former student, Kyle O'Tain, who is like a brother to me. He is miraculous and has the spirit of a champion. Kyle needed a lung transplant and was hours away from death. Just having certain people show up at his bedside gave him strength. People who had no reason to be in NYC came by planes and trains to be remind this unique young man how remarkable he is. I'm so thrilled to say that Kyle got his lungs and even though he still must face the harshest reality of all, Cystic Fibrosis, he can now breathe for the first time in his life. His remaining years will be about the quality of life not the quantity; Kyle understands this and spreads love every moment of his life. He's a hero of mine.

Please sign up to be an organ donor. It's easy to do when you get your driver's license, but you can also have this placed on your I.D. for people who don't drive and live in big cities like New York. Spread Life. Spread Love. Become an organ donor. And while I'm at it, please go to your local school or Red Cross and give blood.

(Thank you...)

I WENT BACK TO THE 'CARDIOLOGIST TO THE STARS' right before we left Hollywood— one year later, as instructed. He quickly came into my room, and with gallant urgency, told me I had a problem. No wonder I couldn't breathe.

"Thank God for the tests!" he said.

"I didn't take any tests," I said quietly.

"What are you talking about?" he asked. "I'm holding your tests right here. These tests clearly show..." His face blanched. I could not have directed it better. His honest horror was absolutely perfect. Cut, print— that's the take!

The 'cardiologist to the stars' looked at the date on the tests and read that they were from *last year*. Yes. He was reading *last year's tests*. *For the first time.*

I realized my cardiologist was merely a TV Executive in a white lab coat. I knew Hollywood was just not for me anymore.

If this was the best I would ever feel physically, it was clear that we had to change the game plan. Immediately. Everything in Hollywood was a reminder of judgmental attitudes, inflated expectations, greed...did I say greed?

Karla and I have spent our lives dreaming; we were ready for another adventure. The screening room in my brain projected that we would 'go to Carolina in my mind.' And soul. It was a rhapsodic, etherial vision of North Carolina. A place where I could *breathe*.

It was the fall of 2002. Lyric was still at NYU; Zephyr was now in the 5th grade. We talked with Zephyr about making this life-change, and he was on board. I went online and bought tickets for a flight to Charlotte. I was finally dreaming again!

But Karla's job was navigating everyone's well-being, and Zephyr would be missing school in L.A. if we left now. So she asked me if we could put off our trip until he had some vacation days.

In a moment of absolute clarity, I turned to Karla and said, "Are you going to save my life by getting me out of here or not?"

Green Acres

OUR INTENTION WAS TO DRIVE through North Carolina, looking for a beautiful places to live near a university: Davidson, Duke, UNC, NC State, NC School of the Arts.

We stayed with our good friend Dee Rinker. in Davidson. Her daughter Audrey, a Duke grad and a phenomenal young woman, nannied Lyric while we shot *Modern Love* in 1989. Dee and her husband Dave (the USC architect who designed the Koger Center) became our close friends. After Dave died, Dee moved to North Carolina.

Dee was a a great sounding board and mentor. She lived on Lake Davidson, where Karla and I went swimming and kayaking with Zephyr,

dreaming about living on a lake. No matter my
limitations, I never stopped exercising after my
second surgery. My goal was to give my family a
great quality of life— and I didn't want to be the
one ruining that opportunity.

Dee called Kay and Frank Borkowski.
Frank was the Chancellor at Appalachian State University. When she told
them our plan, Frank and Kay said "Do not let them leave the state without
coming up to Boone." They invited us to spend three days with them at the
Chancellor's house and take a look around. "It would be a lovely place for
you to teach and Karla and Zephyr will adore it up here."

'Up?' I kept wondering what they meant by 'up.'

Dee drove us 'up' the mountain: 1,000 feet; 2,000 feet; 3,000 feet… We
had lived at 6,800 and skied at 10,000 feet in Park City, but that was thirty-five
minutes from a great hospital and an international airport in Salt Lake City
(important things on Karla's checklist). Boone was two and a half hours away
from anything that looked like civilization to us. When we saw a permanent
sign that read: *Fog Likely Next 8 Miles.*

I thought, 'All year round? Whoa!'

Karla said, "Darling, I think this might be a bit remote."

There was one way up to Boone from Charlotte and one way down without going forty miles out of the way. (Since we've moved, they've widened the 'narrow' road up the hill.) Navigating the narrow winding road cut into mountain probably was a piece of cake for the locals, but huge trucks flew past us heading down the mountain at speeds that took my breath away. (I finally had a reason not to be able to breathe!) This drive was the perfect place to teach the 'Doppler effect' in a sound class. If you were brave enough to de-claw your fingers from the seat of your car, one could record pitch rising in tone as a truck approached our car, and sliding down the musical scale as it passed while its sonic wave lengths changed.

The last thirty minutes revealed the incredible timeless beauty of the Blue Ridge Mountains: heavenly vistas in all directions, with the highest peak Grandfather Mountain in the distance.

Route 321 was the main drag bringing us into Boone, and we were disappointed to find it looking like any other strip mall laden suburban town in America. No official city planning going on here. A local candidate had put up a good fight to ban billboards a few years back, but was voted down because as we were told, "Mountain people are independent. They don't like to be told what to do on their property." Hmm...

None of this boded well for us or our expectations.

When we arrived at the Chancellor's home we were greeted with open arms by the Borkowskis. Frank had been Chancellor at Appalachian State for ten years, enhancing its national and international reputation, taking it from a quaint teachers college to #4 on *US News and World Report's* top public universities in the South. Frank and Kay looked at the world from an artist's perspective— both talented musicians. They saw what we had accomplished at USC and were anxious to have me take a full time position in the Theatre Department. Frank's vision was for me to create filmmaking classes as a bridge between the Theatre and the Communication Departments.

Showing us around the small but well planned campus, students everywhere greeted Frank, stopping to shake his hand and giving him the thumbs up sign— it was obvious he was well loved. This time our first stop was *not* at the football stadium (where they had one of the best Division II schools in the nation). It was so refreshing to go to the different buildings of education without being wooed by the athletic department.

Finally, we arrived at the building that housed the Theater Department. It was... whimsical. Lovely. The Chair and faculty seemed passionate (passionate is not a derogatory term when it comes to teaching). Frank introduced me to the Dean who was thrilled I would consider a position at Appalachian State. He wanted me to keep my 'working professional' status, in film, TV and theater projects, including our New York-bound musical, *Open Heart*— bringing national recognition to the school. Suddenly I felt like I wouldn't mind trips away, knowing I would return to Boone.

Karla wondered if Frank had plans to retire any time soon. If we were going to change our lives and relocate here, it was important to know the man who had the vision, who valued what I could bring to the program, would be there to support me.

Kay said, "Oh no, we plan to stay here at least two and a half or three years."

The smell of the country air was sweet and lacked the 'chromatic brown' smell of Los Angeles. Yes, after all our years in Hollywood, I can say it with certainty: chromatic brown qualifies as an adjective for the scent of LA smog. So the Benson-DeVito clan began a conversation, keeping our options open and our possibilities pure (to quote a Karla DeVito song):

"Are you sure this isn't a bit remote for you?"

"What if something happens to your heart? It's a two and half-hour drive to Charlotte. Impassable in fog, or a blizzard."

"They have helicopters. Don't they?"

"Do we need to buy a gun?"

"We have no friends here."

"Did you say a gun? I don't want a gun!"

"Did you say a helicopter? Helicopters are scary."

"Helicopters aren't scary. Guns are scary."

"I've heard about crystal-meth labs up in dem dar hills."

Then the gut checks became more positive:

"I don't want to make fun anymore. This place - and the people - it's pretty cool."

"They have a great public school system for Zephyr."

"I loved my public school education. Hurray for public schools!"

"Zephyr loves basketball. We'll get Mountaineer season tickets."

"The University is small but Frank has it on a great path."

"Kay and Frank are our friends."

"I still don't want a gun."

We threw out our long list of North Carolina destinations, looking no further than Boone. And that was that.

The gorgeous surroundings of the Blue Ridge Mountains gave us butterflies in our stomachs, legs, any and all places butterflies can exist in adventurers. We experienced this heady feeling before, when we went to South Carolina and Park City.

Telling my family that we were moving again was difficult. For seventeen of the twenty one years Karla and I were married, we lived within a 5-mile radius of my parents. Or should I say, my parents lived and sister lived in a 5-mile radius from me. They were the ones always trying to keep our family close. And I was the restless one who would always seek new adventure. What made this decision more urgent was the need to flee the business that loomed over my every move, every phone call, every trip to the grocery store in Los Angeles. My second heart surgery left me with no physical reserve to push through. I had reached my limit.

I tried to be stoic and foolishly hide most of my problems from my parents— so they weren't acutely aware of my situation. I was in real physical and mental trouble. When I'd mention the creative(-less) forces I had to deal with daily, my folks would remind me I was generalizing and say I would eventually find the right fit. But they had been out of the business for years, so how could I expect them to understand my plight? I'm sure my dad, in my shoes would have done the same. I'm sure of it. He raised me 'right.' My heart felt like it would explode in Los Angeles. Although I would desperately miss my parents and my sister, leaving was a matter of survival.

OUR HOUSE IN TOLUCA LAKE SOLD QUICKLY and when we returned to North Carolina we went looking for a home. Lyric suggested we look for 'cow property.' Cow property? A pet? A cow?

"No, Daddy— *two* cows; they're herd animals. One cow gets lonely and needs a pal."

"But— it's a cow!" (My cowboy friends referred to cows as 'Dumb on four legs.' They didn't know our cows.)

Karla's childhood friend had a dairy farm, and she found this idea appealing. Lyric had already done research on the internet looking for miniature Jerseys. A miniature cow is not like a miniature donkey or a miniature *anything*— there is nothing miniature about a miniature Jersey except it doesn't weigh 800 to 1200 pounds— it weighs 500 pounds! No animal that weighs 500 pounds is miniature, unless it's a miniature elephant. (I would've liked one of those.)

As we were driving down a dirt road with our real estate agent, there were many opportunities to take pictures. It was all so beautiful. Everything. Even a simple fence. We drove up (Up! The angle was so steep I wondered if the car could make it) the hill to a house. Oh my goodness gracious— what a house.

We found a cedar home on eleven acres (cow property!) paralleling the Blue Ridge Parkway, with a barn, a stream, an apple orchard, and one of the best views I had ever seen. It gave us all a sense of peace.

The interior of the house needed a lot of work. I imagined sitting at my desk staring at this remarkable view that changed with every cloud and every ray of sun. I could just look out the window... forever...see Karla and our dogs...(But I was not getting a gun!)

I couldn't believe anyone could be lucky enough to live here. Our 'city kids' were in heaven, running up on down the big hill and into the pasture. Freedom!

Before we put an offer down on the farm Karla asked, "Would you be happy to live here even if you're not affiliated with the University?"

We bought it immediately. I named it K.J. Farms in honor of my

goddess, Karla Jayne. I had been a working professional for thirty-six years and paid cash for the house, so (everyone repeat on the count of three:)

"No-matter-what-ever-happened-to-me, my-family-would-have-a-roof-over-their-heads." (And their cows' heads, too.)

Could we be so lucky? My heart felt... at ease.

Every time the sun moved, the view was radically different and more

inspiring. The Blue Ridge Mountains were alive with color. The sunsets were glorious.

I finally understood what drives people who are adamant about protecting our Mother Earth. For the first time in my life, it was evident to me why people believed in a higher power— God. The overwhelming humility of being smack dab in the middle of nature at her finest is something I never want to forget. Being alone with the power of the forces of the Earth, taught me so much. The power of the wind (wind power! Why aren't we investing heavily in wind power?), the sun (solar power! Why aren't we investing heavily in solar power?), the rain, and the raw elements were awe-inspiring.

I wanted to exist in this uncultivated, feral environment and experience...everything.

Oh, and did I mention, they sold us a tractor with the house? A tractor! It did not run on solar energy nor was it a Prius Tractor. But the little boy in me went batty when I saw that orange tractor. It turned the grown man into one big fossil fuel guzzling hypocrite.

'This land is your land; this land is my land...'

It was hokey, but I finally understood what being an American means. It's not New York and Los Angeles. Not at all. It's here, there and *everywhere!*

C.M. Harris bought this property in 1961 and built the house himself in 1991. He gave me tractor driving lessons. He wouldn't hand me the keys until I understood everything about the big machine because as he put it, "Even the best farmers die in tractor accidents. Every day. That cannot happen to you. I won't allow it."

The tractor had not been driven all winter and a mouse had nested in the engine. We didn't know this until we were out in the open field and I was in the tractor seat and the mouse couldn't stand the heat and the sound of the engine and found sanctuary *in my lap*. Now, as a New York city kid, anything that remotely looks like a rat is my enemy. At first, I froze, poised to throw a quick right hand down at the mouse's head, crushing it instantly. Of course, my follow-through would've done damage to me— but I'd already had my children. C.M. guffawed.

I looked down at the mouse and just as I was about to end its life, the mouse looked up at me. I looked into its little eyes as its nose wiggled and it seemed to... thank me for being a soft place to stay while the tractor was destroying its nest. In one breath, my relationship with this mouse changed. The mouse wasn't my enemy— it was alive, and had every right to stay alive. It was doing me no harm. As a matter of fact, I had such a change of heart I thought the little guy might enjoy a tractor ride. And that's exactly what happened. The mouse and I had a wonderful tractor lesson. After the lesson, the mouse decided to retreat to the safety of the tall grass and find a new home. In the silliest of ways, I'd found a new home, too— and a renewed love of all creatures, not to mention that big ol' Kubota tractor.

"Oh, and one last thing. No takin' it up the hill, keep it in the flats of the pastures."

I had to ask, "You're saying *no one* has ever taken a tractor to the top of this hill?"

He could not lie. "Marvin Storie has done it. But he's been working this land all of his life. Don't you try it, ever!"

C.M. was a good man, but had no idea he was dealing with an actor who had done dangerous stunts in a lifelong career. Afraid? Of a tractor? Really— what could go wrong?

Working at my desk looking out at Mother Nature's 'best side,' it was impossible not to be prolific. Mother Nature didn't need plastic surgery— she was gorgeous and much appreciated.

Who needs a muse when you have Mother Earth? And, speaking of a muse, isn't that Karla... ...way down there? I can see my muse! Just like I imagined...

The stress was gone and the birds were singing. Whoa, did you hear that? The birds are really singing! Bird watching became my new hobby.

Yes, the guy who lives for football season, now lives to bird-watch. (Okay, I still ordered DirecTV sports...I couldn't go cold turkey)

They sang to me.   They came to me.

It was as if they knew I would never, ever hurt

them and they trusted me!   I began to make

friends with them.

The star of the bird show was 'my' cardinal. He had a habit of showing up whenever I was down.

Somehow he knew, and he would drop by. I would have to feed my new friend. When I was feeling a bit... blue (ennui? Screw it: *depressed*), I'd just look out the window and my cardinal would show up.

I learned how to imitate his call and he would come when I would whistle and sing his song.

If this life isn't good for the heart, I don't know what is.

Karla and I were riding on a 'Carousel of Love.' If you don't believe me, listen to the song!

I LEARNED HOW TO USE THE 'BUSH-HOG' (attached to the back of my tractor with the large blades that cut acres of grass) so well that I was able to create my own 'tractor art': I wrote Karla's name copying the way she signs her signature using the Earth as my canvas! And I could do it 'freehand' with the bush-hog as my brush. In the fall:

in the winter:

All year round.

For everyone, every small plane that flew overhead, and even for the passenger flying on a big jet who happened to look down, I wanted them to see what Karla

(and The Beatles) meant to me.

My heart was already feeling better.

One day I was in the barn changing the bush-hog to a fertilizer spreader, I noticed something moving, peripherally. I quickly snapped my head and this time, it wasn't a mouse. It was a large, shiny black snake about four inches in diameter and at least six feet in length. No matter how evolved I had become, I will never make friends with a snake.

Suddenly, I wasn't feeling so 'at-home' anymore, staring at this very healthy reptile. I was holding an empty, 50-pound fertilizer bag— just a limp piece of plastic. Like an episode from *Green Acres*, I began to wildly swing the bag at the snake, as if it were a weapon (that would blow away in a gust of wind). The big black snake looked up at me, very unimpressed. Bored with me, he slowly slithered away. Now I was on 'snake alert.' I did learn that black snakes are very valuable to farmers. They 'eat the critters that eat yer crops, an' they kill copperheads which kin kill you.' I eventually had a couple of run-ins with copperheads, but they wanted as much to do with me as I did with them.

There was a new harmony on K.J. Farms. One day as I was writing I saw a black bear cross in front of my window. I had my camera handy to take pictures of deer and their fawn, a family of twenty-two wild turkeys, and just about every bird in North Carolina. I was so impressed with the bear, that I wanted to follow it and get a better shot. I grabbed my camera and ran outside. The bear went over the fence and into the forest near the Blue Ridge Parkway. I sprinted to the fence, scaled it, completely gasping for air, but I had to get a close-up of the bear. And then, I heard Karla's voice, as if she were sitting on my shoulder.

"Robby— it's a bear. B-E-A-R, *bear*. Climb back over the fence and get inside the house as quickly as you can."

I nodded appreciatively to the phantom Karla on-my-shoulder (John Denver had 'Sunshine' on his shoulder to make him happy— I was much more blessed), retraced my steps, and sprinted back toward the house.

The Infamous Tractor Accident

I had only been a farmer for three and a half weeks when I took the tractor to the place C.M. told me to never go: the top of the hill. It was on May 29, 2003. I remember that day because it is Karla's birthday.

I became 'the fool on the hill' who didn't listen... the stuntman in me actually thought I could pull it off.

When it came to my tractor, I most certainly did not park my ego in the barn. C.M. said Marvin Storie had bush-hogged the hill, so why couldn't I? It was Karla's first birthday in our new house

and I wanted our vast lawn to look like

Yankee or Dodger Stadium.   What could be more beautiful? Ever since I was a kid, when I walked into a baseball stadium I loved the sight of a perfectly groomed baseball field. If anyone on this planet deserved 'groomed grass' on her birthday, it's *Karla Jayne DeVito.*

Karla and Zephyr went on a field trip with his new fifth grade class to the New River. I ran down to the barn, started up the tractor, and headed up the hill. The first two runs down the hill were perfect. The smell of the fresh cut grass was hypnotic. And most people say I must have been hypnotized to go back up that hill. As an avid skier, this hill was a black diamond and the tractor was taking to the moist, dewy grass beautifully.

On the third time down, the tires lost traction on the grass, and the back wheels locked. I learned a new term that day— when your tractor's back tires lock and you go flying down a hill, it's called 'ball hooting' (think 'yaw' but in southern mountain farmer lingo). The sheer weight of this gigantic farm machine sent me barreling down the mountain at a speed no tractor should reach. I did not panic. I assessed the situation and used my skiing logic. If this were a black diamond I'd just keep my shoulders straight, heading down the hill. There was plenty of pasture at the bottom to slow me down before crashing through the fence. All I had to do was keep the wheel straight and enjoy the thrill of the ride.

Just then, my front wheel hit a huge ground hog hole, twisted sideways and I found myself airborne! The massive tractor flipped end over end, high above the field below. Again, I didn't panic but tried to find the horizon (as if that mattered or could help me). I remember the sequence of words going through my mind: 'Horizon, sky, impact; horizon, sky, impact; horizon, sky, ugh.' The 'ugh' stood for the last moment of impact. The declivity of this particular hill was deceiving; I always looked at the hill as steep, but I didn't realize the true quality of the drop until I was the one being dropped.

The tractor rolled, flipped, fell, tumbled, skipped, plummeted and finally landed with such force, that it 'stuck the landing' like an Olympic gymnast. It not only stuck the landing, it was stuck 4 feet into the dirt, stuck. I did a mental body check and to my surprise, I was only slightly hurting. The strange thing about that was that I wasn't sure exactly 'what' was hurting.

I got out of the tractor and surveyed the hill and the damage. I'd never be a groundskeeper at Yankee Stadium, I thought. 'Look at the tractor size divot near second base!' The groomed grounds of the hill were now a mess based on the accident. I had to fix it! It was Karla's birthday and this was my plan and it had to be carried out perfectly (she deserved the best!)— now, there was a 4-foot hole in the middle of the 'infield.' The first thing I had to do was fix the exhaust pipe on the upside-down tractor. So I pushed with all of my might and 'righted' the 'wrong' tractor. Good! That was a start. I grabbed the exhaust pipe to bend it back in place until I realized it was as hot as the sun.

"AHHHHHHHHH!"

Now everything that was slightly hurting before was getting more and more intense, not to mention the burns I now had on my stupid hands for trying to fix an exhaust pipe on a tractor that was still running.

I had to get back on the tractor and do my best to make everything look better than okay before Karla got home.

I mowed for another 40 minutes until the pain was so intense that I could hardly move. I pinpointed the most excruciating pain: my left shoulder. It must be dislocated, I thought. I knew all of my plans for Karla's birthday were not only dashed— I was condemned to reality. She was going to be furious with me for even attempting to get the tractor to the top of the hill. I put the tractor away, took off my shirt and wrapped it around my hands and tried to straighten the exhaust pipe, because nothing says 'tractor accident' more than a buckled and bent exhaust pipe— even though I was completely forgetting the 4 foot hole in the middle of the hill where the tractor finally came to a stop.

When Karla and Zephyr returned home from his field trip, Zephyr saw the deep hole in the ground from a quarter mile away. "Mom, look at that hole! Do you think Dad's in the hospital?"

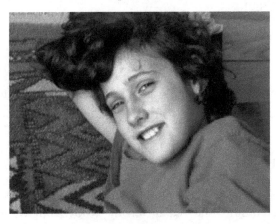

To which Karla replied, "Of course not, sweetheart." She drove up to the barn and saw the tractor parked neatly inside and said, "See. Daddy's fine. If he was hurt the tractor would be in the field."

I drove myself to the hospital.

The admitting nurse said, "Hey— Robby Benson! C'mon in. Don't be shy."

She sized me up: Overalls. Grass stains. Tractor oil. A whole lot of hurt.

"So, didja ball hoot?"

"Ball what?"

"Tract'r accid'nt?"

"How can you tell?"

"Yu'gotcha a roll bar."

"Yes! I do. How did you know?"

"Wore y'seat belt, didja?"

"Wow. You're good."

Then she looked me in the eyes and said, "Y'flipt it."

Embarrassed as if I was the city-guy in *Green Acres* I looked down. (Learning the North Carolina accent is actually pretty easy: just know your clitics: C'mon/Y'flipt.)

"How many times y'flipt?" she asked.

"I think it was two. And a half."

"Yer a lucky man. Usually the next words ya hear after 'He flipt the tractor' are, 'and the funeral is… ' Let's get a doc in to take a look atcha. Ya wan me ta call your wife?"

"No! I'll call her when I'm done."

It took three strong doctors pushing and pulling to pop my shoulder back into place. Nothing showed up on the X-rays, but when I was still in excruciating pain ten days later they did a CAT scan and saw the cup of my shoulder was broken in three places. Because I felt like an idiot for getting in the tractor accident in the first place, I asked the orthopedic surgeon on-call what he was doing that afternoon.

"Huh?"

"Can you operate today?

"Uh, no."

"Tomorrow?"

"Uh, no."

"How does Wednesday look for you?"

"Uh, yeah. I guess I could do Wednesday."I was a problem-solver from Hollywood. I had a problem. I wanted to solve it.

Explaining to Karla...   ...well— I'll do it in movie terms:

Imagine the wide shot!

You see the entire hill and here comes the tractor coming right at you! And without CGI, it flies over the lens! Awesome shot! (Not such an awesome birthday present. I also found out something I never knew about Karla. She's not a fan of groomed fields. She thinks weeds are beautiful.)

I had surgery on my shoulder on Wednesday. It didn't go well. One of the screws used to keep my shoulder in place was too long and was coming out of my back. So Karla insisted that we go down to Charlotte and see the sports medicine people who work on the Carolina Panthers. They took X-rays and other imaging tests and saw that my cup was shattered and the screw was too long but I had also torn the ligament and muscle off my shoulder and it had taken up a new living space in my bicep. The Sports Medicine Doctor would try his best to pull that back up and re-attach it to the shoulder when he operated on me, but no promises on that one. Unfortunately, he couldn't operate until the cup with the screws had healed and he could get the screws out and could start from scratch.

A ton of people told me I should sue the surgeon who did the initial shoulder surgery in Boone, N.C. But, how could I ever do that? I basically forced my way onto his schedule (let alone was the fool who rode a tractor down an 'E' ticket ride back at the homestead, having been specifically told and warned not to take the tractor up the hill). He did his best. Yes— he was a hand surgeon and didn't do shoulders, but *I picked him*— he didn't pick me.

I was in pain for about three months until the Carolina Panther surgeon decided that my broken cup was healed and ready to be operated on. It was quite an ordeal. I heard he had my body flopping all over the table when he was trying to get that long screw out of the bone. But he fixed my shoulder. I looked at it as if I was still doing films and this was just another stunt. No problem. Let's get it fixed and move on. And that's what happened. I still can't hold the phone up to my ear with my left hand because my left shoulder can't take it for more than 30 seconds but hey— whose fault is that? Unfortunately, I had to chalk up two more major surgeries to my list of hospital stays based to my stupidity.

I did lose all tractor rights going up the hill.

And a cow? Well, we learned about miniature Jersey cows... Our remarkable neighbors, the Storie family, quietly decided to take the Benson family under their wing in all things farm related.

Lyric's miniature Jersey yearling which she named "Run Lola Run" and our little four month old bottle fed bull calf "Vincent's Starry Starry Night" finally arrived from Virginia. Their first night in our pasture we heard plaintive mooing echoing through the valley all night long. When we looked down in the morning little Vincent was gone. The Stories knew before we did. They showed up in our pasture with a group of nine people and spent twelve hours with us searching for our wayward Vincent. Marvin Storie raised cows and he said it was only natural: Vincent went looking for his mother's milk. Our cow penning team on foot found Vincent two miles away across The Blue Ridge Parkway in another farmer's herd of cows. Twelve hours spent helping their new neighbor. In L.A. you'd be lucky if a neighbor spent five minutes looking for your lost dog.

North Carolina Mountain hospitality Storie-style came again when a huge tree from the Blue Ridge Parkway fell over onto our driveway. We just happened to be looking out our window as it fell and it was a spectacular sight. (I'm always looking at things like a director and how it would photograph, rather than the immediate fact that we were trapped on our hill with no way in or out.)

Within minutes, without us making a single phone call, Marvin Storie and a truck full of men appeared down where the fifty foot tree fell. Using chains and chainsaws they cut the tree into moveable pieces. Before we could walk down the hill they were stacking the wood to dry for use in the coming winter. For our use. Not theirs. There was absolutely nothing in it for them; except the peace they felt *helping others in need*.

But the story of our first months in Boone, N.C. represented my heart having to face two more major surgeries— which meant more trauma and more anesthesia. I started to know what someone like Brett Fauvre felt like every time he got up in the mornings...

Open Heart

I DIDN'T MIND LEAVING THE BEAUTY AND PEACE of our family home in the Blue Ridge Mountains to shoot a television episode or two in Los Angeles, knowing I was keeping up my working professional status as a professor and adding to our newly downsized income.

Only a few weeks after Karla and I moved to Boone we were saddened that Frank Borkowski left his position as Chancellor of Appalachian State for personal reasons. But I was not naive. I summed it up shortly into my first year at USC in Columbia: "There's as much backstabbing in academia as in show business— only the stakes are so much lower."

When I got the call to direct *8 Simple Rules for Dating My Daughter* starring John Ritter, I wasn't sure what to expect on set. I knew he was a talented physical comedian, and I loved his dramatic crossover performance in *Sling Blade*. But it was the beginning of the second season on his show, and sitcom actors can be set in their ways. The day work began I asked him to try something a little different, and I got a rare and welcome response: "Sure. Let's try!"

We were kindred souls—riffing on outrageous ideas. We started completing each others' sentences. With a little work (reeled in from outrageous to hysterical) my time with John Ritter ended up being some of the most satisfying moments in my entire directing career. Like me, *he wasn't afraid to fail;* he wasn't afraid to *try* something that was surely doomed if not performed with 100 percent commitment. John gave that 100 percent with complete joyous abandon. Oh, how I loved him.

Karla and I laughed about the irony of us moving 3,000 miles away to finally find my perfect creative partner in television comedy. (And of course, thinking back— my parents were right. I did find my perfect fit...) I only had the opportunity to direct two episodes of *8 Simple Rules*— but they may have been the best ten days I've ever had on a sitcom. A week later on September 11, 2003, John died of an aortic dissection, likely caused by a undiagnosed congenital heart defect. I was not there that week, but I had the honor and privilege of directing the last two episodes of *8 Simple Rules* John Ritter completed.

THERE IS NO GEOGRAPHICAL BOUNDARY FOR TALENT and I had a few gifted students in my classes at App State. I noticed I had problems getting up one flight of stairs just to get into the theater department's building. My breathing was becoming more labored.

I tried playing basketball with some of the faculty members but I found myself at mid-court blacking out, still standing, but not knowing where I was when I came back to my senses, while a bunch of old hackers would say, "We're too good for the *One On One* movie star!" I couldn't jog, let alone run. As a matter of fact, I became so symptomatic, sometimes I could barely walk, but I never missed a day of work...

Open Heart, the musical we had been working on since 1999,

was picked up by fantastic producers.

It would have its New York premiere at the historic Cherry Lane

Theatre, directed by my great friend Matt Williams, and developed and produced by Artistic Director Angelina Fiordelissi (a

remarkable woman).

It would star Karla DeVito, Stan

Brown (my former student at The University of South

Carolina; a man who could sing better than any male singer I had ever been on stage with) and... me.

I took my own advice: 'Surround yourself with smarter and more talented people.)

I was overwhelmed; so excited and pleased, but I was a mess physically. I needed another surgery and knew it— but the musical, and everything it represented, was so important to me.

I really didn't know that my second surgery was a calamity. As far as I knew, I was in need of a third. I didn't grok my place in the overall scheme of life and death. I only knew I had to keep moving forward and try to overcome all obstacles in order to get better. But honestly, I didn't even know what 'better' meant. Hell, I just learned what grok means. (Great word...)

The audiences loved the show. *Open Heart* dealt with the importance of that last minute in a person's life. Time. If we knew exactly when we were going to die, would we treat life differently? Not a new subject matter, but I was hoping to put a comic spin on it, along with some very cool music.

Even Paul Newman and Joanne Woodward made a special trip to come see our show. (Amazing people... I was so lucky to work and get to know them and become friends during *Harry and Son*.)

Paul Newman was an extraordinary man. I was so honored that he and Joanne came to a performance. When we were backstage afterward, he told me that *Open Heart* truly touched him and he wanted to go out for drinks and discuss the show. This meant the world to me. But I was in such bad shape physically, struggling for every gulp of air, that I made some asinine excuse as to why I couldn't go out with them. I'm still angry at myself for not finding the energy to do it and talk with Paul... I have so few regrets, and that is one of them.

THERE WERE TWO VERY REAL PROBLEMS I had during this run of the show:

1) *I could not breathe*— and my character *never* left the stage in the 90-plus minutes of the show. So I mapped out certain sections (strategically) where I could turn my back to the audience without them knowing it, and gasp for air before I had to sing. It's really tough having to sing when you have no air supporting your voice. Very tough... but I learned a lot from *Pirates* and my other Broadway shows.

2) We sublet an apartment from CraigsList that was a three-floor walk-up. The only problem with an 'advertised' three-floor walk-up in New York was that if the brownstone was made of *duplexes*, you may have the third 'floor' apartment, but it was now a six-floor walk up. So after every show, every night, not being able to breathe and coming home from giving every ounce of energy to the show and the people who came to see our show, I had to walk up 6 flights of stairs with a bum heart, doing a show called *Open Heart*. It was an ironic (funny) almost-killer scenario.

I returned to Boone exhausted after our New York run.

The next order of business was for Karla and me to focus on my heart — *again*. We found an amazing hospital in Charlotte called Carolinas Medical Center and a bright and gifted cardiologist, Geoffrey Rose from The Sanger Clinic. Dr. Rose calmly explained our options, and we were wise to place our trust in him. He recognized my symptoms and had me undergo a **valvuloplasty** to try and open up my pulmonic valve by Dr. Hadley Wilson.

The test showed that insufficient blood was flowing through the valve and the balloon was unable to widen the valve.

I needed surgery to replace my pulmonic valve (the one with the cadaver valve on it— okay, pulmonary homograft). Karla called LA to get all my records and the 'cardiologist to the stars' got on the phone and put in his 2 cents, telling her it had to be calcification causing stenosis of the pulmonic valve; that after two heart surgeries, my body's reaction was responsible for creating the constricting hardening of the valve. Whatever the reason, it was definitely time for the valve to be replaced. Yup— open heart number *three*.

The ride from our house at the end of the dirt road on top of the hill

was over two and a half hours to the hospital in Charlotte. Lyric's cow Lola ('Run, Lola Run!') was going to give birth any second and only Karla knew what to do if the calf was breach and how to save the calf and Lola, I decided we couldn't chance losing the calf. I would drive down to Charlotte alone and meet the surgeon recommended by Dr. Rose.

Dr. R. Mark Stiegel was tall, strong and rugged, but had the hands of a pianist. He also had an accent so thick that if judged by stereotypical first impressions he might be the last person a Northerner would want as his open-heart surgeon. Moments after meeting him I had complete faith in this amazing man. I was worried what Karla's impression would be if she were to meet him *briefly* the day of my surgery, and not get the chance to see he is quite brilliant. (She loved him.) We talked and I was able to discuss things a bit more in-depth now that it was my third open-heart operation. I liked his answers and his honesty.

Lola needed no help and the beautiful calf was born (Violet)

and we built a shed for mother and

daughter in the pasture,because we could get some very cold weather, then gave Vincent (our bull) back to the breeder, otherwise we would be having a calf every year. We had two magnificent animals Lyric trained to harness and take for walks.

Now a lot of farmers might think we were insane. We weren't. We just wanted to give these two cows the best life possible and Lyric and Karla did just that. And Zephyr had fun.

MY HOPES FOR MY THIRD OPEN-HEART SURGERY were very simple: survive (visualization) and when I would awaken, be able to breathe again.

The surgery went well. After the closing, Dr. Stiegel quickly came out in his scrubs to speak with Karla and twelve year old Zephyr.

"I've never seen anything like it," he said, shaking his head, and explained "the pulmonary valve [replaced during the Ross Procedure surgery in 1998] *had been sewn on incorrectly.*"

"The valve was bent, constricting the opening to about this big: the size of a split pea. I tried but couldn't even force my pinky finger into it."

There was no calcification causing stenosis.

"How could the surgeon have done this?" Karla asked, thinking about the six and a half years of suffering I had endured since that operation.

"Open-heart surgery is more than science, it's art." Dr. Stiegel gently explained. "You have to visualize everything— and have the experience to know how placement will be impacted by the closing."

WHEN I WOKE UP FROM MY THIRD OPEN-HEART SURGERY, I immediately realized:

I can breathe.

I had asked them not to tie my hands down (and my hands were not tied down) and I had asked them to put the Foley catheter in my bladder after I was put to sleep (which they did) and the nurses in the I.C.U. were compassionate and cared about each and every one of us. (I might not have been able to see, but my hearing was perfect.)

Unfortunately, all of the TV's in the I.C.U. were tuned to the Fox Channel, blasting the news that Bush had just been re-elected. (I was trying to be open-minded, but it's hard when you're down to such base emotions, just hours after surgery.)

Then I got the 'good' news: *this* operation was a success, but in the previous Ross Procedure (as my surgeon had explained to Karla), my pulmonary homograft had been sewn so tightly that it buckled and the valve crimped when it was put back into my chest— very much like a water hose when it zigzags on itself, buckling the hosepipe tubing, and no water can get to the nozzle.

In other words, *there was a reason* I couldn't breathe the moment I was out of surgery six and a half years before— and there was a reason I could breathe *perfectly* the moment I awoke from this surgery. (It's a relief to find out you're not crazy…)

People told me I should've sued because my second surgery had a *major effect* on my earning power in show business. It not only affected me, it affected my children's life. But after waking up and being able to breathe for the first time in six and a half years, I wasn't going to spend one more minute on anything negative. Time to start anew. Time to conquer this wonderful world!

And I personally don't believe in suing. I believe in moving on and seeing the beauty around us; smell the flowers, avoid the thorns. I want to take that time and energy and invest it in love.

Unfortunately, if surgery is as much *art* as it is science, I turned out to be a bad piece of art.

(Dr. Frankenstein: 'It's aliiiive!')

You know you've found someone special when they love you...
even if you look like this.

AFTER MY EXCELLENT SURGERY at Carolina's Medical Center, I decided to help

them with a 5K charity run called The Cupid's Cup to benefit people who didn't have the resources to get the treatment they needed for their heart (or their loved one's heart). Karla and I helped sponsor and co-chair the event. It was a wonderful success and still continues near Valentine's Day every year in Charlotte raising money for people who can really use it.

If you live in the area and like to run, please check it out.

I ran a disgraceful time of 24 minutes, but "a very good time for a three-time open-heart patient"— at least that's what Karla tells me. (Who can

disagree with that?) We had a magnificent life now. (Yes! Magnificent, even after 3 open heart surgeries.) I co-coached Zephyr on many of his basketball teams (I was the court jester: I'd make the kids laugh no matter how badly we were getting spanked); I had built a home studio in a closet so I could do voice over commercials from home rather than flying to New York or L.A. and I continued to work on the *Open Heart* musical orchestrations. But I missed teaching and sharing the knowledge and passing it forward...

Not long after my 50th birthday, I went to New York to meet with the NYU search committee. My hopes weren't too high, because the opening was likely to be filled 'from within.'

What I didn't know was that the committee thought I was a 'perfect fit,' although, as the department chair Lamar Sanders later told me, the committee said "It's never going to work— he's too good to be true." Their words, not mine. I wouldn't be so kind...

In the spring of 2006, Karla and I made a quick trip New York to meet with our publishers, Samuel French, about *Open Heart*. I had the morning free before we left, and met Lamar for breakfast. We talked about NYU, and Lamar asked if I would be interested in a future position.

"Sure, call me any time."

Then in August, Lamar rang me up. "You told me to call any time. Would you like the job?"

Back To New York

SOMETIMES I THINK OF MY HEART, the imperfect but remarkable engine of my body, and realize how, through all my years and all my surgeries, it has never failed me. It has allowed me to have adventures in life.

After a lengthy discussion with Karla and Zephyr, I took the position offered to me by Chair Lamar Sanders and Dean Mary Schmidt Campbell to teach at New York University's Tisch School of the Arts in The Maurice Kanbar Institute of Film and Television. And we moved to New York City (even though our home was still in Boone, North Carolina). In New York, we lived in faculty housing and I was teaching at NYU, Tisch School of the Arts in The Maurice Kanbar Institute of Film and TV.

NYU is a wonderful University. I had talented students who were at NYU only because they wanted to be filmmakers. I also had the pleasure of working with faculty who became friends. I admire the Chair of the Department, Lamar Sanders, whose first question to any problem was always 'Are the students' best interests being served?' The faculty and staff are one of the best I've ever worked with and they supported me completely. I had the good fortune to teach varied courses during my stint: Television Production; Directing The Camera; Directing The Actor; Developing The Screenplay; Advanced Filmmaking (a year-long course where each student begins with a short script of their own; and we, as a class, develop the script into a shooting script, which includes everything that goes with getting a film off the ground: fundraising; insurance; crewing; preproduction and finally, production and dailies. And usually, there is a finished film— notice how at NYU we say 'a finished *film*'— not a finished 'product'— which is why I have so much respect for NYU).

Every time I looked out at the students, I saw my daughter's face (a former NYU film student) and I remember how she told me the classes were long, she didn't have time for breakfast. So I'd set up a 'craft service' table in my classes with fruit and granola bars. A small price to pay to keep these young students alert, especially during advanced filmmaking classes that

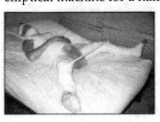

lasted up to nine hours long.

I'd wake up at 5 and workout my heart on the elliptical machine for a half hour. Never an excuse to

stop exercising. Never!

Okay, maybe once in a while…

The calibre of talented students accepted into Tisch School of the Arts Filmmaking program is the best in the country. Teaching them the skills of filmmaking can be easy; a no-brainer. Asking your students to always 'try' is quite another issue. Asking them to show their unbridled passion, and be willing to fail in front of their peers in order to learn, is asking a lot of a young person in the arts. It's simpler to hide behind 'eccentricities' when studying the arts. Getting past that 'wardrobe' and digging deep to help them find their true artistic passion is the key to my style of teaching something as unquantifiable as art. If I were going to ask them to be vulnerable and give 100% without cynicism, I owed it to them to give my all in each and every class and never allow cynicism into my behavior as well.

Sometime in the early winter months of 2007 (loving my job at NYU and was in awe at how much *I could learn from my students*— thrilling!), I had a 'heart-to-heart' with my son Zephyr.

It was the first time I realized that coming from the farmlands of North Carolina and leaving all of his friends

and basketball buddies behind,

New York City was making him feel… miserable.

I grew up in New York City. It's easy to see the brilliance of the city

and   at   the   same   time   to   despise

its crankiness; the city's filth and irritability. New York City has a personality: the only way to describe its characterizations is to say that the city is schizophrenic. I 'got it.' Zephyr was approaching 15 years old. Karla and I only had him for three more years... We recognize the value of urgency.

The answer to this dilemma was easy (it had complex consequences, but the right answer was easy).

We would leave New York City and NYU and move back home to the farm. This would be the best thing *for our family*, and Karla and I *always* did what was best for our family, or at least we always *tried* to do what was/is best for our family. (As long as each decision begins with that premise, we know we are bound to make good decisions.)

Karla and I felt good about the decision, and immediately informed Lamar so he could find a replacement and not be left looking foolish since he was championing me to be the new head of the television department. I would finish my year, but we would move back to our home. Lamar understood the mind of a teenager. And he had a daughter close to Zephyr's age. We packed up and moved out of New York and headed back to our farm.

ON AUGUST 28, 2007 MY NOVEL, **Who Stole The Funny?**, was published by HarperCollins. When it made the bestsellers' list of the *Los Angeles Times*, I received a congratulatory call from Maureen O'Brien, my editor and great supporter. She told me, "No matter what, from this day forward you will always have the title of 'best selling author.'"

I guess to the publishing industry, that platitude meant prestige and money. I don't think I will ever be a true capitalist. I only want what is fair. And I want it for everyone. I despise greed, yet I have been its willing accomplice.

My favorite *Who Stole The Funny* review was in *The Wall Street Journal*. It was not an all-out rave, but the reviewer understood the book, what I was trying to accomplish, and knew my weaknesses as a novelist. Her critique has helped me be a better, wiser writer.

> "*Who Stole The Funny?* benefits from Mr. Benson's deep knowledge of his subject matter both the shallow snake pit of TV comedy and the angst of a perfectionist director... Mr. Benson labors overtime— and succeeds— in making us care... I can see the novel joining college reading lists and not only in Mr. Benson's film classes. There are plenty of books on acting and directing, on semiotics, auteur theory and Stanislavsky's method. But not many are likely to

present so many appalling and reality based teachable moments."

— Barbara D. Phillips, *The Wall Street Journal*

Whenever I sat down alone in a room with a blank piece of paper, it was never about the money, just the satisfaction of expressing myself creatively. The icing on the cake is being able to share it in a form that reaches people.

I once told Karla, "Why be one of thousands protesting something you feel passionate about as an individual, when you can create something as an artist that reaches millions?"

Similar to the impact of my incorrectly sewn on pulmonary valve being the intense catalyst for writing my musical *Open Heart*, I had something to say when I sat down to write *Who Stole the Funny?* I spent over 10 years directing television and finally an incident in 2004 began the marination process that culminated in the release of my first novel. Beginning, middle, end. If nothing else, as an artist I do know how to finish.

I started to see that I was getting tired more easily... not a good sign. New beds, new strip malls, new jobs, new hours, new environments... Many, myself included, just chalked it up to age. I was getting older. Everything that happens to me doesn't have to be blamed on a deficiency in my heart.

It was life... pure and simple: I began feeling my age. (Mentally was another story; mentally I felt like I was 25; that didn't go over well with my body.)

I WAS CALLED BY MY OLD FRIEND Larry Mortoff who was producing a feature film in Nashville, Tennessee. He told me two other directors had been fired and the film was in the last weeks of casting and preproduction. "Please do me a great favor, and come to Nashville" to direct **Billy: The Early Years** — the story of the young Billy Graham becoming an evangelist.

I may have lived in the Bible Belt for a few years, but I was raised as a non religious Jew; what did I know about evangelicals? He said the writer-producer had shot a documentary on Billy Graham, was a personal friend of the Graham family, and would help me with my religious learning curve.

Every new project brings hope, and I had a brainstorm for our family. Zephyr was at a point in his life where he realized unless he wanted to coach, basketball wasn't going to be his life mission. Karla and I asked him, and with his high school principal's blessing I told Zephyr, "I want you to pack for 3 months of *work*. You're going to be my assistant. I don't want you to bring a single schoolbook or think about school for one second. I'm going to *teach* you everything I know— I'll be your teacher; or at least try." (*Try* is a big word in our family. I judge others and myself by how hard they/I try. The *effort* is so very important to me.)

"Zephyr, if I'm location scouting and you have to pretend you're an actor in the scene, and I'm checking my framing for a shot, then you stand where I tell you to stand. I'll always take care of you, but the days and nights will be long. Moviemaking is not glamorous. It's *tedious*."

Zephyr was excited to be my new assistant. I said, "Yes" to the producer. Zephyr and I got in the car and began our journey to Nashville,  a new adventure for our family and a new escapade for my heart! Creativity! Inspiration! What could be better for the heart? Not just my heart, but *all of our hearts!* (Yet another move… into hotels and motels for more than three months.)

The first (and most wonderful) thing that happened in Nashville was meeting the crew. Because I came to the film late, as a favor for my friend, I met a crew already in place. (For anyone thinking of shooting in Nashville, there are great, skilled people there.) I also became one lucky director— I was sent several reels for DP's from LA, and by instinct chose the perfect man...   David Rudd instantly became an artistic soulmate. We are like brothers. We bounce ideas off of one another and neither of us care who gets credit or how the idea would spiral into another idea. Working with David Rudd actually has given my film-life a shot of adrenaline, igniting a new *hope* inside me that was

dormant,   just waiting to spew ideas again. (If I have any say in the future, I never want to make a film without my creative soulmate, David Rudd.) We did our preproduction in Nashville at light speed, spending some time in Los Angeles casting the lead role of Billy, and to see if we could get Martin Landau for a pivotal role in the film. Mr. Landau and I hit it off immediately and I loved working with him.

And did we ever find the lead... Armie Hammer walked into the audition and possessed everything I was looking for in the character. And he did something I think I've only seen twice in my life: gave an audition that was absolutely perfect. It was... brilliant. Even in the land of "BRILLIANT," where the word is so overused that brilliant can mean 'the steak was medium-rare, take it back,' I actually saw true brilliance. Armie was not immediately embraced by the producers because the pompous casting director had the 'balls' to say that Armie "always comes in second. He's just not a star."

My advice to that casting director is to (get out of casting) wait a few years and then eat your 'BRILLIANCE' medium-rare, with a heaping side of your own words, and please don't forget to add the bitterness.

Armie Hammer has since become a bonafide movie star. So how's that for 'always finishing second?'

 I begged Karla to come to Nashville, wear age make-up and play Billy's 65 year-old secretary in the film. I needed someone to nail two moments in the movie, and Karla was everything I hoped for.

A frantic last minute phone call got our best friend Cliff Bemis to fly in and replace a controversial non actor/real preacher. He would play one powerful scene at a tent revival, inspiring Billy to change his life.

Cliff grounded the film and gave a stellar performance.

Working with Armie, Kris Polaha, Stephanie Butler, Lindsay Wagner and the entire cast and the crew on this film was a joy. The script was... well, let's say maybe the two other directors were not fired. Maybe they quit. It was preachy and expositional— all 'tell' and very little 'show'— but everyone working on this film did everything they could to bring it to life.

And Zephyr not only assisted me, he took the initiative to run lines with the cast and assist anyone who needed help at any time and in any department. Seeing his effort, the crew chose 'Way to go Zephyr!' for the back of the *Billy* t-shirts. Zephyr fell in love with the family business, and got his SAG card. He loved the creative process.

While I was working on editing the film in L.A. and post production in NYC, Karla and Zephyr flew to Fairfield, Iowa, where the good people at the brand new, gorgeously constructed Stephen Sondheim Theater, were beginning rehearsals for my musical *Open Heart*.

I flew in just as Iowa was hit with the 500 year flood.

The talented director Randal K. West, who was also the artistic director of The Stephen Sondheim Center for the Performing Arts, had a terrific summer program for college interns. This was the first time I had the opportunity of hearing my music the way I had written it, with a chorus of twenty singers and dancers and terrific new orchestrations by musical director Justin Hill for a big and very talented band— all too expensive to pull off in New York. How exciting to see my musical up on its feet, the way I envisioned it in my mind!

Audience members would meet us in the street and hold in-depth conversations about the text of my show. The community in Fairfield, Iowa— the home of Maharishi University— understood my piece better than I could ever have imagined. We received standing ovations every performance of our two-week run.

Then I had to immediately go back to L.A. to begin a very fast post-production schedule on the film I had just directed. A certain producer had gone ahead with *Billy* as if he had the Graham family's cooperation to make the film on the life of 'a young Billy Graham.' I was later astounded to learn that nothing I had been told was in writing. No matter how we cut the film to make it a better movie, the next thing we would find out was that some of our producers were 'making nice' with not only the Graham family members, but preachers all around the country, having them come into the editing room— to make changes. It was insane. Artistically, it was a tug of war for every single frame. And even though I lost in the end, I can still appreciate what we all accomplished. As the film now sits on DVD, I can say, it's beautiful to look at, and I'm very proud of my cast and crew. The experience was a bit heart-breaking— and I mean that literally as well as figuratively. After what we thought were the last of the Graham 'family changes' editorially, I went to New York for the final mix.

Suddenly, the music in the film had become an issue as well. I had a temp score with period songs which contributed to the authenticity, but one of the titled producers was also the 'music supervisor.' This was nothing but an opportunity for an opportunist. In other words, the album had nothing to do with the film artistically. Absurd *modern* country songs were being placed in a

period film. Sad. And painful. My heart... This is what one gets for coming in, last-second, to direct a film— I should've known better. (Truth is— I'd do it again. The pre-production and production was wonderful, and my son got an education of a lifetime.)

Then from New York's mixing stage, I moved back to Boone, North had blossomed into a young man who was now interested in the arts.

What better place to be if you are interested in the arts? New York. *Again?* Again.

I let NYU know I was available again, and because of the good graces of Chair Lamar Sanders, and Dean Mary Schmidt Campbell, I was offered my job back in the fall of 2008. We moved back to New York. This time, faculty housing was down in the financial district. Water Street.

It was a phenomenal experience; NYU had apartments in a building for faculty and graduate students way downtown and this was a great opportunity to learn a lot about a part of the city both Karla and I never had the chance to discover.

The first bus that left Water Street for Tisch was at 6:05 a.m. That was

my bus. All of my classes were going extremely well and life was good for all of us.

Then, *my worst nightmare.*

We found out Karla needed thyroid surgery. Even if it wasn't cancer, Karla's vocal cords could be damaged from the operation. Now, for the first time in our marriage, I was the medical advocate. She had the surgery in October and we waited for the results. Karla came through the surgery like a champ with perfect vocal chords and most importantly, when the biopsy finally came back— no cancer!

Meanwhile, Zephyr went to a school for performers (working young people) and he would come and be my 'ringer' in the classes that needed

actors at a moment's notice. He not only helped my students enormously, but he was becoming more and more of a spontaneous thinker and his work still maintained honesty. He was also learning and *listening* in every class. Then he would go off to his own normal

education. What a beautiful way to learn and soak up a ton of life. And for me, to have my son there didn't make me feel like I was a 3-time open-heart patient who was spending quality time with other people's children but not my own. He was there with me. And when I was asked to direct my next film, he was right there with me again.   Karla was healing, Lyric came back to help our family heal. I took a deep breath and counted my blessings. Family. Love. What else is there...?

Out of left-field, I received a phone call from a friend about a film to direct. I had dropped all agents and managers long ago— I wanted to see if it were possible to work in show business and not deal with the B.S. and backstabbing of Hollywood. I was working as much as I wanted to work: when people needed me, or wanted me, they found me. No more B.S.

This movie had to do with The New York Yankees and their move to the new stadium; leaving the ghosts of the old stadium behind— and then during demolition of the old Yankee Stadium, the George Steinbrenner character realizes that the new stadium is missing something: it's missing *the legends*— the 'ghosts.' So a wonderful, very human device is used in the film to get the ghosts to cross 161st street and take up

residency in the new stadium, making it whole again. I would direct and David Rudd, my new partner, would D.P.

My participation began in October of 2008. Just my luck, the producers were in the real estate business and 'other ventures.' None of them had ever done a film before. Business... was their business. Like raw meat in the Serengeti, certain greedy vultures descended for a feeding frenzy. These new producers were taken advantage of and they began to learn the hard way — no matter what I'd say, or how David and I might warn them. But still, *the film could be wonderful.*

I felt it was a lovely opportunity to tell a very human story (with the help of a few ghosts). Soon we would begin to shoot the Old Stadium and get our effects plates. The 'Old Lady' was coming down. And we had to capture it on film.

The deal breaker for me? NYU students *must* work on this feature film. For that deal point, I took a huge pay cut (that was meaningless to me) in return for the production to hire and *pay* my students— those who were ready to contribute to this film.

I had my lawyer put it in writing, *in my contract,* that at least fifteen of my students would be paid to work on this feature. The agreement was such

that the students would not work xeroxing papers or getting coffee; my students would P.A. in all of the areas they were interested in. I had a couple of students who were interested in the camera department because at NYU they had taken more 'camera' classes; others were interested in lighting, etc. David Rudd put them to work in the camera department as P.A.s, and *if* they could 'hold their own' and prove they *deserved* to be there, they would get more and more responsibilities thrown their way. But much more importantly, they would be learning from the best. I even had the opportunity to hire a wonderful writer, Ezra Sacks, the head of the writing department at NYU, to do the rewrite.

In May 2009 we were doing 2nd unit shooting. My students worked! They were paid! This was *almost too good to be true*. It was.

We were deep into pre-production when a terrible rumor began circulating like Global Warming. Certain vendors were not getting paid. And worse, David Rudd's weekly check not only bounced, but his wife and young children were in the apartment that the production was providing, when the landlord unlocked the door and showed it to a 'future renter.' How future? Next month. The economy was imploding and so was our film. Production department heads began jumping ship and taking other jobs— all in a matter of hours.

It was one very long year of...passion, heartache, and finally, *heartbreak*. Another in-your-face example of time slipping away...

And the death begins...

After a year of 24/7, hard and very creative work, the film was demolished, too.

Zephyr and I had the opportunity to see the death of a stadium and the death of a film. So did many of my students.

My deepest disappointment was that my students did not get the chance to work; to learn; to be taught by professionals in the skilled departments they wanted to pursue; to make contacts for an entire film— only for second unit. Still, a few did so well on the 'second unit shoot' that they impressed the right people and moved forward professionally, on to other jobs. More notably and enormously significant, they all had a unique, 'box-seat view' of a film folding, right before their eyes, yet they weren't crushed in the verbal and career debris. It was educational, fascinating yet not detrimental or damaging to them.

What an education! I began my next class with: "This is show business. This happens. And you were not hurt by it, only disappointed. So, in a way, if the film could not be made, what an amazing opportunity it was for all of you to see your professor, who was the director, lose a job in a matter of hours. It's a great experience without the heartache." (My heartache was a very different story...)

WE RECEIVED TERRIBLE NEWS about Karla's Aunt Marilyn; she had fallen and hit her head, and because she was on Coumadin (an anti-coagulant, anti-clotting drug), she had cranial bleeding. To survive, she needed emergency brain surgery. Not only was Marilyn best friends with her sister Vivienne (Karla's mom) but Aunt Marilyn was a second mother to Karla. I came to love Marilyn as a cherished, treasured member of our family.

All of this weighed heavily on us. But, because of everything Karla had learned from going through her mom's death, and all of my surgeries, she became the 'expert advocate' and flew to Illinois. She wasn't afraid of hurting feelings or concerned about how she was perceived. Only one thing mattered to Karla: to make sure Aunt Marilyn got the best care possible.

Marilyn's brain surgery was miraculous— she came out of it like a champ. The surgeon predicted ghastly results, but Marilyn proved them all wrong.

A sadistically evil parable that only real life can write: as Marilyn was recovering so well, she was then diagnosed with lung cancer. She quit smoking at 55, but the tobacco companies arrived on cue to haunt her. As Marilyn got stronger, she decided to fight like mad to win this battle, attacking her cancer with chemotherapy and radiation. Then on the day she was being driven to her *last* session, she 'threw a clot' and had a devastating stroke.

Marilyn survived the stroke and was eventually put in a health-care dwelling where 'she would either die or recover.' Karla flew back and forth to Illinois.

Karla did everything she could to make the nurses aware that her aunt was a *person* who had needs that weren't being addressed. She went to the store and got child-like materials; poster-board, glue, markers... and designed a poster with photographs of Marilyn, in chronological order, telling the story of Marilyn's accomplished life. This simple poster awakened the dulled emotions of the caretakers and forced them to realize that Marilyn wasn't a piece of meat lying in a bed. By humanizing Marilyn to the staff, Karla made a difference for everyone, *and every patient in that facility*, hopefully, until this very day.

When it became clear that Marilyn was not going to survive, Karla brought the family together and rallied them to get Marilyn home, where she could be in her own home and live out the rest of her life in peace. And where she could die surrounded by people who loved her dearly.

Hospice care. Something we should all understand if we're lucky enough to have choices.

During this same time, when Karla would fly back and forth to her Aunt Marilyn in Illinois (I would do my best to come, too), her best friend and

'best woman' at our wedding,

Billie Best, found out her husband was dying.

Years earlier, Chet had been treated with full-spectrum radiation to cure Hodgkin's disease and twenty some years later that cure was killing him. Billie was now his caretaker and advocate. *Hospice.* Chet wanted to die with dignity and die at home, and Billie made that possible.

BECAUSE OF MY HEART, we treat my 'death' with a sense of humor. The only way for us to handle my life-long open-heart surgeries in a healthy way was to laugh at it. But now there was nothing funny about death. We were constantly reminded how precious is each moment, each breath, each heartbeat.

Karla and I began thinking about our own future. Neither of our children were interested in living on the farm in Boone. It suddenly seemed too far away to have our peaceful retreat.

It was time to leave my friend behind.

The Quest

IN THE SPRING OF 2009, while I was working on the Yankee film, we had to make yet another move, from faculty housing in the financial district at Water Street to faculty housing on Bleecker Street in the Village.

More boxes;   more tape— a closet for my
sound studio and my office!

Maybe, thinking back in time, those film people were wrong: I was
authentic— *I was the epitome of **King of the Gypsies***.

In late July, Karla and her friend Billie Best had gone back to North
Carolina to prepare our house in Boone for sale. We were surprised by how
quickly it sold, I went back to dispose of some of our belongings, put others in
storage, and pack the rest. I had my last checkup with Dr. Geoff Rose in
Charlotte just before the closing on October 23.

Selling the house in Boone was an astonishing stroke of good luck, but
now I faced a life-long dilemma: When I fell in love with Karla, I had made a
promise to myself that I would never let a day go by where my family didn't
have a roof over their heads, free from debt. And the reason I made that
promise to myself was because of the very reason I couldn't breathe— at any
moment, something could happen to me and I wanted Karla, Zephyr and

Lyric to always know they had a home. And now— we didn't. Yes, selling Boone was an astonishing, yet ironic stroke of luck.

We were both thinking of places where we could downsize and still live the loving and artistic life we had always hoped to live. For the time being, that would mean continuing to live out of boxes in our small Greenwich Village apartment. We had both been trained to make decisions quickly; this didn't mean foolishly, this meant we accelerated the decision-making process and came to a conclusion— and then tried to live by it.

When the Yankee film fell through that October, Karla and I had some free time. Since I wasn't due back at NYU until second semester, it seemed like now was the time to look for a place for our new beginning. It could be anywhere...

We decided to look at the spectacular Pacific Northwest. The colors and the cities (Portland, Seattle) were remarkable.

The trees and flowers and the abundance of life that was growing everywhere, and the spectacular beauty was beyond compare.

Then we were educated by my 'sad' friends about the '100 Days of Gloom.' Rain and weather appealed to both Karla and me, but we were told over and over that it was drizzly *endlessly,* and sometimes— "If you're lucky— you *may* actually see the sun. It can be very depressing. You'll probably want to blow your brains out."

Oh dear…

"But the coffee's great!"

We spent Thanksgiving with my family in California, and when we got back to New York, we still had a week before I had to be back at NYU. So we visited the 'best man' at our wedding— which was almost 29 years ago! My 'best man' lived in Massachusetts; his name is Dan Berlinghoff. (Calling Dan 'the best man' at our wedding is like calling Secretariat 'the best horse' in the stable. Dan is the man I aspire to become.)

Massachusetts. We would also be in close geographic proximity to Karla's best friend Billie, who had a beautiful farm in the Berkshire Mountains, so we decided to visit in a very small window of 'off-time.'

You mean there's— fake time...?

Time...

We were falling in love with Massachusetts— and it didn't hurt that 'the best man at our wedding' was now also a realtor. The life of being a Broadway conductor, pianist and chamber musician is a really tough one. I think Dan realized he wanted to try another life and found his adventure on Cape Cod. He is a brilliant, exceptionally gifted musician; a remarkable pianist. Aside from his moral fiber, Dan's Juilliard-trained musicianship is mesmerizing; he can write computer software; and he is a real estate agent who cares about the lives of the renters and buyers. He... tries!

Karla and I asked Dan and his terrific partner Julia MacLeod Ruffino if it were possible to look at some houses. The very first house we found was a perfect fit for our family. We couldn't believe it. We would be downsizing, but it was so lovely and homey. And best of all for me: Karla liked it and she would have the proverbial and literal 'roof over her head.' I could keep my promise while still a mortal being.

We get old(er):

The inevitable: *Age.* Father Time. Err, Mother Time. He/She catches up with all of us, eventually. That sounds like a generalization, but we are the only species on the planet (that we know of) to understand and contemplate our own death. This could be a very profound chapter, but I'd like to stay on the comic side of the 'waiting line.' I am now in my late 50's and for me, this is the timeline where I need my contact lenses to find my glasses. And I need my contact lenses with my glasses to find my drugstore reading glasses. For me, multi-tasking successfully means showering and peeing at the same time. To shower and brush my teeth is an accomplishment. Not because I can do both — because I remembered to bring the toothpaste. I think this is the time in life where many of us (especially me) should have a blinking sign on our

foreheads that reads: "EXPECT DELAYS." I'm very appreciative of road signs that I can identify with, like "BLIND DRIVE AHEAD."

'Oh, how nice..' There are others out here driving who are just like me.'

Being a product of Hollywood, I am proud to age gracefully, and I like my wrinkles and gray hair. But there are a few things that are truly frustrating. When I began to buy anything with the words: Prep (or) ration (or) H— without embarrassment— I realized I had hit a new plateau in my life. One day in the check-out line, as we were discussing which best over-the-counter medicine we should buy for acid-reflux, a very nice elderly man asked me for my autograph. His daughter wasn't sure which film she knew me from but her daughter knew me from *Beauty and the Beast* and told me where to get the hemorrhoid cream. Great. All demographics in his family now know...)

Then it hit me: I'm getting old(er). I still think young, and although my birth year may be the oldest in the room, it doesn't mean I have to 'act' old. I may still foolishly pick my head up when someone says, 'Hey, kid— come here,' and then realize it gave me a crick in my neck, but acknowledging and embracing my age does not mean buying a walker; it means that I should never stop walking. Or trying.

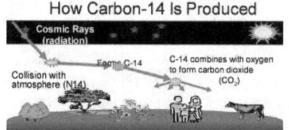

I didn't need carbon 14 testing to know my age; I didn't need a birth certificate. I felt young, but there seemed to be a direct correlation (in my life) that everything— *everything* affects my heart in one way or another; more benignly to more intensely— but it all affects the heart. From feeling acute compassion for a tragedy-stricken stranger in a news program, to seeing Karla cry in private when she lost her aunt. The physiognomy-rings around my personal tree trunk, my age-features have nothing to do with my maturation signature, which comes from my 'heart.'

I still did stupid, dumb, young things.

One day in March 2010, while running on a treadmill, I decided I would run a sub 6-minute mile. This was an act of foolhardiness from a 'now-jogger' who runs a 7-minute mile for exercise; I should have known better. In my teens I used to work intervals so that my fast-twitch muscles could eventually handle (after weeks, maybe months) taking 10 seconds off my base-line mileage time.

But now, thirty-five to forty years later, *what* in my brain tells me I can run a full minute faster than I've been training at for over a year? Maturity? No. Hope? Maybe. Magic? Hopefully. A memory of what running without effort *used* to feel like? Yes— a frantic search for that fleeting memory.

Every step I took had an effect on my heart. I came to understand that frustration; love; food; a blow to the head; every chemical I must swallow in pill form; every sentence and how I design my words; every feeling my wife feels; every pain my son has; every hope my daughter dreams; every day that my mom and dad get older; every single day that I don't see my sister... everything has a consequence on the heart. Many times it's a very abusive punishment— pummeling, drubbing, chastising— everything has an effect on the heart. But sometimes it can be a soothing love— or passion, sympathy, productivity, relaxation, effectiveness, moderation— Moderation? What's that? Then I realized:

I take everything 'to heart.'

It's fascinating how many words we use everyday that are associated with the destruction of the heart. From heartache, heartbreak, and of course, heart attack to heartworm. Sometimes we 'wear our heart on our sleeve' and sometimes we do something 'after one's heart.' Sometimes we let things 'go to one's heart' and sometimes we have a 'heavy heart.' I tend to do everything with 'all of my heart' and with 'heart and soul.' But no matter what anyone says, we are never: 'heartless'!

INSIDE MY KING OF THE GYPSY-LIKE BODY, my ascending aorta was swollen to the point of needing repair, my aortic valve needed replacing, and there was significant stenosis on the pulmonic valve. This according to the results of tests that came back on April 17, 2010. My symptoms were more obvious now than ever before. I knew I was once again in serious trouble.

I wanted more time, more life with my wife, best friend, and my partner in this world that we know. I wanted to fight for more time with my children; even if they were off in their own worlds, I wanted to be alive to know that they were now independent and striving for happiness.

At NYU, I was learning how to teach without a single student or faculty member catching me gasp for air. Here were my plans: get to school before anyone else; pick strategic moments to turn my back and write something on the white-board or look for a non-existent piece of paper so no student or faculty member could see my fight: 'tonight's card': Me vs. Heart Failure.

I had finally come to terms with mortality. Even if they fixed my heart, I believed I was going to die soon. In the time I have left could I tell the people I love, in plain words, without frightening them, that I loved nothing more than being their husband, their father, their brother, their son? Why is this so difficult for me? Why am I such a non-evolved human being? Why? I must change that! Now. In the *present*.

THE QUEST FOR THE GREAT DOCTORS and surgeon and hospital continued. Karla and I did our homework (again) and found great doctors and surgeons in New York. I was given a recommendation to go see Bill Clinton's cardiologist.

But over the last 16 years I had been told many, many times, that 'for the best cardiac care, The Cleveland Clinic is the place to go.' Cleveland? Cleveland over New York? New York with surgeons who operate on Presidents? Cleveland over Los Angeles and the 'cardiologist to the stars?' Cleveland? Isn't that the best joke in *Tootsie,* when the director asks the cameraman how far back can he zoom *out* because the shot is on (the comparatively unattractive Dustin Hoffman in drag) Tootsie, and the cameraman responds, "How's Cleveland?" Isn't Cleveland where the lake started on fire? Didn't LeBron James run away from Cleveland?

Our dear friend Steve Popovich was one of the greatest music executives of all time. He created Cleveland International Records and signed the iconic songwriter Jim Steinman and his partner Meat Loaf when no one else would touch *Bat Out Of Hell*. (Sales to date: 44 million... and counting.)

Steve had heart issues, and because of the kind of man he is, Steve did thorough homework and came to the conclusion that the best place for cardiac care was in his own back yard: *The Cleveland Clinic*.

I met with a famous New York cardiologist who was very nice... incredibly competent (an understatement), yet there was another issue with me: New York City was not the place I wanted to awaken after my *fourth* open-heart surgery. I love New York, but if I were to wake up from surgery hearing curse words, people yelling and cabbies honking their horns endlessly in complete futility— well it was not my idea of a healing environment.

Steve Popovich gave us his cardiologist Mike Koch's phone number and said he was awaiting our call. I had a meeting with the President's cardiologist in less than 10 days. Who in their right mind would cancel that meeting and go to Cleveland? Dr. Koch walked us through his recommendations and told us Dr. Brian Griffin at The Cleveland Clinic was an outstanding cardiologist. I wanted to speak to him on the phone. Would he agree to do that? Would he have the time?

Part of the mindset at The Cleveland Clinic is, 'We'll find the time. And if we can't find the time, we'll make the time.' Not just for me— *for everybody*. Now, finally— my kind of place! The words: 'for everybody' really meant something very special to me. This was a place where your name or your celebrity didn't matter. Your illness mattered. Bravo!

The name of one surgeon kept popping up in every conversation about the Cleveland Clinic: Gosta Pettersson, M.D., Ph.D.

People spoke about this man in terms of the miracles he had performed. Some surgeons take cases that make their 'batting average' 1.000 percent. No fatalities. Dr. Pettersson takes cases to *save people's lives*. He takes the cases *other surgeons wouldn't touch*.

I also kept hearing about how The Cleveland Clinic handles their patients and the patient's *family*— 'the patient and the family come first at The Cleveland Clinic.'

Where is this place? Disneyland? Oz? Wait— did you say... 'Cleveland?'

I learned that this attitude came straight from the top. Delos M. 'Toby' Cosgrove, M.D., is the chief executive officer and chairman of the Board of Governors of The Cleveland Clinic, and I read an article by Ceci Connolly in *The Washington Post* about him. In big headlines:

Head of Cleveland Clinic Is Attacking Big Mac
And in Hospital Lobby, McDonald's Fights Back

"A heart surgeon who has cleaned out a career's worth of clogged arteries, Cosgrove didn't think Big Macs, supersize fries and inch-thick, six-cheese pizzas belonged in the lobby of a hospital renowned for its cardiac care. So he decreed the fast-food joints had to go."

I also heard that the head of The Cleveland Clinic was openly against smoking. This is an area that hits close to home.

As an actor, I made a decision to never use a cigarette as a prop. It's a great prop, too. It gives the actor 'history' from the second he or she walks into the room. A cigarette tells us something about the character before the first line is spoken. But, not for me. I'm not 'squeaky clean'— I just don't want to inhale hot, fiery smoke into my lungs that's addictive. And I certainly wouldn't want an audience member doing it because I did it in a film. Nope— just not for me.

I'll get off my soapbox with these overwhelming statistics from the American Heart Association: In the United States, an estimated 24.8 million men (23.1 percent) and 21.1 million women (18.3 percent) are smokers. *These people are at higher risk of heart attack and stroke:*

Among whites, 23.5 percent of men and 20.6 percent of women smoke (2008).

Among blacks, 25.6 percent of men and 17.8 percent of women smoke.

Among Native Americans, 24.3 percent of Native American adults smoke.

Among Hispanics, 20.7 percent of men and 10.7 percent of women smoke.

9.9 percent of Asian adults smoke.

WHY SMOKE? WHY?

No employee of any kind may smoke on the grounds of the Cleveland Clinic. (And the Cleveland Clinic takes up an entire zip code.)

I HAD NEVER MISSED A DAY OF WORK IN MY LIFE and now I would be missing two classes in both courses I was teaching. There was a strange sense of shame in that; I felt I was letting my students down. I still oversaw everything that happened in those two classes— and I desperately wanted to be there— but I physically had finally had all my body could take.

Chair Sanders, Dean Campbell and my students were amazing and helped me get through this very difficult time. And so did the internet. Every chance I had, I was online trying to help my students in any way I could, until typing became problematic. (Once a marathoner and now, no endurance and too tired to type... Humility: the great equalizer; always magnifying my shortcomings. Death isn't as demanding— I guess it needn't be. Life is demanding.)

After discussing Dr. Cosgrove and his views on healthcare, Dr. Pettersson's abilities and his goal to take on extremely difficult cases, and Dr. Griffin's expertise and willingness to always talk to us and help us understand the gray areas, The Cleveland Clinic— and everything we were learning about it— seemed like an extraordinary hospital. We also learned that they were ranked #1 in cardiac care in the United States by *U.S. News and World Report* for sixteen years. There became little doubt in my New York/ L.A. mind that The Cleveland Clinic was the place for me. But still— the cardiologist who worked on Bill Clinton? Come on, that's got to be a no-brainer. And I knew my mother would be... happy. (I mean, whose mom wouldn't want their son to have Bill Clinton's cardiologist?)

Finally, I decided I'd listen to my own heart. Forget all this baloney. I'm going to *Cleveland!*

The Cleveland Clinic

WE IMMEDIATELY GOT ON A PLANE, flew to Cleveland and the most remarkable thing happened. Our adventure with the Cleveland Clinic *began at the airport*. There was a very extraordinary man, Mustapha Bounit, who had emigrated to America from Morocco— waiting at the airport to pick us up and take us to the hotel. A hotel that is literally 'connected' to the hospital. Mustapha would not allow me to lift my luggage. I asked him why. "Because," he said, "you need heart surgery. You cannot put more strain on the heart by lifting this luggage. I cannot allow you to hurt yourself." (Huh?) I looked at Karla and wondered if the slogan (a dictum that would cause the most cynical patient to provide an instinctive smirk) 'The patient and the family come first'— were *not* empty words. Could this motto actually begin with this compassionate man, Mustapha, at the Cleveland Airport?

I expected and hoped for... 'wonderful things'... but was this some kind of joke? Was someone going overboard because they liked me in a film? My mind was so small and slightly pessimistic that I kept thinking, it must be because he liked one of my movies or wanted an autograph. But then again, I am a bit of a has-been. Does he know this— or have my films taken this long to make it to Morocco? Then when we were in the car and I asked him what the photo album on the floor of the backseat was, he said I could look at it. The photo album was filled with six years of pictures; pictures of Mustapha posing with different patients, as they came to the hospital and as they were leaving to go home, always with a very proud Mustapha in the photo, smiling as if this may be the most important photo ever taken.

"So, who are these people?" I asked.

Mustapha became passionately animated as we drove toward Cleveland. He genuinely explained, 'They are patients who come here and are very sick. It is important that I remember this from the second they get off the airplane. The journey was probably very tiring for them in their condition."

He drove so safely yet at the same time was filled with excitement and energy. 'These people in the pictures, these patients are very vulnerable people who come to the Cleveland Clinic and they are extremely sick. The wives or husbands— sometimes they must come along— everyone is afraid. They are frightened because they don't know how the surgery or treatment will affect them. So, I *must* take very good care of them. They need help immediately. They don't come from Cleveland. They may come from anywhere in the world. I must make them feel safe and feel at home right away in this new city. It is like with you and your wife. You are sick and that is scary for your wife. I don't want you to be scared. I want you to feel like everything will turn out right and it does here! I see miracles. Every day!"

Let me emphasize— this stranger was our *driver*. After 5 minutes, he was no longer 'our driver'— Mustapha was our *friend*. A friend who was reassuring us that everything will be okay. He had no idea that I had ever been in a film, and he certainly didn't want my autograph. He was going to make sure that we got from the airport to the hotel without incident and he believed it was his job that we feel better when we arrived at the hotel.

Mustapha told us he came to this country in 2000. He scrubbed floors, cleaned toilets. He saved up enough money so that he could fulfill a need that he perceived to be valuable to the patients and the families who came to the Cleveland Clinic: someone to reassure them and help them from the moment they got off the plane.

Mustapha did not speak English in the year 2000. But, by taping *Judge Judy* and watching it instead of sleeping after moonlighting on sometimes four different jobs at once, he learned English, little by little. (His English is flawless.) I was so fascinated with a trait that I admire so much in people, 'hope' and the willingness to *try* with every ounce of energy, that I asked him what his goal in life was. His answer was so pure.

"I want an office in The Cleveland Clinic. It can be a broom closet. I don't care. I want to help people from the moment they get off the plane. If their families need to see a movie or get a carton of milk, I want to get it for them or drive them to a place where they may need to think or be away from the hospital— and then when everyone is healed and feeling better, I want to help them get back to their home."

I wished I was making a film— I wanted to hire this man. He would be invaluable to any film— in any department! But then I thought, this is unique. Mustapha is that rare man everyone hopes they will meet and become friends with; this cannot be 'the way of the Cleveland Clinic'. That would be... silly.

Silly. I was in for the shock of my life. *Everyone I met that day,* from the bellhop to the person who checked us in at the front desk of the hotel, to the waiter in the restaurant in the hotel that was connected to The Cleveland Clinic's mantra; (how could this be?) they were all compassionate! This was an exceptional environment— a place, a feeling I had never felt before. I kept waiting for the 'pie in the face.' Aha! The TV in the hotel room wasn't working.

"Hi, I'm here to fix the TV. We're changing some of the cables. It will only take a second. Is now a good time?"

"Um..." I reached into my pocket for a tip as the gentleman was leaving.

"Oh, no sir. That's unnecessary. I just want your TV to work. Have a wonderful evening."

He left me with a few dollars in my hand that I could've stuffed into my open mouth.

The next morning I was to begin with meetings and tests with doctors and X-ray machines, etc. Same ol', same ol'. Our problem was, The Cleveland Clinic is a very large place. How early should we leave? How do we get a map so we'll know where to go? (I was so exhausted, I could barely think, but the director in me wanted to be prepared.) The phone rang. Karla answered the phone.

On the other end of the phone was a woman named Francine Pate. When I knew we would be coming to The Cleveland Clinic, I was very nervous about the travel, the bigness of it all and to be honest, getting lost in the shuffle— and I didn't want Karla to have to do endless amounts of work to find offices, blood labs, etc. I asked if there was someone I should speak to from the Cleveland Clinic and I was put in touch with Francine. Francine held the title of: Manager, Executive Patient Services.

The hospital had so many people flying into Cleveland from around the world, they needed people with diverse skills to help the patients in many ways; some as difficult as getting a schedule together of when the MRI would be, and when the meeting with the Cardiologist would be, and how to get from one to the other, and if there was enough time to get from one to another, and would the patient who had to fast for the blood test be hungry after giving blood, and is there enough time to get from the lab to the restaurant to the doctor's office. This kind of planning on a film is critical— it is not easy or simple— not when you're dealing with sick people. At this hospital, we filmmakers should take lessons from Francine and her staff.

Francine told Karla to meet us down on the 3rd floor, right at the elevator and she would help us from there. And "don't forget to tell Robby not to eat anything after 10:00 o'clock."

Francine helped us all day (leaving us to help other patients— then all of a sudden, she was back. Who knows how many people she helped that day?) But Francine refused to be just 'a guide' or a person to make sure we weren't late for appointments. Francine... *cared*. It happened effortlessly, but Karla and I immediately trusted Francine. She just became... a *friend*.

We listened to all of the doctors we met with, asked all of the questions that were on our minds, and the doctors took the time to answer the questions. If we didn't understand, they were not annoyed or constantly checking their watches, they would keep explaining any and all things until we felt secure and understood everything they were explaining to us.

I asked Francine one day if she could sum up what she thought her job description was at The Cleveland Clinic.

"How do I describe what I do? Actually, it is quite simple. I treat the patient as I would want myself or a family member to be treated. In other words, respectfully and with genuine care. I respond promptly to questions, concerns or areas of concern. I am a small part of a wonderful Clinic team where *details* are so important; my goal is to assist in *any* manner— to reduce the stress of coming to a large facility for serious medical conditions and who knows, maybe for complicated surgeries. The payback for me is in seeing the miracles that are performed every day by our outstanding surgeons, giving hope where there was no hope and curing so many. The other benefit for me is meeting new and wonderful people and (in many cases) forming wonderful friendships. Does this help? Did I answer your question?"

I looked at Karla in awe. My response was to get a giant bullhorn. I wanted to stand on a cartoon mountain so that *everyone in the entire universe could hear me.* As a patient who has been pummeled by the system and by endless medical procedures, all I was encountering were experts who wanted to make those very specific incidents in my life a thing of the past; and they wanted me to start with a clean slate and show me how it really should be done.

Of course— I was sick, a bit scared (though I was now a true veteran) and very vulnerable; as I've been many times in the past. I could have a life-ending experience in front of me and we all knew that. Just like in the past. But no one was being secretive, patronizing or aloof— I was meeting people who were at the top of their game. Even the people who take blood have a nickname (the best were called the SWAT Team) because no matter what condition your veins are in, they not only find ways to take your blood— an 'event' I'm an expert at— without the patient *feeling* any pain. That was their goal!

When I would be waiting to see someone, I would be asked if I was willing to fill out a form that had to do with 'How long was your wait?' or 'Were you treated respectfully?' As I was trying to fill out the first questionnaire, my number was called. This place cannot be as good as I'm experiencing; there must be horror stories— it's a hospital. I haven't even had my surgery yet. I'm not some dimwitted convert ready to drink the Kool-Aid.

We met with my cardiologist, Dr. Brian Griffin, and his staff (the nurses and the administrative people who all had the same attitude: 'How can we help?'). I am still amazed to such an extent that even writing about our experiences, I keep trying to find times where things went wrong so it's more dynamic to read— to write. (Nothing so far.) Dr. Griffin answered *every* question we had.

Even more remarkable was his ability to go to his computer and look at the tests I had taken *earlier that morning* and go over the results until both Karla and I understood the intricacies to every detail. He was a warm, kind man. The person anyone would want as their uncle. (Does that make sense? It will after I ask him to be my uncle.)

That morning I had an angiogram/echocardiogram— and every single nurse, every doctor, every tech person that I came to respect told me:

You don't want a 5th open heart surgery Robby...

I thought, why not? I'm an old pro. I know what to expect. What I never really took into account was that my heart, not my mind, was going through these surgeries. They all told me that if Dr. Gosta Petterssen was my surgeon, I probably would never need a fifth surgery. The consensus seemed clear; to avoid a fifth surgery, I would need a mechanical valve, and with that came rat poison— err, Coumadin. (The chemical is used in rat poison, causing death by internal bleeding.)

I loved all veggies and salads, even sometimes juicing green drinks. How would that work with Coumadin? Karla realized if I was going to be on Coumadin for the rest of my life we were going to need some great nutritional advice. Did the Cleveland Clinic have an expert? The chief wellness officer and chair of the Wellness Institute of the Cleveland Clinic is *New York Times* #1 best-selling author Dr. Michael F. Roizen. Karla had read several of his wildly successful "YOU" books, co-written with Dr. Oz.

We made an appointment and brought a concise list of questions so we wouldn't forget anything. I brought a tape recorder and said I wanted to ask him some questions. Would he mind?

"Sure. Go ahead. I'll do the best I can."

Many of our questions had to do with the use of Coumadin because my life was going to change radically if I were to have a mechanical valve— and with a mechanical valve in the aortic position, I needed a blood thinner so I didn't 'throw off a clot' and that meant rat poison— err, Coumadin— every day. (I make jokes about it, but in certain heart patients Coumadin's blood-thinning ability saves lives.)

Dr. Roizen: "Coumadin is what we call a 'blood thinner'. What it really does is stop some of the coagulation pathway by depleting certain factors. Consequently, you can oppose it with certain factors such as green leafy vegetables. Many of these green leafy vegetables are rich in vitamin K. You can boost your Vitamin K factor with certain green leafy vegetables and deplete your system of coagulation with Coumadin. If, God forbid you were to hit your arm while on Coumadin you would bleed more. So it is a very dangerous thing for people who do extreme sports. It's a dangerous drug for bike riders who don't wear helmets."

"I know you are a big proponent of Omega 3. Is it permissible to take Omega 3 while on Coumadin?"

"Yes— as long as you use DHA rather than fish oil. DHA is the active component of fish oil for the heart, it is the EPA component of fish oil that is the anticoagulant in fish oil— but DHA gives you all of the benefits for the head, all the benefits for the eyes and most of the benefits for the heart doesn't interfere with anticoagulants. It has 15 calories in 600 milligrams. Coumadin, because of its very potent anticoagulant effect has a lot of impact on other parts of the body. Heparin not only has the anticoagulant effect but it can often have an allergy to platelets. It can attack your own platelets. Some medicines have a short-term effect like Coumadin and other medicines may have a long-term effect like Heparin."

"Let's say I eat a little bit of broccoli every day and I stay consistent and we're able to balance the Coumadin. Is it okay to eat this leafy vegetable as long as I'm consistent?"

"You've brought up the key point. Do not avoid leafy green vegetables and vegetables and foods that are good for you and all of your organs, but— it is important *to stay consistent.* Eat the foods every day at the same time so your physician or Coumadin Clinic staff can get an appropriate reading to keep your Coumadin levels stabile. Lutein, very important for eyes and joints and the brain, has nutrients that you need— you want to get that in your diet. Broccoli and all of the cruciferous vegetables, watercress or arugula have one of the compounds that have an anti-breast and anti-colon and anti-prostate effect for cancer. You want the good foods— and work with your physicians so you get the proper balance of all of the good nutrients that wonderful and healthy foods give you without negating the effects that Coumadin gives you; that you need for your mechanical valve. You must be consistent. If you are consistent you can eat the good foods that will keep your body strong with the nutrients that come with those foods. One of the key components is working with your physician and the team you have to get a stable level. Don't eat all of your leafy vegetables on one day of the week and then not for the rest of the week; eat your salad, let's say, everyday at lunch. That way your physician will get stable and proper reading, the therapeutic range— the right range for you— this is very important— for *you*— because everyone is different— but you can still get the proper nutrients that good foods can give your body. There are new medications that are being developed that will help people who do not have the opportunity to work with a lab and a Coumadin team or live near a hospital where they can get their Coumadin monitored, so they will someday soon be able to take this new medicine that is being developed and there will be a lot more freedom to the way they live their lives when it comes to the foods they eat. We're working on this. Hopefully... hopefully it will be available soon."

SOON, WE WOULD MEET WITH OUR SURGEON. (I always say 'our' because he might as well be operating on Karla. We are a team, period— and always will

Cardiovascular Imaging Outpatient Center and Echo Lab

be.) One of the ironies of our lives is that I did voice over commercials for GE ("Imagination at work") for about two years, and every time I was going to have heart surgery, a GE machine was used to help save my life. I could honestly say, "I believe in this product!" This is a state-of-the-art ultrasound echo machine.

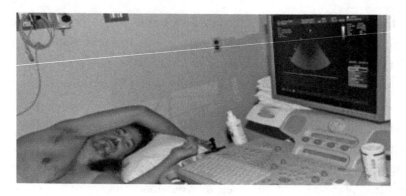

When your life is hanging in the balance, you realize that companies like GE are literally helping to save your life— all jokes and *cynicism* go flying out the window. I usually just close my eyes and dream...

Before we met with the surgeon, Dr. Gosta Pettersson, we were told 'he is one of the best heart surgeons in the world.' Dr. Hillel Laks at UCLA was on that list. These surgeons *touch our hearts...* We use the phrase in poetry, sometimes in our daily lives, but these surgeons touch our hearts in the most literal way. Someday there will be a way to quantify the tenderness, the expertise, the quality that comes from gifted surgeons who do this delicate operation and what impact their work has on the psyche and future of the patient, far beyond the physical.

Dr. Pettersson is tall, thin, pale and has a smile that reminds me of life, death; experience, an attempt at happiness, profound sadness and... humility and knowledge. All in one smile. As a director, I wanted to bottle that smile and show it to actors— study its every wrinkle, crinkle, and how every director must follow the creases at the end of the smile, and use the cheeks as a map on the way up to the source of the smile— the origin of expression— *the eyes.*

Karla did most of the talking at first, asking questions that we've discussed as a couple so many times: 'From the results of the tests, what were his surgical intentions? How would he deal with the aortic valve? Would he really try the Reverse Ross Procedure and take my original pulmonary valve off of the aortic position and put it back to its original home, in the pulmonary position? Is that possible?'

I just stared and listened to the man with the elegant Swedish accent who would soon have his hands in my chest. Everyone had told us that we would like Dr. Pettersson as a person as well as a miraculous surgeon. The phrase that seemed to follow every description of this surgeon was 'down to earth.'

Yes. He was. Down to Earth— and brilliant.

He spoke to us as if we were out on a park bench, and he was quietly, seriously, but with an honest amity, explaining the fate of my heart. Dr. Pettersson did so with a gentle devotion, ardor and commitment that had both Karla and me listening to his every inhalation, swallow, consonant— becoming more and more impressed with his detailed descriptions so that nothing would come as a surprise to either of us. We felt calm, yet he was discussing the stuff of horror films. Blood, incisions, and even cooling my body by putting me on ice and stopping the blood flow to the heart and the brain for 21 minutes— completely off the heart-lung machine. We were captivated.

When he finished I wanted to jump up like a Studio Executive and say, "I'll buy that script! I want to make that movie!" Then I remembered, this was my movie— and I had already 'bought it'…

We left Dr. Pettersson's office with every question answered to our satisfaction and not one false moment. Even the needle on my show business B.S.-meter never moved. *Everything was honest*. It was quite daring, audacious — bold, to try the 'Reverse-Ross,' but I honestly believed he was trying to give me the best future-life possible. He made a point that this had absolutely nothing to do with him and his reputation as a surgeon. Everything had to do with me. *The patient*. Making me *better*. And my family. Giving Karla and me more time to be together in this lifetime.

Karla and I waited in the hotel room for an opening in his schedule because he was in such demand and my operation was so complicated that he wanted to make sure everything was perfect.

At the hotel, we had a surprise visitor. Lyric came to stay with us. She not only made us both feel better and was always cheerful, Lyric filled the room with light.

I tried to walk on the treadmill down in the hotel gym but it was really pathetic. I don't know if I was doing it for exercise or if I was walking to prove to myself that I was a machine and this surgery was basically a 'valve' job— a lube job. There was nothing *really* wrong with me, I thought. Then I'd see an 80 year-old man next to me running and I looked into the gym mirror— overweight because I couldn't exercise; bloated from certain medications, and walking at a pace that was slower than Dick Cheney on a bad day. Crap! Crap! Crap! I was so angry. Why can't I beat this? Why doesn't my heart work? I had finally come to the 'Why me?' moment and I would not allow it to linger. I got off the treadmill and went to the stationary bike. I rode for 30 minutes. At the setting of "1"— but I still rode for 30 minutes. I *tried*. I stopped complaining and I tried.

While I was waiting for my operation date, I kept in touch with my students via email and tried to help as much as possible.

THE NIGHT BEFORE MY SURGERY I shaved myself, because I didn't want to be shaved by a stranger this time. I took every hair off my body that I knew had to be hairless and clean for the surgical work that would follow: my torso and my groin, too. I even got into the whole shaving thing and shaved under my arms and most of my legs. I wanted to look like an Olympic swimmer. If I could never be an Olympian, at least I could look like one— Maybe I'd look like Mike? No, not this time either.

Finally, I didn't have any hair to make for 'drag' in the pool of my Olympic surgery. I then did what they wanted me to do; I showered with a special soap, instead of the old, very cold Betadine that used to be swabbed on me after the dry shave in the morning.

I didn't eat. It was another long night just wondering if it were to be my last night. I just wanted to hold my wife, and both my children. By now, Zephyr had finished his senior year of high school early and come to Cleveland, and so had my mom and dad. Even my sister was there. I was nervous, not scared— the feeling I felt before I went on the *Ed Sullivan Show*— a feeling I hadn't felt since I was 14 years-old.

On May 25, 2010, the early, dark morning of the surgery, I had to go through the same routine again. At 4 a.m. I had to shower and wash with a special soap.

At the Cleveland Clinic, they allow your loved ones to stay with you longer than at any other hospital I've ever been to.

Then, off we went.

They wheeled me into an elevator. A clean elevator.

They wheeled me into the operating room.

It was cold.

They asked me if I wanted a blanket.

I said, "Yes, please."

And, unlike in the past, this request was immediately granted. I now had a warm blanket on me.

There were two people staring at me in operating room garb along with paper hats and masks. I could only see their eyes. 'What caring eyes,' I thought. Not a hint of falseness; just compassion.

Someone told me they were going to give me an I.V. They gently checked my hands and arms and found the best possible place to insert the I.V.

I waited for the I.V. to be inserted.

"I thought you were going to put in the I.V.," I mumbled quietly.

"We do that when you are asleep. There's no reason for you to go through any more pain than is necessary. Even for an I.V." someone in a mask said with a very gentle quality in their male voice.

"Are you scared?" the lady looking down on me asked quietly.

"No." Then I thought, I don't have to fool these guys. "Yes. I guess I am."

"We're going to give you something to help with anxiety."

"Okay."

They did.

And it worked.

I looked around and there were more people coming into the operating room.

"Good morning," someone said— not in a condescending way. It was... just a nice thing to say.

"Good morning," I said back.

"Are you feeling more comfortable?" the nice female nurse who never left my side said. And then she did something I'll remember for the rest of my life. She took my hand.

"I want you to squeeze my hand if you're a bit nervous."

I didn't want anyone to see, but I really squeezed her hand.

"I understand," she whispered back to me.

She put her other hand on top of mine and now was completely giving me the kind of honest support that I thought only family members give to one another.

"How do you feel now?" a voice said. I knew it was coming from someone to the left of my feet but I wasn't sure who actually asked.

"I've had a few of these operations and I'm ashamed to tell you, but I might have a high tolerance to some of the drugs."

It wasn't but a beat of three when I heard a voice ask me, "How about now?"

Oh dear Lord— I was no longer anxious and there was no such thing as fear, until I looked around to answer and saw everything in the room, and everyone in the room.

The nurse who was holding my hand whispered, "You're going to do really well. We're going to take really good care of you."

Then a man about to place a plastic mask over my nose and mouth said, "I'm going to put this mask on you and all you have to do is breathe normally."

"If I could breathe normally, then I'd better get out of here now."

They laughed. Oh, thank you! If it was the last thing I did on this planet, I made someone laugh.

And that is the last thing I remember from the operating room.

THEY WENT TO WORK and diligently, miraculously, performed a Reverse Ross Procedure.

In medical terms, here is what they did that made the operation elaborately complex:

(According to my chart:) First, they performed a median sternotomy (or in my case, a *re*-sternotomy or, 're-re-re'), which basically means the first important thing that happened was that they made a vertical incision that begins about 6 inches above the belly button and goes upward to the sternum and then they split or crack the sternum, to divide it. Then, they performed an ascending aorta replacement with a 26-mm Hemashield graft using deep hypothermia circulatory arrest and retrograde cerebral perfusion. The right atrium was opened and a retrograde cardioplegia cannula was placed in the coronary sinus and the heart arrested with cardioplegia. This is where they cooled me down and stopped the heart and made sure there was no damage to the brain while they worked on the ascending aorta which, as they had told me, had an aneurism. My understanding of an aneurism and the medical interpretation for the ascending aortic valve in the heart are two different things. When I hear the word 'aneurism' I think of something that has burst. In my case, and in its simplest terms, they want to get to the problem *before* it bursts. They continued and performed an aortic root *re*-replacement with a composite graft including a 25 mm On-X valve and a 30mm Hemashield graft. Then the surgeon performed an aortic autograft pulmonary root replacement — which is basically the 'Reverse Ross.' They then placed the mediastinal drains so that the fluids could drain from my body. (The mediastinal drains are the dreaded drainage tubes I have discussed.) In other words: it's miraculous. Dr. Gustav Pettersson is a remarkable surgeon but I am so grateful to everyone else who was in that room.

WHEN I BEGAN TO REGAIN CONSCIOUSNESS after my chemical sleep in the ICU, I tried to get the attention of anyone because the breathing tubes were still down my throat. I only had this discomfort for about 60 seconds— someone was there almost immediately, and before I knew it, the tubes were out of my mouth.

With my contacts out, I squinted to see my surroundings. As blurry as it was, I could still see that this was an open area, not the carceral environment I was used to from past operations. I thought, 'How smart. I can get a sense of everything and I don't feel claustrophobic. I don't feel like a prisoner.'

A man looked down at me. "How do you feel?"

I did a quick diagnostic check and was absolutely blown away by my answer, "I actually... don't feel too badly. I mean, I hurt a little but... this doesn't feel like any other operation I've ever had."

"Good. I'm going to give you this button," and he placed the small tubular device in my right hand "and if you feel like the pain is getting a bit too much, all you have to do is squeeze the top. You can't get too much pain medicine because you're only allowed to have so much every few minutes, so never worry that you're giving yourself too much. We want you comfortable."

The next thing I knew, Karla was there. She looked great.

"You look great," I said.

"So do you," she smiled. She had a worried look on her face but when we locked eyes, she seemed to be comforted. Maybe she saw that when I looked into her eyes, I felt comforted too.

"Everything went perfectly. I spoke to Dr. Pettersson and he was able to do the Reverse Ross procedure on you. Your pulmonary valve is 'back home' and looks fantastic— and your new mechanical valve is working perfectly."

Mechanical. Valve. Frankenstein. Coumadin. Rat poison. 'Rat Boy' was going to be my new nickname. A newfangled lifestyle. I guess I can be a Pollyanna and say, 'A new adventure,' but my genetic, physical instincts were always to take action in a crisis; to throw my body in front of someone who was falling and take the hit, be their buffer. Now, on Coumadin, how was I going to reprogram myself? And let people fall? It's not in my DNA.

The next thing I remember in the ICU was seeing my beautiful children. They were on either side of me. I thought, 'Wow. What amazingly brave kids, to come into the ICU and pretend that it's not creepy; to act as if they were coming into the bedroom just to sit and have a chat. I was so proud of them. They made me want to talk to them, sit up and show them I wasn't a sickly old man ready to die— I was a vibrant 54 year-old dad who was going to get out of this hospital and be a part of their lives for a long, long time to come.

I remember telling them jokes and making them laugh. I remember telling one truth after another. Not truths hidden within language and body language— truths that cut to the core.

Suddenly I was opening up to my daughter and telling her how proud I was that she had completely fought her physical demons on her own and she had won. I saw the pain; I saw her agony. She had bulging disks in her back; herniated disks from horseback riding; she had injuries from being a competitive skier as well as a competitive horsewoman (both English and

Western); she was a phenomenal figure skater and many times as a young little girl on skates, performing to "Send in the Clowns," I would see her practice and fall hard on the unforgiving ice.

And Lyric, who on her own, without medication, by exercising every day and by practicing T.M. (something I always had doubts about, but could now see what it can do for people who truly practice it properly and *try*): Lyric had completely healed herself.

By herself. By trying. There wasn't an ounce of 'give up' in her being.

I remember that because of whatever drug I was on in the ICU, I was able to turn to my daughter and tell her things that my own screwed up defense mechanisms couldn't seem to say: "I'm so proud of you, Lyric. You did this all by yourself. Do you know how miraculous that is? Do you know how courageous you are? I'm so proud of you. I love you so very much. I think T.M. is wonderful."

I could see that she was taking this all in; I could also tell that both of us knew I was on a lot of medication, and it was truly pathetic that it took a lot of medication for me to be so honest and loving. What is wrong with me? Why can't these same words come out when I'm *not* on medication yet still believing every word. Why, without medication, was there some sort of *qualification*, some stipulation that worked its way into my sentences acknowledging her courage?

Then I remembered Zephyr was on my other side. I had to tell him how much I love him, too. I kept understanding the premise: I'm on drugs— drugs that are helping you tell the truth. So don't blow it— tell the damn truth, and later work on your pitiable, wretched and weak brain— and all of the hurdles and stop-gaps that don't always allow the purest truths to come out. But for now, do what is right. *Tell the truth.*

"Oh, Zephyr... you're the best son any father could hope for. I know that soon you will pass me by— all of my accomplishments that really mean nothing in the scheme of things. You'll do better than me— and you will be a better man than I am. You may already be... but if you're not, if you're still an apprentice to what is right in life, you will be a far greater man than I am."

I remember I really had Zephyr and Lyric laughing. I can't remember what I said that was funny— or if they were laughing at my over-the-top sincerity. To just be able to come out with a sentence that was absolutely truthful was liberating. The 'truth serum' opened my reinforced gateway to my love for both of them— and it was all confirmed with devoted and stanch squeezes of their hands. I'm so lucky that no matter how it came from my mouth— my truths transpired honestly, and I can remember them and write them now so that when my children go their own ways, maybe one day they'll pick up this manuscript and re-read how much I loved, honored and respected them.

Everyone who came into the ICU was a bit blown away by how talkative I was; how coherent I was. I could see the surprise on their faces. My sister laughed and said, "Robby hasn't talked that much since high school!"

Now it was my turn to prove that all of the past three surgeries had taught me something. I asked for the breathing machine— and the ICU doctor was a bit surprised that I asked before he gave it to me.

I used that inhalation plastic toy as if it were the Superbowl of all events. I used it every few minutes. I got used to the maximum chest pain as fast as I could. I checked how it hurt when I leaned to the right; to the left, when I used my stomach muscles to try and sit up; when I pretended to cough.

I knew that pain was the main obstacle that most open-heart patients try and avoid and in avoiding it, they stay motionless, which is the worst thing you can do after surgery. Within reason, you must begin to move your body parts. And, the way I deal with pain is that there is a pain I call the definitive, ultimate pain. I try and go hunting for it as soon as I can. It's a safari for pain. Once I make up my mind and find what I believe to be 'the worst possible pain,' then all of the other pains are relative.

I find that pain is only a minor part of a patient's unwillingness to help themselves: it's the *unknown* that is really the culprit: how much worse is this pain going to get? For me, once I find that supreme pain situate, I'm ready for some football!

Later in the day my mom, dad and sister came back into the ICU to say goodbye. They were flying home. I know they saw me in my actual room, but I only remember shadows...

I made it to my room pretty fast— not in record time for me, but still pretty fast. I was now on Lasix, a drug they give to horses to reduce swelling and it stops the horses from retaining fluids. As a guy who grew up around horseracing, I felt a silly delight that I was on the same drug that many of the horses I had bet on also used. (I usually lost...) I learned that the more surgeries one has, the more scar tissue and the more liquids and fluids build up in the system. They need to be removed with Lasix and through the infamous tubes coming from my abdomen, which drain the fluids into a bag hanging on the side of my bed. I stared at the see-through heavy plastic bag. It was a pinkish color. Because of the Lasix I had to urinate like... well, a racehorse.

There came a time when I asked if they would take the Foley catheter out of my bladder, through the urethra and out of my damn penis. "I'm tired of abusing my penis." (I made the nurses laugh.)

They had to wait a while for two reasons: 1) the bag that was collecting my urine was taken to the lab and they were checking on things like electrolytes, infection, muscle breakdown and kidney function; 2) they wanted to be sure that I could walk to the bathroom— and in doing so, be able to collect all of my urine in a device that looks like a plastic prototype that didn't pass muster with the company that makes pitchers for lemonade.

Each nurse that I had was *exceptional*. All of them cared about my well-being but also cared about helping Karla, Lyric and Zephyr, too.

Little by little my body was cleaning out the amazing drug cocktail of anesthesia that put me to sleep and then made my ICU stay like a vacation in a science fiction film where you feel great— even when you hurt. Now I just hurt. The only thing on my mind was when and how are they going to pull out the drainage tubes? Then I realized, I only had *one* drainage tube. That was an innovation since my last surgery six years ago, and from what the nurses were telling me, removing it didn't hurt like the old days.

They gave me Metoprolol, a beta-blocker to help the heart heal. I never did well on beta-blockers so after a few days, they switched to an alternate medicine and I never even knew it. I just felt better. There was someone constantly coming into the room to take blood. For some reason, I had a high white blood cell count.

At the time, I was on a myriad of medications: Simvastatin which is in the class of statins which lower cholesterol, but since my cholesterol counts were in the good range, I was taken off this medication when I left the hospital. Omeprazole, 20 mg capsules were given to me by mouth. This is a medication that treats ulcers because if I had to be on a blood thinner, I definitely didn't want bleeding in my esophagus or lining of my stomach. I was given one baby aspirin a day to also thin the blood. It was 81 mg. Very small but strong enough to do the trick. They prescribed a Lidocaine patch (700 mg) for my wound as added pain relief, but I found it to be uncomfortable. They knew, from my second surgery, where I woke up in the ICU feeling something was wrong (and it was), I might require anti-anxiety medication post-op, so I was prescribed Lorazepam tablets at 0.5 mg. It was comforting to know they were available if needed, and that they actually listened to my prior medical history.

Because of the pain meds and the anesthesia, our bowels seem to 'go to sleep' and it is very important to have bowel movements without grunting and putting pressure on the newly-wired sternum, so Sennosides at 8.6 mg. tablets were given to me orally, twice daily. This medication is derived naturally from Senna, a natural herb extract that is safe and is a time-tested laxative. Along with the laxative they gave me a stool softener called Docusate sodium at 100 mg. Even though it can be the subject of many good juvenile jokes, this is an extremely important medication, believe it or not.

Finally, they gave me Warfarin (Rat poison! I find it ironic that the first three letters in this medication spell *war*) at doses beginning at 5 mg. but with pills that were 2.5 mg. doses. Warfarin or Coumadin, is basically going to keep me alive.

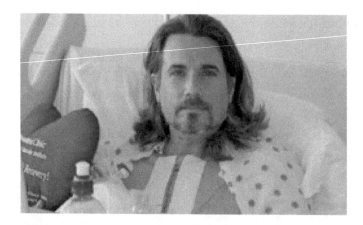

I got up as soon as I could and we'd put the drainage tube bag on the I.V. pole so I could walk the halls. The hallways were great places to walk and I saw other patients doing the same.

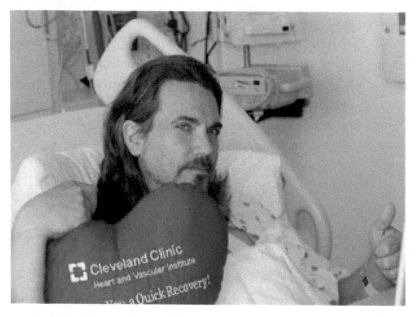

I faced my moment of truth again: the dreaded removal of the drainage tube. Two kind nurses were talking to me; I was sitting up and knew it would come any second. Their ability to take my mind off of the 'pulling of the drainage tube' would never work with someone like me— whoa, it's out!

It hurt a little. Was that really it? Then, with a smile, the nurse removed my pacemaker wires. Okay, it wasn't fun— but remembering back to my other surgeries, those procedures were the stuff of nightmares. But not here, at The Cleveland Clinic.

It was over.

We all had made it.

Valuable Life Lessons? *Life* is a Valuable Life Lesson...

A New Beginning

FINALLY, AFTER THE LONGEST STAY I had ever had in a hospital, nine days, I was released on Thursday, June 3— and I don't count the day I was released because... I don't want to! (Or as my dad once said when my mom told him he was being a little cranky, "I'm 80 years old. If I want to be cranky, I'll be cranky!")

We had been living at The Cleveland Clinic for over a month and knew the hospital almost inside out. It worked like a clock.

What is necessary is acknowledging the team, from Mustapha the man who met us at the airport, to Dr. Koch who was on the phone with me and Karla immediately after we told our friend Steve Popovich that I needed another open-heart surgery. *It was all a team effort.*

Dr. Brian Griffin, my cardiologist, was as intelligent a man as I had ever dealt with but more importantly, he immediately made Karla and me feel *safe*. Dr. Griffin didn't waste time with us; he would just stay until he was sure we understood what was happening inside my chest, and what would happen in order to fix it. And, he is a gentleman. A *gentle* man. In every sense of the words.

Dr. Griffin had a young assistant, Dr. Krishnaswamy who was a great help to us as well. He would explain things in terms of sports so that I could understand it better— but never in a condescending way. When I returned to The Cleveland Clinic for my post-surgery follow up tests, I ran into him in the hallway. He is such a force of goodness, there was no way of missing him,

even in a crowd. We learned what our new life-adventure with Coumadin was going to be like from Dr. Mike Roizen,

who is the hospital's wellness expert and is also the best-selling author of the "YOU" book series with Dr. Mehmet Oz. I discussed the

effects of cardiac depression with Dr. Leo Pozuelo. Our discussions were honest and frank— but again, there was a *respect* that he and everyone at The Cleveland Clinic exuded. He invited us to attend a conference about the effects of cardiac depression on the patient, the *2010 Heart-Brain Summit*. In his mind, as with so many others, there is no secrecy at The

Cleveland Clinic; it's a pool— a pool of *knowledge*— and everyone, even the patients, were encouraged to participate.

From past experience I understood that surgery is more than a medical procedure; it is an art form. Dr. Gosta Pettersson is an artist who performs his art under life and death situations. He is also co-author of the book, *You Have Touched My Heart,* with Johannes Mollehave.

I had the opportunity to ask him about certain issues I didn't understand, the first being the Ross Procedure (where the pulmonary valve is removed and put in the aortic position and a cadaver valve replaces the pulmonary valve).

Dr. Pettersson began by saying, "Let's elaborate about the Ross Procedure. The Ross Procedure to begin with is a simple principle where you take the best valve the patient has and put it in the most important position. We take it out of the pulmonary position and put it into the aortic position. The valve goes from a low-pressure position and goes into a high-pressure position."

"This principle has two weaknesses. One, you take it from the low pressure and put it into the high-pressure position. Not all pulmonary valves can stand up to the high pressure. The majority do fine in the aortic position. Before we are born, the pressures in the two ventricles are in essence identical; they both serve the systemic circulation, and it's really first at birth that they separate— the right side becomes the low pressure and the left side becomes the high pressure— so it's really a wonderful operation. The weaknesses are the low pressure to high pressure and how the valve reacts; and the second issue is we have to use a cadaver valve in the pulmonary position— and that has a limited lifetime. If you're lucky the failure mode is such that it's really non-consequential; and if the rest of the heart is perfect and normal, you can live with a bad valve or even no valve in the pulmonic position."

"Many people have invested a lot in trying to save the pulmonary valve in the aortic position. The idea of reversing it or trying to fix the pulmonary valve in the aortic position is understandable, but I have operated on enough patients, and you have the risk of having two bad valves in your heart. I have been less impressed with how good these failed pulmonary valves are in the aortic position— I have been able to repair some, but these failed pulmonary valves in the aortic position have not been as good and as reliable as I would like them to be to take a fairly high risk of needing another operation down the line."

"The Reverse Ross Procedure comes out of experience with many other operations. For example, human cadaver valves in the aortic position is a fairly common operation, but that also results in re-operation; it has a limited lifetime. So what we used to do for those patients is put the valves inside the existing failed human cadaver valve. That didn't turn out to give the patient a very good valve— they got a small valve in a bad conduit— so I started to take this failed human valve completely out. Then I learned how to take the whole root out, very nicely and safely, and to clean everything out and go back to the original pathology. So the Reverse Ross came as a consequence of a lot of experience with re-operations."

We discussed the art of being a surgeon and he literally blushed and said, "Whatever you do is imperfect... prosthetic valves aren't perfect, so you have to find good compromises, and I think the older you get, the more important safety becomes to you... the *safety* of the *patient*... and to do, what you are, deep down inside, convinced is the right thing to do— what I would do to myself if I were operating on myself or to family members. Safety."

"Actually, there are very simple rules. And when you violate those rules, you go home with a conscience that is not perfect. With this job, there is always concern... you always have 'bad conscience' because you're never quite perfect. You try so hard to be, but we're never quite perfect. And remember, nobody ever calls a surgeon with good news. When I get a phone call, it's always about... bad news. Someone needs me to help them. It's very hard for me to sleep because I go over each part of the operation, since I first began, always asking myself, 'Did I really answer this question correctly or did I perform this part of the operation perfectly and what should I have done to make it better.'"

I was fascinated with the part of the operation where they cooled my body down so that they could work on the ascending aorta.

I asked Dr. Pettersson if he could describe the procedure for me:

"What we do is to cool down the patient completely so that the brain metabolism almost stops. It doesn't stop completely— there is still a time-dependent damage that you do to the brain— the time you have available to stop the circulation without brain damage is about four minutes. That time goes up as you lower the temperature of the body, and when you come down to 16 or 17 degrees (Centigrade; the conversion is 61-63 degrees Fahrenheit), you can say you have 30 to 45 minutes— and I only need 12 to 15 minutes of time, so it's very safe."

"Is the heart ever out of the body?"

"No," he smiled graciously, allowing us to learn at whatever speed it took. "The heart is never out of the body. The heart is stopped with an ice-cold blood base solution that has a high concentration of potassium that paralyzes the heart. There are a few blood cells in this solution so it can oxygenate the blood. We can stop the heart for four or five hours and it's in essence as good as when we started after a couple of minutes of recovery."

The most important question I had for Dr. Pettersson had to do with the heart-lung machine, which he says is very, very safe in today's world.

He continued, "You get the slow activation of the blood. The white blood cells for instance. The white blood cells respond to injuries in the body — and they get a little confused. (He began to laugh at the simplicity of the discussion, but he loved that we were interested and was so happy to explain things to us.) They know, the white blood cells know that something is going wrong. They understand that something bad is going on and they become activated, but they don't know where the problem is. So these activated cells get deposited everywhere in the body and they release their enzymes and toxic substances— and that's why you get this, what we call 'general inflammatory response' to the heart-lung machine. Not necessarily linear but more exponentially time-related. How bad your response to the heart-lung machine is also age-related; so the older the patient, the worse they tolerate the heart-lung machine and the more difficult it is for them to reverse this effect afterward. You can see that afterwards you are a little mentally impaired, your lungs are not so good, your liver is not so good, and your kidneys are not so good— but if it's a short operation you will recover quickly. There will be minimal permanent damage."

I asked Dr. Pettersson if he visualized his work before he began his operations, the same way many 'jocks' might visualize athletic moves— even winning — before each game.

"I've always been that way, but now I visualize more after the operation, thinking about what I did and how it turned out, and what I didn't do perfectly, and why didn't I see that, and that... I think that is more important."

"I had one patient who was having her fifth re-do, and it was very complicated. I went over and over everything I had to do, counting the minutes, again and again, and it took me weeks before I could see it clearly in my mind and could do her the justice she deserved. It was only after talking to her a couple of times that I felt truly committed to her. If we don't do the operation, there is... nothing for her. And I could not accept *not trying*. I wanted to help her; give her the best life possible."

"It's... getting over the fear of killing people... truly loving people, but getting over that fear in order to save them. I operated on her after thinking and thinking about each step of the procedure, and the operation was a success..."

He became very quiet. For a moment I thought he was going to get emotional but then he pulled himself together, and honestly, after hearing that story, I knew that somehow I had found my way to the right man to operate on my heart. The man who gave me more time with Karla; with my son and daughter; with my friends and family. I somehow found the right man.

IT'S DIFFICULT TO COMPREHEND a place like The Cleveland Clinic, where even though the world is at war, there is a zip code in Cleveland where everyone is trying to help one another. Everyone shows a simple goodness to one another. Everyone is genuinely compassionate. As my daughter said when she was little, and we always mimic her in her small voice, 'Where is this place?' Well... it's in Cleveland. And dammit, it should be in every city in our civilized United States of America.

Someone needs to sit down with Dr. Delos Cosgrove, the President and Chief Executive Officer of The Cleveland Clinic and hear how he runs his hospital; and what his values are; and what he holds near and dear to his heart— especially since he is an accomplished heart surgeon as well as a brilliant administrator. He is a man who believes that everyone, himself included, should be on a one-year contract. He is a man who believes his doctors should be salaried and not rewarded by the quantity of patients each doctor sees, but by the quality of medicine each doctor gives to his and her patients. He is a man of innovation; he invented the system in which the blood that is lost by a patient during open-heart surgery is re-used rather than wasted. He supports a system where everyone discusses successes and failures. He believes that the patient and the family come first. I am so fortunate that I was steered in the direction of this place; this man; and the doctors, surgeons, nurses and staff at this remarkable hospital— and this comes from someone who has seen too many hospitals.

My hope is that one day soon, Mustapha will get his office so that he can feel part of the same system I felt so close to; a system driven by humanity, not dollars; a system structured on decency, integrity, honesty and compassion. It's **The Cleveland Clinic Model of Care**.

It's a hope that the ways of The Cleveland Clinic will someday be the template for our healthcare system in America.

I FINISHED THE FIRST DRAFT OF THIS MANUSCRIPT in less than three months from the day they sawed me open.

It isn't easy to get up every morning and hurt; every day it seems like I start from scratch. But it sure beats *not* getting up every morning. And I refuse to complain— but every once in a while when the ticking from that damn mechanical valve is louder than the percussion in my music it pisses me off. But, I'm getting the chance to compose music. So no complaining.

Coumadin, exercise, the right diet, peace-of-mind, creativity, music, friends, family, love— and then there is Karla. It all begins again— the cycle to stay healthy and enjoy life. What a gift I was given.

I went back to work again as an actor for the first time in years, on my good friends' Peter and Leslie Tolan's NBC pilot, *Brave New World*, in 2011.

Even though the network didn't pick it up, I was glad to be in front of (instead of behind) the camera , acting in a comedy with talented kids and old

friends, including Ed Begley Jr., whose dad

watched out for me so long ago on Broadway in *Zelda.*

Karla and I wanted to spend time with our children, now adults, who are finding their way in the world. We believe when it comes to our children, all creative thoughts should be free-flowing and respected. We never put down or scoffed at an idea our kids had— we nurture their dreams with our love. It works (for us).

Zephyr just finished writing his first feature— a terrific screenplay that he's working to get off the ground. Zephyr is a remarkable young man. He has the skills to be a powerful storyteller, but more importantly, he is compassionate, tender and understanding of others. Both of our children are successful no matter what they choose to do. They *give* to the world, they don't 'take, take, take.' (And both of our children make music.)

After devoting eight years to silence and the study of higher states of consciousness, Lyric, our peace warrior, came home and asked if we'd like to make an album with her that rocked out. We were thrilled!

Making **Lyric's Love Light Revolution**, with her was a blast for our entire family. Lyric sang like a champ, I composed the music and engineered (thanks to years of mentoring, tutelage and friendship from my buddy Ross Wissbaum), and Karla and I produced— resulting in an album that nurtured Lyric's exquisite and astute poetry. It's what Billie Best coined as an 'eco-psychedelic transcendental hip-pop celebration'— and you can hear the entire album on iTunes!

the debut album by Lyric Benson

LYRIC'S LOVE LIGHT REVOLUTION

I WAS INVITED TO SPEAK at The Cleveland Clinic's 2nd Annual Patient Experience: Empathy+Innovation Summit. On May 23, 2011— almost a year to the day of my fourth open heart surgery— I gave the keynote address before an audience of 700 healthcare professionals from across the country meeting to exchange ideas on improving the patient experience.

I have my problems, I have my flaws and I have my demons— sometimes my 'life music' is dissonant and the dissidents in my soul threaten to go on strike. But my beautiful family (and the people at The Cleveland Clinic)

have given me the precious time and ability to try and live a *productive* life.

Epilogue

WHEN I MET KARLA IN *Pirates of Penzance* on Broadway, we used to sing, 'Take heart.' Why has it taken 56 years to learn how to nurture my own heart even though I would sing the lyrics 'Take heart' eight shows a week?

Why didn't I *truly* listen to Thornton Wilder's advice in *Our Town* when the stage manager (in my case, Hal Holbrook) suggests to Emily, "...that saints and poets sometimes fully realize life as it is lived."?

Where was my mind when Emily simply, yet poignantly states, "Oh, earth, you're too wonderful for anybody to realize you."?

Was I merely a puppet repeating, reciting written words? An actor, lying still as if dead, yet alive and surely deaf? Why didn't I absorb the deliberate inspection of humanity in Mr. Wilder's uncomplicated, straightforward, effortless wisdom? Why, after life and death surgeries, had I been taking my heart, my life, for granted?

Why not 'take heart' as Gilbert and Sullivan would have us do, and bloom, blossom and flourish with the bouquet of a principled, virtuous human existence, rather than choose to do battle with the universe? Does life reside only in memories; are we merely spectators of our own lives as we think back? Why be a forward thinker if I cannot think in the *present?* Life is happening *now.* Can we be that one 'straining star' trying to make something of ourselves, as Mr. Wilder so purely, basically states?

Now my heart finally beats in tandem with my soul reminding me to ('take heart') *always* make choices based on 'goodness.' Not for my personal benefit— but for the benefit of others: our planet; the benefit of mankind; for the benefit of my children and their lives, and their children's lives, and for the benefit of *now.*

I do know that one saying that has become a cliché must be inspected: 'the quality of life.' I found that in all of my years of having heart surgeries, I could still have an exquisite quality of life. That was up to me.

Now I take the time to appreciate the beauty around me…

Man need not be stupid.

I am a man who moves forward, who truly believes that he can make a positive difference in this world— that despite the odds, there is much life to be lived and enjoyed.

This can be you… I hope this is you.

I still do not find life 'easy'— but I have at least *discovered* it. And it took 56 years… how sad. But allow me to start anew: how spectacular!

I'm not dead... yet!

Acknowledgments

Posters & Stills

The author would like to thank the many individual artists and photographers whose images have been selected from the productions listed below and his personal archives for inclusion in this book.

"JORY"
Courtesy of AVCO-Embassy Pictures

"JEREMY"
Courtesy of MGM-UA

"DEATH BE NOT PROUD"
Courtesy of American Broadcasting Co.

"PIRATES OF PENZANCE"

Courtesy of New York Shakespeare Festival.

"TWO OF A KIND"

Courtesy of Columbia Broadcasting System

"RUNNING BRAVE"

Courtesy of Buena Vista Pictures

"HARRY AND SON"

Courtesy of Orion Pictures Corp.

"CALIFORNIA GIRLS"

Courtesy of American Broadcasting Co.

"RENT-A-COP"

Courtesy of Kings Road Entertainment

"WHITE HOT"

Courtesy of Scotia International Filmverleih

"MODERN LOVE"

Courtesy of Columbia Pictures

"BEAUTY AND THE BEAST"

Courtesy of Buena Vista Pictures

"EVENING SHADE"

Courtesy of Columbia Broadcasting System

"THUNDER ALLEY"

Courtesy of American Broadcasting Co.

"ELLEN"

Courtesy of American Broadcasting Co.

Songs from *I'm Not Dead... Yet!*

available on **iTunes Amazon CDBaby**

"Forever"
From *Open Heart – The Musical*
Music and lyrics by Robby Benson

"Run To You"
From *Open Heart – The Musical*
Music and lyrics by Robby Benson

"Problems"
From *Open Heart – The Musical*
Music and lyrics by Robby Benson

"Good Guys Win"
Music and lyrics by Robby Benson

"Mr. Weinstein's Barbershop"
live recording
Music by Robby Benson
Lyrics by Jerry Segal

"Why Not Me?"
Music and lyrics by Robby Benson

"Falling"
Music and lyrics by Robby Benson
Duet by Stan Brown and Karla DeVito

"I Believe In Fate"
live recording
Music by Robby Benson
Lyrics by Jerry Segal

"Baby Boom"
Music by Robby Benson
Lyrics by Karla DeVito and Danny Lawson
Vocals by Karla DeVito

"Nobody Makes Me Crazy" (Like You Do!)
original demo
Music by Robby Benson
Lyrics by Karla DeVito
Vocals by Karla DeVito

"Classic Problem"
Music and lyrics by Robby Benson

"Bang My Drum"
Music and lyrics by Robby Benson

"If I Had The Wings"
From *Open Heart – The Musical*
Music and lyrics by Robby Benson

"Vivienne's Theme"
Music by Robby Benson
Piano solo by Sterling Smith

"Let Me In"
From *Open Heart – The Musical*
Music and lyrics by Robby Benson
Vocals by Robby Benson & Karla DeVito

"Carousel Of Love"
Music and lyrics by Robby Benson
Vocals by Karla DeVito and Robby Benson

"Paint A Picture"
From *Open Heart – The Musical*
Music by Robby Benson
Lyrics by Jerry Segal & Robby Benson
Vocals by Karla DeVito

"Let's Get A Colonoscopy!"
Music and lyrics by Robby Benson

"My Heart Is The Sun"
From the album *Lyric's Love Light Revolution*
Music by Robby Benson
Lyrics by Lyric Benson
Vocals by Lyric Benson

and our newest song:
"Open Your Heart"
From the upcoming album *Karla 58*
Music by Robby Benson
Lyrics by Karla DeVito and Robby Benson
Vocals by Karla DeVito

BIO BENSON
Benson, Robby.
I'm not dead-- yet!, or, "The
corpse moved" :a medical memoir
08/18/2022

CPSIA information can be obtained
at www.ICGtesting.com
Printed in the USA
LVHW022152150722
723616LV00016B/906